Winter Olympic English

Winter Olympic English

2016년 12월 25일 초판 인쇄
2016년 12월 30일 초판 발행

지은이 안필규 · 이철 · 최은영 · 구자혁 · 류승구 · 강보렴 · Stephen Lindhorst
펴낸이 이찬규 | **펴낸곳** 북코리아 | **등록번호** 제03-01240호
전화 02-704-7840 | **팩스** 02-704-7848
이메일 sunhaksa@korea.com | **홈페이지** www.북코리아.kr
주소 13209 경기도 성남시 중원구 사기막골로 45번길 14 우림 2차 A동 1007호
ISBN 978-89-6324-531-7 (93740)

값 18,000원

Winter Olympic English

Pilgyu Ahn · Chol Lee · Eunyoung Choi · Jahyeok Koo · Seunggu Lew · Bowryum Ghang · Stephen Lindhorst

Bookorea

Preface
머리말

이 책은 2014년 10월부터 2016년 2월까지 강릉원주대학교에서 시행한 예비특성화 프로그램인 "2018년 평창 동계올림픽 인재양성사업"을 기반으로 만들어졌다. "2018년 평창 동계올림픽 인재양성사업"의 목적은 영어영문학과, 중어중문학과, 일본학과에서 선별한 우수한 학생들에게 영어, 중국어, 일본어를 집중적으로 교육하여 2018년 평창 동계올림픽에 다녀갈 외국인들에게 통역을 해 줄 인재를 육성하고 영동 지역 소개를 담은 통 · 번역 책자를 제작하는 것이었다.

"2018년 평창 동계올림픽 인재양성사업"을 효율적으로 수행하기 위하여 영어영문학과에서는 4명의 교수가 책임자 역할을 맡는 조장이 되고, 각 조마다 강사나 대학원생의 멘토(mentor)와 15명 남짓으로 선정된 우수한 영어영문학과 재학생들을 멘티(mentee)로 모집하여 2018 평창 동계올림픽의 통 · 번역에 관련된 업무를 효율적으로 개시하였다.

여러 자료들 가운데에서 동계올림픽과 동계패럴림픽의 종목에 관한 자료가 이 책의 목적에 가장 부합될 것이라는 의견이 모아져서, 각 조는 개별적으로 멘토와 멘티가 상의하여 수집한 자료들을 바탕으로 우리말과 영어로 원고를 작성하였다. 그 후 각 조에서 만든 자료를 바탕으로 영어영문학과 지도교수들과 원어민 Stephen Lindhorst 교수가 감수와 편집을 맡아서 그 결과물로 한 권의 책을 만든 것이다.

프로그램이 시행되고 이 책이 나오는 기간 동안 한 조를 맡았던 이철 교수가 해외 파견교수로 결정되면서 구자혁교수로 바뀌는 우여곡절 끝에 프로그램은 무사히 완료되었고, 모든 자료는 잘 정리되어 외국인뿐만 아니라 우리나라의 초보자들에게도 도움이 될 만한 한 권의 책으로 정리된 것이다.

처음부터 끝까지 계획을 세우고 정리를 도와준 강보렴 선생에게 이 글을 통하여 심심한 감사의 표시를 전한다. 뿐만 아니라 강의와 연구에 바쁜 와중에도 프로그램이 종료되는 순간까지 각 조를 지도하고 책의 제작에 도움을 주신 이철 교수, 최은영 교수, 구자혁 교수, 류승구 교수에게도 감사의 마음을 전한다. 그리고 처음부터 끝까지 꼼꼼

하게 자료를 읽어준 Stephen Lindhorst 교수 또한 이 책이 출판되는 데 커다란 도움을 주신 분이다. 또한 묵묵히 프로그램 운영에 최선을 다한 영어영문학과 참여 학생들에게도 감사의 마음을 전한다. 마지막으로 어려운 여건에서도 이 책을 출판하겠다고 결정한 북코리아의 이찬규 사장님과 임직원 여러분들에게도 고마움을 전한다.

2016년 12월 20일
집필자 대표 안 필 규

Contents
차례

Contents

II
PARALYMPICS THE SUMMER AND WINTER GAMES ENGLISH CONVERSATION GUIDE — 187

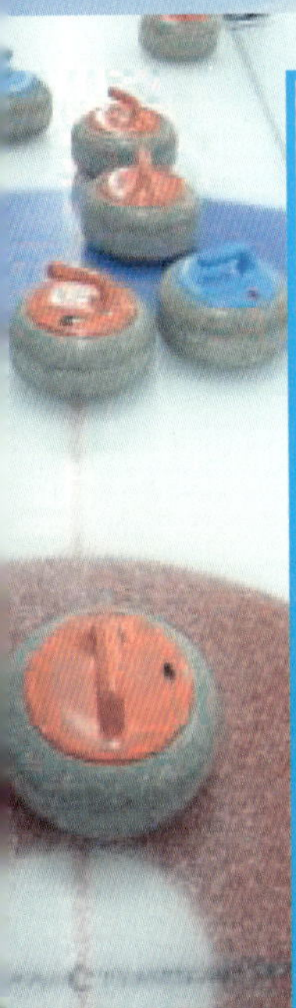

I

Pyeongchang 2018 Winter Olympics

01 ALPINE SKIING
알파인 스키

EVENTS

MEN'S EVENTS	WOMEN'S EVENTS
Alpine combined men	Alpine combined women
Downhill men	Downhill women
Giant slalom men	Giant slalom women
Slalom men	Slalom women
Super combined men	Super combined women
Super–G men	Super–G women

An Introduction to the Game

Alpine skiing developed near the mountainous regions of the Alps in the form of skiing down steep slopes. The sport is named after the hometown of Austrian born Hans Schneider, the founder of modern skiing. The first official alpine skiing game was the Arlberg Kandahar Championships in 1928. Athletes were ranked according to a combined score in two events, the downhill race, and rotation. Alpine skiing was adopted as an official Olympic sport in the 1936 4th Winter Olympic Games held in Garmisch- Partenkirchen, Germany.

Official alpine skiing includes 6 games: downhill, slalom, giant slalom, super combined, super-G slalom and alpine combined. Downhill is a game that emphasizes speed. Slalom records the fastest skiing time coming down shorter turns with narrow set poles. The giant slalom has poles set at a wider width than the slalom. Super combined is a speed race that combines one downhill or Super-G run with one slalom. Super-G slalom consists of wider poles, while demanding greater speed. Alpine combined is a combined game of downhill and slalom. This game is held separately only at the Winter Olympics and World Championships.

"What is Alpine Skiing?"

Joe : Did you know that the 2018 Winter Olympics is going to be held in Pyeongchang?

2018년에 평창에서 동계올림픽이 열리는 것을 알고 있었니?

Karen : Yes! I'm excited about the Pyeongchang Winter Olympics.

What **events** are you looking forward to?

응! 평창 올림픽이 엄청 기대된다! 너는 무슨 종목이 기대되니?

Joe : I'm looking forward to alpine skiing!

나는 알파인 스키가 기대돼!

Karen : Alpine skiing? Oh, I've heard about it, but I don't know it well.

알파인 스키? 아, 들어는 봤는데 잘 모르겠다.

Joe : Basically, alpine skiing is skiing **downhill** on a **steep** mountain **slope**. There are six types of games. There's the **downhill**, **slalom**, **giant slalom**, **super combined**, **special-g slalom**, and **downhill combined**.

기본적으로 알파인 스키는 가파른 산비탈을 활강하는 스키야. 알파인 스키에는 6가지 종목이 있어. 활강, 회전, 대회전, 슈퍼대회전, 슈퍼 복합, 복합 종목이 있는데, 모두 가파른 경사면을 활강하는 형태로 이루어지지.

Karen : Oh really? What is the difference between the six games?

그러니? 그럼 6가지는 어떻게 달라?

KEY WORDS & EXPRESSIONS

event: 종목
alpine combined: 알파인 복합 경기
downhill: 활강 스키
world championship: 세계선수권대회
steep: 가파른, 비탈진
slope: 경사, 비탈, 경사지
slalom: 슬랄롬, 회전 경기
giant slalom: 대회전 경기
super combined: 슈퍼 복합
super giant slalom: 슈퍼대회전 경기

Joe : Downhill is a game that emphasizes speed. Slalom is skiing down a short course with sudden turns in the fastest time possible. Giant slalom is a combined game of downhill and slalom. The gates are wider and so are the turns. Super combined is also looking for speed while making one run in a downhill or super-G and one slalom. The super-G slalom is an advanced version of the giant slalom with even wider gates and faster time requirements. Alpine combined is a combined game of downhill and slalom. But you can see the alpine combined only at the Winter Olympics and World Championships.

음, 활강은 스피드를 중요시하는 경기야. 회전은 정해진 코스를 짧고 급격한 턴으로 빠른 시간 안에 미끄러지는 경기야. 대회전은 그보다 더 넓은 회전 폭을 갖는 활강과 회전을 복합한 경기이고, 슈퍼대회전은 대회전을 발전시킨 경기로서, 턱이 적고 일부 구간에 넓은 게이트가 설치되는 경기지. 알파인 복합은 활강과 회전 등 다른 특성을 가진 종목을 한 경기로 치르는 것이야. 그러나 이 경기는 동계올림픽이나 세계선수권대회에서만 볼 수 있는 경기지.

Karen : That sounds awesome! Now I must see the game!

엄청 재미있겠다! 이번에는 꼭 봐야겠어!

Joe : Hey, let's go watch the game together.

그래, 알파인 스키 경기하는 날 같이 보자!

The History

Alpine skiing which began as a type of transportation in regions near the Alps evolved into a sport measuring the speed of downhill skiing on a steep slope. However, due to the dangers involved with this sport, a wide variety of safe downhill skiing techniques and technology have been developed. For example, Norheim's toe-and-heel strap was invented to fix skis onto the skiers to prevent them from separating while skiing down steep hills. Other skiing techniques, such as turning techniques, were added as the sport began growing in Europe in the 1920s.

The European leisure activity began its journey of becoming a sport with Austrian born Hans Schneider establishing the modern skiing system. Also, the first downhill race was held in 1911 in Switzerland. In 1913, Arnold Lunn of England established rules for the downhill and slalom, allowing the first slalom race to be held in 1922. The sport became organized in 1924 when the International Ski Federation (FIS) was founded. Then the Arlberg Kandahar Championship in 1928 marked the first official game. This was followed by Arnold Lunn's official game rules for the downhill and slalom in 1930. The formulization of an organized sport led to the adoption of alpine skiing as an official Olympic sport in the 4th Winter Olympic Games in 1936 held in Garmisch – Partenkirchen, Germany.

Top Athletes

Didie Cuche was born on August 16, 1974 in Switzerland. Didie is a famous star recording 21 wins in the World Cup over 19 years. His prime was in his thirties and he is the oldest athlete to win all three events(the downhill, super giant slalom, and giant slalom) in the World Cup. He retired in 2012.

Didie Cuche는 1974년 8월 16일 스위스에서 태어난 Didie Cuche는 19년 동안 월드컵에서 통산 21승을 기록한 간판스타이다. 그는 30대에 전성기를 맞아 활강, 슈퍼대회전, 대회전 세 종목에서 월드컵 최고령 우승기록을 가지고 있다. 그는 2012년에 은퇴했다.

Ted Ligety was born on August 31, 1984 in the United States. He won two gold medals in the combined event in the 2006 Turin Olympics and in the giant slalom race in the 2014 Sochi Olympics. His major event and strength is the giant slalom, which he has continually won in the Olympics.

Ted Ligety는 1984년 8월 31일 미국에서 태어난 선수로 2006년 토리노 올림픽의 혼합 종목과 2014년 소치 올림픽 대회전 종목에서 금메달을 땄다. 그의 주 종목은 대회전으로서, 올림픽에서 연이어 우승했다.

Lindsey Vonn was born on October 18, 1984 in the United States. She won a gold medal at the 2010 Winter Olympics to become the first US winner in the women's downhill event. She also won six consecutive years in the World Cup downhill section, four times in the Super G event, and three times in the combined event.

Lindsey Vonn은 1984년 10월 18일 미국에서 태어나 미국 여성 최초로 2010년 동계올림픽 활강 종목에서 금메달을 땄다. 또한 그녀는 월드컵 활강 부분에서 6년 연속 우승하고, 슈퍼G 종목에서는 4번, 혼합 종목에서는 3번 연속 우승하였다.

* Photo from Wikipedia

"How did it all start?"

Joe : Hey! What are you searching for?

안녕? 뭐 검색하는 거야?

Karen : Right now, I'm looking into alpine skiing.

나 지금 알파인 스키에 대해 찾아보고 있어.

Joe : Alpine skiing?

알파인 스키?

Karen : Yeah! Alpine skiing, the sport where you have to speed down a steep slope. It developed from regions near the Alps.

응, 알파인 스키. 알프스 산맥의 산악 활강에서 발전한 종목으로 가파른 경사면을 활강하는 형태의 스키 운동이야.

Joe : Oh, I see. But why?

그렇구나. 그런데 왜?

Karen : I've always wanted to become an alpine skier.

사실 내 꿈이 알파인 선수가 되는 거야.

Joe : Really? I didn't know that!

진짜? 꿈에도 몰랐어!

KEY WORDS & EXPRESSIONS

Search for: (인터넷상에서) 무엇을 검색하다

speed: 속도를 내다

gold-medalist: 금메달을 딴 선수

forte: 강점

twist (something) into something: 무엇을 변화시키다, 무엇을 새롭게 하다

take off: 출하다, 시작하다, 도약하다

who would have ever thought of: 무엇에 대해 누가 생각이나 했겠냐

figure: 생각에

unraveled from there: 거기서부터 시작되다

nitty-gritty: 핵심, 자세한

Karen : Yeah, I wanted to be a great athlete like Ted Ligety!

응. 나는 Ted Ligety 선수처럼 멋진 선수가 되고 싶어!

Joe : Ted Ligety, the **gold-medalist** at the 2006 Turin Olympics and 2014 Sochi Olympics? Didn't he continue winning the giant slalom events at the Olympics? The giant slalom is definitely his **forte**.

Ted Ligety는 2006년 토리노 올림픽과 2014년 소치 올림픽에서 금메달을 땄어. 올림픽 대회전 종목에서도 계속 우승을 했지. 대회전은 확실히 그의 주 종목이야.

Karen : He is such a great athlete. If I continue to work hard, maybe I'll be able to achieve my dreams!

아주 훌륭한 선수지. 나도 노력하면 꿈을 이룰 수도 있을 거야!

Joe : So, what have you got so far?

지금까지 무엇을 알아냈어?

Karen : One thing is that it's a fairly new official sport. It began as a transportation method that people began to **twist into** a fun leisure activity in the early 1900s. But it really **took off** in the 1930s when the official rules were made and it was accepted into the Olympics.

한 가지 찾아낸 것은, 비교적 최신 스포츠 종류라는 것이야. 사람들이 교통수단에 재미를 붙여 1900년대 들어 여가 활동으로 변신시킨 거지. 그런데, 본격적으로 출발한 시점은 1930년대야. 이때 공식 규칙이 확립되고 올림픽 종목으로 채택됐으니까.

Joe : It does have a shorter history than other Olympic events. **Who would've ever thought of** making this into an official sport?

다른 올림픽 종목들에 비해 역사가 짧아. 그런데 누가 스키를 공식 스포츠로 만들려고 생각했을까?

Karen : I have the answer for that! It was Hans Schneider, an Austrian. He is the founder of the modern ski system. I **figure** everything **unraveled from there**, but Arnold Lunn got into the **nitty-gritty** by drawing up the rules for the games.

내가 그 질문의 정답을 알고 있지! 오스트리아 출신 한스 슈나이더야. 그가 현대적인 스키 시스템을 개발했지. 거기서부터 모든 것이 출발했다고 봐. 그러나 아놀드 런이 경기의 규칙을 만들면서 스포츠의 세부적 부분을 창출해 냈지.

Equipment and Gear

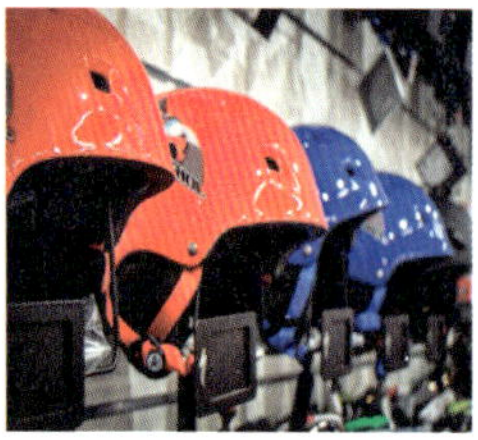

Helmets 헬멧

Helmets are a solid device designed to protect the skier's head from injuries. Helmets are mandatory during the games.

선수의 머리를 보호하도록 고안된 단단한 장비이다. 경기를 할 때, 헬멧 착용은 의무적이다.

Wrist straps 손목 끈

The wrist strap is a strap that is attached to the handle of the pole. It prevents skiers from losing the poles during use.

폴 손잡이에 부착되어 있는 끈이다. 스키 선수가 이 끈을 손목에 둘러서 폴을 놓치지 않게 해준다.

Skis 스키

The ski is a long stick that differs in length, width, and shape, and is designed to slide over the snow. The bottom sides of the skis are carefully polished to suit snow conditions so that the ultimate skiing experience can be obtained. The long groove in the skis improves glides and stability on downhill and straight paths.

눈 덮인 지면을 미끄러질 수 있게 설계된 긴 막대로서, 길이와 폭, 모양이 여러 가지이다. 스키의 밑바닥은 최상의 스키를 탈 수 있도록 여러 가지 눈 상태에 맞게 섬세하게 광택을 낸 부분이다. 스키 바닥에 길게 난 움푹한 자국은 활강이나 직선 코스에서 미끄러짐과 안정감을 좋게 해준다.

Ski boots 스키 부츠

Ski boots are made of plastic or a composite of materials. They are attached to the bindings of the ski.

플라스틱이나 복합 재료로 만든 단단한 부츠로서, 스키의 조임쇠 부분에 부착한다.

Gloves 스키 장갑

Ski gloves cover and protect the hand and wrist against cold and bad weather. They are padded but flexible. They are made to provide a better grip on the poles. They also have a forearm guard that protects skiers when passing the gates.

추위와 궂은 날씨에 대비해 손과 손목을 덮어 보호하는 싸개로 패딩 처리 되어 있으나 유연하며 손잡이를 잘 잡을 수 있도록 만들어져 있다. 또한 선수가 게이트를 통과할 때 팔을 보호하기 위한 팔보호대가 붙어 있는 경우도 있다.

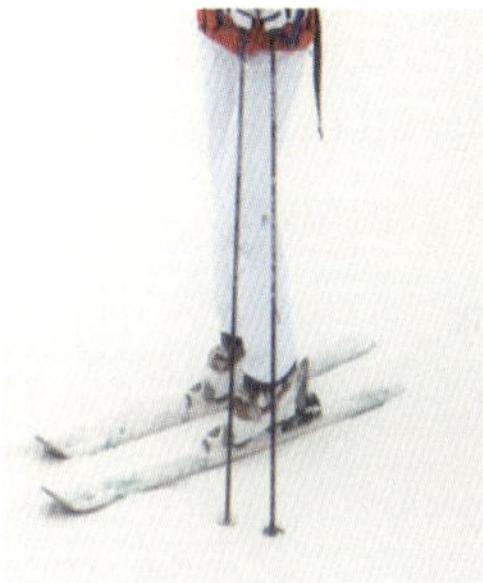

Poles 스키 폴

Ski poles are a metal or a composite fiber rod with a handle and a basket. They are used to maintain balance and are used in rotations. The basket prevents the poles from getting stuck in the snow.

손잡이와 빠짐 방지 고리(basket)가 달린 금속 또는 복합섬유 소재의 막대이다. 스키 폴은 균형을 유지하고 회전을 할 때 사용한다. 빠짐 방지 고리는 스키 폴이 눈 속에 너무 깊이 빠지는 것을 막아준다.

Ski suit 스키복

The ski suit is a one-piece garment that fits tightly onto the body so air resistance is reduced and speed is increased.

공기 저항을 줄여서 속도를 높여주는 몸에 딱 달라붙는 일체형 의복이다.

Goggles 스키 고글

Ski goggles protect the eyes from the sun's rays and other risk factors. The filtered lens optimize distance perception.

태양광선과 위험요소로부터 눈을 보호하는 장비로서 필터를 사용한 렌즈는 거리 감각을 최적화한다.

What is this contraption?

KEY WORDS & EXPRESSIONS

Ski poles: 스키 폴
Rotation: 회전
Basket: 빠짐 방지 고리
Have a look: 구경하다
Groove: 홈, 바닥홈(스키용어)
Downhill: 활강

Joe : What are these?

이게 다 뭐야?

Karen : I am going to start learning alpine skiing next week. So I bought the necessary equipment.

내가 다음 주부터 알파인 스키를 배우기로 해서 필요한 장비들을 좀 사봤어.

Joe : I knew you wanted to become an alpine skier, but I didn't think you would actually go out and buy all the equipment.

네가 알파인 선수가 되고 싶어하는 것은 알았지만, 정말로 나가서 장비를 살지는 몰랐어.

Karen : Yes! I am going to work hard and become a great skier!

응! 열심히 배워서 훌륭한 선수가 될 거야!

Joe : Are those long sticks called ski poles?

이 긴 막대는 스키 폴이라고 하는 건가?

Karen : That's right. They are used to maintain balance and are used in rotations.

응. 이게 바로 스키 폴이야. 스키 폴은 균형을 유지하고 회전을 할 때 사용해.

Joe : What is this on the bottom of the ski pole?

그런데 스키 폴 아래 달려있는 이건 뭐야?

Karen : It's a basket. The basket prevents the poles from getting too deep into the snow.

그건 빠짐 방지 고리야. 스키 폴이 눈 속에 너무 깊게 빠지는 것을 막아주는 역할을 해.

Joe : Oh, I see. I've never seen skis this close before! Is it okay if I take a look?

아 그렇구나. 그런데 나는 스키를 이렇게 가까이서 본 게 처음이야! 구경해도 되지?

Karen : Of course! Have a look!

응! 구경해!

Joe : Wow. What's this long indentation? Why is it there?

우와. 스키 바닥에 길게 난 움푹한 자국이 있네. 왜 이런 거야?

Karen : Umm. It's called a groove. It improves the glide and stability when on a downhill or a straight path.

음. 그건 바닥 홈으로서, 활강할 때나 직선 코스에서 활주와 안정감을 좋게 만들어주는 역할을 해.

Joe : Amazing! Are you beginning lessons next week? Work hard!

정말 신기하다! 다음 주부터 수업한다고 했지? 열심히 들어!

Karen : Thanks.

고마워!

SPORTS FACTS

ALPINE SKIING

- First contested date in the Olympics :
  1936 Garmisch-Partenkirchen Winter Olympics
- Place of origin :
  Europe-Alps region
- Types of events :
  Downhill, Slalom, Giant Slalom, Super Combined,
  Super G-slalom, Alpine combined
- Type of arena :
  Snow event stadium
- Race time :
  Downhill: approx. 2 minutes
  Slalom: approx. 40~60 seconds
  Giant slalom: approx. 60~90 seconds
  Super G-slalom: approx. 1~2 minutes
- Country with most medals :
  Austria (114)
- Athlete with most medals :
  Kjetil André Aamodt (four gold, two silver, two bronze)
- Youngest medalist :
  Traudl Hecher (she won bronze at age 16)

해 석

An Introduction to the Game

알파인 스키는 알프스 산악지방을 중심으로 가파른 경사면을 활강하는 형태로 발달하였다. 그 이름은 근대 스키를 정립한 인물인 오스트리아의 한스 슈나이더가 태어난 지명에서 유래됐다. 첫 공식적 알파인 스키 경기는 1928년 아를베르크칸다하르 대회로서, 활강과 회전 경기 점수를 합하여 순위를 정했다. 1936년 독일의 가르미슈 파르텐키르헨에서 열린 제4회 동계올림픽 경기 대회에서 활강과 회전 종목의 알파인 스키가 정식 종목으로 채택되었다.

공식 알파인 스키의 종목은 활강, 회전, 대회전, 슈퍼복합, 슈퍼대회전, 알파인 복합 종목 총 6가지가 있다. 활강은 스피드를 중요시하는 경기다. 회전은 정해진 코스의 짧고 급격한 턴을 빠른 시간 내에 마치는 경기다. 대회전은 그보다 더 넓은 회전 폭을 갖는 경기다. 슈퍼복합은 활강 또는 슈퍼대회전과 회전 경기를 함께 하는 경기다. 슈퍼대회전은 대회전을 발전시킨 경기로 턱이 적고 일부 구간에 넓은 게이트가 설치되는 경기다. 알파인 복합 종목은 활강과 회전 등 다른 특성을 가진 종목을 한 경기로 치르는 것이다. 동계올림픽대회와 세계선수권대회 등에서만 별도로 경기가 치러진다.

The History

알파인 스키는 유럽 알프스 지방의 산악 활강에서 발전한 종목으로, 가파른 경사면을 활강하는 형태의 운동이다. 안전한 활강을 위해 폭이 넓은 스키가 개발되었고, 적합한 기술도 발전하였다.

오스트리아 출신의 한스 슈나이더가 근대 스키 체계를 정립하였고 첫 활강 경기는 1911년 스위스에서 열렸다. 1913년 영국의 아널드 룬이 활강, 회전 경기의 규칙을 만들면서 1922년 첫 회전 경기가 개최되었다. 국제스키연맹(FIS)은 1924년에 창설되었고, 첫 공식 경기는 1928년 아를베르크칸다하르 대회가 처음 열렸을 때 선보였다. 1930년 아널드 룬이 활강과 회전 경기 규칙을 공식 제정하였다. 1936년 독일 가르미슈 파르텐키르헨 올림픽에서 알파인 스키가 정식 종목이 되었다.

02 BIATHLON
바이애슬론

EVENTS

MEN'S EVENTS	WOMEN'S EVENTS	MIXED EVENT
10km men	10km pursuit women	Mixed Relay
12.5km pursuit men	12.5km mass start women	
15km mass start men	15km women	
20km men	4X6km relay women	
4X7.5km relay men	7.5km women	

An Introduction to the Game

Biathlon is a combination of the root word **bi (two)** and **athlon (athletics)**. This sport brings shooting and cross-country skiing into one game. Biathlon is known as one of the two modern winter games.

In this modern winter sport, the athletes carry a rifle while riding skis as they travel a given distance. Thus, it is fair to say that it is a complex game consisting of shooting at a shooting range and skiing.

Biathlon, a sport requiring excellent shooting skills and physical fitness, was adopted as an official Olympic sport in the 1960s.

Talking about the Game

Joe : Hey, do you like skiing?

너 스키 타는 것 좋아하니?

Karen : Of course! I can't wait for ski season this year.

당연하지! 올해 스키 시즌이 참 기대돼!

Joe : How about shooting rifles?

그럼 사격은?

Karen : I like it. Why do you ask?

사격도 좋아하지. 그런데 왜?

Joe : Oh, then there is an Olympic event you might love.

네가 좋아할 만한 올림픽 종목이 있어.

Karen : What is it?

무슨 종목이야?

Joe : It includes both shooting and skiing. The game is called biathlon. You ski down to a shooting range and shoot. So it's a sport that looks for both shooting and skiing skills.

스키와 사격을 모두 하는 게임이야. 바이애슬론이라고 하지. 스키를 타고 내려오다가 사격장에서 총으로 사격을 하지. 그러니까 사격과 스키 실력을 동시에 요구하는 스포츠야.

Karen : So, I can enjoy both shooting and skiing in one game? Cool! Are there only male athletes?

그럼 한 경기에서 사격과 스키를 동시에 즐길 수 있는 거야? 멋지다! 그런데 남자 선수들만 있는 거 아니야?

Joe : They have women's events. the women's event was adopted as an official sporting event in 1992 in the 16th competition held at Albertville. So now it's more interesting than ever, since it has male, female and mixed events.

그렇지 않아. 1992년 알베르빌에서 열린 16번째 대회 때부터 여자 경기도 정식 종목으로 채택되었어. 그리고 남녀 혼합 경기도 있으니 정말 흥미로울 거야.

Karen : You found the perfect Olympic sport for me. Thanks.

나한테 딱 맞는 올림픽 종목을 찾아줘서 고마워.

KEY WORDS & EXPRESSIONS

shooting: 사격
rifles: 사격 총
shooting range: 사격장
sporting event: 스포츠 경기
mixed event: 남녀 혼합 경기

The History

Skiing originally developed as a winter transportation method in Northern Europe. Then combat troops started using skiing not only as a means of transportation, but combining it with firing rifles transforming the two skills into a single sport. It began with Swedish and Norwegian guards in the late 18th century, when soldiers from Norway opened fire at Swedish borders. The simultaneous shooting and skiing technique gradually developed from a military fighting method into a type of sport. This is why biathlon is also known as a sport for soldiers.

The first world class tournament was held in 1958. It was adopted as an official Olympic sport in the Winter Olympic Games during the 8th Congress for men's events, while the 16th Congress in 1992 accepted the women's.

Since 1979, South Korea has formed five Modern Biathlon Committees for the Olympic Committee. The Five Modern Biathlon Federation was organized after 1982. This resulted in the first participation of South Korea in the biathlon events during the Sarajevo Winter Olympics in 1984. Then in 1998, biathlon was reorganized into the Biathlon Federation, renewing itself from the Five Modern Biathlon Federation.

Top Athletes

Ole Einar Bjoerndalen was born on January 27, 1974 in Norway and is a professional biathlete. He has won thirteen medals in the Winter Olympics, making him the most successful athlete in biathlon.

Ole Einar Bjoerndalen은 1974년 1월 27일 노르웨이에서 태어났으며 프로 바이애슬론 선수다. 그는 동계올림픽에서 13개의 메달을 획득하면서 바이애슬론 종목에서 가장 성공한 선수로 간주된다.

Ricco Groß was born on August 22, 1970 in Germany. He began biathlon at the age of thirteen and has won many gold medals in the Winter Olympics and the World Championships. He has currently retired from competing. However, he actively continues his love for the sport as a biathlon commentator and as a coach.

Ricco Groβ는 1970년 8월 22일 독일에서 태어났다. 그는 13살인 어린 나이에 바이애슬론을 시작하였으며 동계올림픽과 세계선수권대회에서 많은 메달을 획득했다. 그는 현재 은퇴했으나 바이애슬론 관련 해설과 코치 활동으로 스포츠에 대한 애정을 이어가고 있다.

Sven Fischer was born on April 16, 1971 in Germany. He began his career in biathlon at a very early age, becoming a district champion in the fifth grade. He experienced a kneecap injury further into his sports career, however, this did not prevent him from winning four Olympic gold medals, two silver, and two bronze.

Sven Fischer는 1971년 4월 16일 독일에서 태어났다. 그는 어린 나이에 바이애슬론 선수로 활약했으며 5학년에 지역 챔피언으로 우뚝 섰다. 추후 무릎 부상을 입었음에도 불구하고 4개의 올림픽 금메달, 2개의 은메달과 2개의 동메달을 획득했다.

* Photo from Wikipedia

"How did it all start?"

Joe : Karen, I've been wondering.

카렌, 궁금한 게 생겼어.

Karen : What is it?

말해 봐.

Joe : Was skiing and shooting always a combined sport?

처음부터 스키와 사격이 합쳐져 있었어?

KEY WORDS & EXPRESSIONS

have a sense of: 무엇에 대해 직감이 있다

let me guess: 내가 맞춰보지

try if you can: 할 수 있으면 해봐라

biathlete: 바이애슬론 선수

Karen : Of course not. Wait, I think I have a sense of why you are asking. Let me guess.

당연히 아니지. 네가 왜 그걸 물어보는지 알 것 같아. 맞춰봐도 돼?

Joe : You can try if you can.

맞출 수 있다면 맞춰 봐.

Karen : You are asking me how skiing and shooting was combined into one sport, right?

어쩌다 스키와 사격을 동시에 하게 됐는지 묻고 싶었던 것 아냐?

Joe : Exactly.

정확히 맞췄어.

Karen : Let me explain briefly, soldiers incorporated a winter transportation method, or skiing into a military combat technique.

간단히 설명하자면, 겨울철에 이동 수단으로만 활용되었던 스키를 군인들이 전투용으로 발전시켰다고 볼 수 있지.

Joe : Oh, so it was developed for combat but later became a sport.

아하, 전투용으로 발전되다가 스포츠로 자리 잡은 거구나.

Karen : That's right. Also, in 1998, the Korean Biathlon Federation was established independently.

맞아. 게다가 1998년도엔 한국에서 바이애슬론 경기연맹이 독립하기도 했지.

Joe : I didn't know there were Asian biathletes, let alone Korean biathletes. I always thought of it as a sport with more European athletes.

나는 바이애슬론 종목에 동양 선수들이 있는지, 그중에서도 한국 선수들이 있는지 몰랐어. 항상 유럽 선수들이 주류인 스포츠로 생각했으니까.

Karen : I know what you mean, since skiing itself is a means of transportation in the winter in that part of the world. The fact that Korea established an independent league out of a sport grounded in a foreign military tactic is quite amazing.

스키 자체가 유럽에서 겨울에 이동 수단으로 쓰였기 때문에 네가 무슨 말 하는지 알겠어. 외국 군인들의 작전 수단에 뿌리를 두고 있는 스포츠로서 한국에 독립적인 연맹이 있다니 정말 신기한 것 같아.

Equipment and Gear

Poles 스키 폴

Used to maintain balance and gain momentum. Poles used in biathlon are much longer and stiffer.

몸의 중심을 유지하고 추진력을 얻기 위한 스키 장비. 바이애슬론에서 사용하는 스키 폴은 일반 스키 폴보다 길고 단단한 것이 특징이다.

Skis 스키

To direct movement and endure force, skis in biathlon are generally shorter and stiffer. The tip and tail of the skis are curved, the former curved less for speed, and the latter shaped to prevent wear.

움직임을 이끌고 다양한 힘을 견디기 위해 바이애슬론에서 사용되는 스키는 대체적으로 그 길이가 더 짧고 단단하다. 스키의 팁, 즉 앞부분은 일반 스키보다 구부러짐이 덜하고 꼬리 부분은 마모 현상을 줄여주기 위해 휘어있다.

Ski bindings 스키 바인딩

Ski bindings let skiers attach boots onto skis. They also disconnect the boots from the skis to reduce the risk of hazardous outcomes upon falling or impact.

스키와 부츠를 연결시키며 스키를 타다가 위험한 상황이 오거나 외부의 충격으로 인해 넘어지는 등의 상황 시에 스키와 부츠를 분리하여 위험을 예방하기 위한 장비이다.

Rifle 소총

The .22 caliber rifle is used in biathlon. It generally weighs 3.5 kg and can shoot up to 50 meters. The rifle can hold up to four clips or magazines and is held on the back of skiers with a harness.

바이애슬론에서는 .22 구경 소총을 사용한다. 소총은 약 3.5kg이며 50m까지 쏠 수 있다. 소총은 4개의 클립이나 탄창을 장착할 수 있으며 하니스라고 불리는 끈으로 등에 매도록 되어 있다.

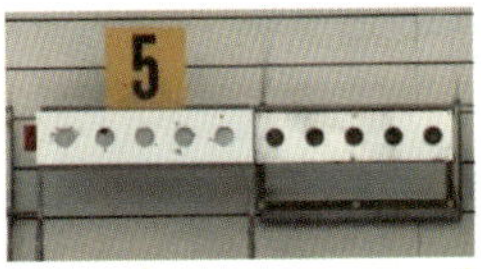	**Target 표적** The target consists of 5 round marks that are 11.5cm in diameter for standing and 4.5 cm for prone targets. The black target marks are covered by a white metal plate when hit. 표적은 5개의 둥근 점이 있다. 서서 맞추는 표적의 지름은 11.5cm이며 누운 자세는 지름 4.5cm이다. 정확히 맞출 경우 하얀색 철판이 검정 점을 가린다.

What is this contraption?

Joe : Why do you need those long sticks to ski?

스키를 타는 데 저 긴 막대기는 왜 필요한 거야?

Karen : Long sticks? Oh, you mean the poles. Those aren't sticks, they're poles.

긴 막대기? 아, 폴을 말하는 거구나. 저건 긴 막대기가 아니라 폴이라 하는 거야.

Joe : Yes, poles. What are they for? The pointy end makes it look like a weapon.

그래, 폴. 뭐에 사용하는 거야? 끝이 뾰족해서 무기같이 보이네.

Karen : Skiers use them for walking, turning, and balancing on hilly courses.

폴은 스키를 타는 사람들이 걷거나, 턴을 하거나, 비탈길을 오를 때 균형을 유지하도록 도와주는 역할을 해.

Joe : What's the ring at the end?

끝에 이 링은 뭐야?

Karen : It prevents you from getting stuck in the snow. One tip, different poles are used for different types of skiing techniques. So the shorter ones are used when doing skills and techniques, while the longer ones are used for standing, moving or walking.

폴이 눈 속으로 너무 깊이 박히는 것을 방지해. 팁을 하나 주자면 사용하는 기술이 달라지기 때문에,

KEY WORDS & EXPRESSIONS

pointy end of the+N: (명사)의 끝
hilly courses: 비탈진, 언덕진 길
get stuck: 어디에 빠지다, 끼다
essential: 필요한, 필수적인
when it comes to: 무엇에 관해 서라면
risk of accidents: 사고의 위험
.22 caliber rifle: .22 구경 소총
clips: 총알
loading time: 총알 충전 시간
mark: 표시
target: 표적
penalty: 벌칙

스키의 종류에 따라 서로 다른 폴대가 사용돼. 폴대 손잡이를 잡았을 때 스키 기술 등에 적용할 때는 약간 짧은 것이, 그리고 서 있거나 움직이거나 걸을 때에는 약간 긴 편이 도움이 된단다.

Joe : Skis are essential for skiing, so pick ones you like.

스키 판은 스키를 타려면 당연히 필요한 장비이니 맘에 드는 걸 고르면 되겠다, 그렇지?

Karen : There are many things to consider when it comes to skis. The shorter the skis, the safer. The longer the skis, the higher the risk of accidents. Normal skis are about 10 to 15cm shorter than your height. More advanced skiers prefer shorter skis, about 20cm shorter than their height.

스키 판도 고려해야 할 점이 많아. 스키 판이 짧을수록 안전하거든. 그러니까 스키 판이 길수록 사고의 위험이 높아지는 거야. 보통 자신의 키보다 10cm~15cm 정도 짧은 길이를 선호해. 상급 정도의 수준이라면 20cm 정도 짧은 스키 판을 많이 사용하지.

Joe : Skis 20cm shorter than your height is probably apt for athletes skiing quickly down slopes and shooting a rifle, don't you think?

빠르게 내려와서 총을 쏴야 하는 선수들에겐 20cm 정도 짧은 스키 판이 적당하겠네?

Karen : Yes! Also ski bindings that connect the boots to skis have to stay on tight. In case you fall on a fast slope, you need to separate your skis from your boots.

그렇지! 그리고 스키와 부츠를 연결해주는 바인딩도 꼭 있어야 해. 속도가 나는 경사에서 넘어졌을 때 부츠와 스키를 분리해야 하거든.

Joe : I see. What kind of rifle do they use?

그렇구나. 그럼 소총은 어떤 걸 써?

Karen : They use .22-caliber rifles. And they use a rifle with a minimum pressure of 1kg on shooting.

.22 구경 소총으로서, 방아쇠의 최소 압력이 1kg인 소총을 써.

Joe : Can clips be shared in the shooting?

총알 클립은 사격 대에서 나눠주는 거야?

Karen : No, participants each carry their own clips. The rifle holds four.

아니. 선수들은 각자 자기 탄알 클립을 가지고 있어. 소총에 4개를 장착할 수 있어.

Joe : Reducing loading time before shooting is also considered a skill.

사격 대 앞에서 장탄 시간을 줄이는 것도 선수의 능력이라고 볼 수 있구나.

Karen : And you must hit all 5 marks on the target from a 50m distance.

그리고 50m 밖에 있는 표적 5개를 꼭 맞춰야 해.

Joe : If you fail, then what?

못 맞추면 어떻게 되는데?

Karen : 1 minute is added to the record or you ski a 150m course as a penalty. This is fatal since recorded time determines your ranking.

1분의 시간이 기록에 추가되거나 150m가량의 벌칙코스를 돌아야 해. 시간이 순위를 결정하는 바이애슬론에선 정말 치명적이지.

Joe : Thanks, I think I am going to have more fun watching the biathlon now.

고마워, 덕분에 앞으론 바이애슬론을 더 즐겁게 시청할 수 있을 것 같아.

Karen : The pleasure was mine.

별 말씀을.

해 석

An Introduction to the Game

바이애슬론은 '둘'을 의미하는 '바이(bi)'와 '운동경기'를 뜻하는 '애슬론(athlon)'의 결합어로서 서로 다른 종목인 사격과 크로스컨트리 스키가 결합된 경기이다. 바이애슬론은 동계 근대 2종 경기라고 말하기도 한다.

이 경기는 라이플 총을 메고 스키를 이용하여 일정한 거리를 주행하면서 중간에 있는 사격장에서 사격을 하는 사격과 스키의 복합 경기이다. 바이애슬론은 사격 실력과 체력을 가리는 스포츠로 1960년 대회에서부터 정식 종목으로 채택되었다.

The History

스키는 본래 북유럽에서 겨울철 이동 수단으로 발달했었다. 그 후에 군대에서도 전투와 관련하여 이동 수단으로 사용되면서 스키에 사격이 합쳐져 '군인들의 스포츠'로 새롭게 탄생했다. 스웨덴 국경 지대와 노르웨이에서 18세기 후반에 두 국가의 수비대가 사격과 스키로 대결을 펼친 것을 시작으로 군인들 사이에서 많이 행해지다가 점차적으로 스포츠의 형태로 갖추어졌다.

1958년에 첫 세계선수권 대회가 개최되었으며, 동계올림픽에서는 제8회 대회부터 남자 경기가 정식 종목으로 채택되었다. 그리고 1992년, 제16회 대회부터는 여자 경기 또한 정식 종목이 되었다. 한국에선 1979년에 처음으로 대한 올림픽 위원회에 대한 근대 5종 바이애슬론 위원회가 구성되었다. 그 후 1982년 대한 근대 5종 바이애슬론 경기연맹이 창립되었으며, 1984년엔 사라예보에서 개최한 제14회 동계올림픽 경기대회에 처음 출전하였다. 그리고 1998년에는 대한 근대 5종 바이애슬론 경기연맹으로부터 독립하여 대한 바이애슬론 경기연맹으로 새롭게 태어났다.

BOBSLEIGH
봅슬레이

03

📢 EVENTS

MEN'S EVENTS
Two–man men
Four–man men

WOMEN'S EVENTS
Two–man women

An Introduction to the Game

Bobsleigh, also known as bobsledge, is an event involving riding a sled that can tilt right and left down an icy track. There are weight specifications for sleds; the two-man sled is set at a maximum of 375kg, including crew and equipment, and the four-man sled, a maximum of 630kg. The average velocity of a bobsleigh is approximately 120km to 140km, and the length of the track is 1,500m.

There are two events for men, the two-man men and the four-man men. For women, there is only the two-man women event.

Bobsleigh was adopted first in the 1924 Winter Olympic Games. However, the women's event was later adopted in 2002.

Talking about the Game

Joe : Hi, Karen. Did you watch yesterday's game?

안녕, 카렌. 너 어제 경기 봤니?

Karen : You mean the bobsleigh game?

봅슬레이 경기 말하는 거지?

Joe : Right. Wasn't it exciting?

맞아. 정말 흥미진진했지?

Karen : But, an athlete got injured.

그런데, 한 선수가 다쳤어.

Joe : Yes, that was a close call.

그래, 정말 아찔했었어.

Karen : Watching the game made me realize that I knew nothing about bobsleigh. Do you know anything about it?

그런데, 경기 보면서 깨달았는데 내가 봅슬레이에 관해서 아는 것이 없더라? 너는 이 종목에 대해 조금 알고 있니?

KEY WORDS & EXPRESSIONS

close call: 위험할 뻔하다
look into: 조사하다
two–man: 2인
four–man: 4인
track: 트랙
weight specification: 무게 제한
sled: 썰매
have never seen: 본 적이 없다
that's expected (to be expected): 당연하다
look at this: 이것 봐
velocity: 속도
I never knew (that): 전혀 몰랐다
goes on (to go on): 이어지다, 계속되다

Joe : Nope, so I looked into it after watching the game. Come here and look at this.

아니, 그래서 경기를 보고 나서, 나도 봅슬레이가 궁금해서 조사를 좀 했지. 이리 와서 이것 좀 봐.

Karen : What's that?

그게 뭐야?

Joe : These are the two types of events in bobsleigh. The two-man and the four-man.

봅슬레이는 두 가지의 경기 방식이 있어. 하나는 2인 1조 다른 하나는 4인 1조야.

Karen : How long is the track?

트랙 길이는 어느 정도야?

Joe : It is 1,500m. Bobsleigh also has two types of weight specifications.

트랙 길이는 1,500m야. 두 번째로, 봅슬레이는 두 가지의 무게가 있지.

Karen : Two? Why two?

두 가지? 왜 두 가지인데?

Joe : Because it has two events.

봅슬레이는 두 가지의 형태가 있어서 그래.

Karen : I see! There's a two-seater and four-seater sled, so there has to be two weight specifications.

알았다! 2인 1조랑 4인 1조. 그래서 봅슬레이가 두 가지의 무게가 있구나!

Joe : Karen, why are you suddenly so curious about bobsleigh?

카렌, 왜 갑자기 봅슬레이에 관심이 생겼어?

Karen : It was my first time watching a bobsleigh game. I had never seen the game before.

봅슬레이 경기를 처음 봤거든. 전에는 한 번도 본 적이 없어.

Joe : That's expected. Bobsleigh is not a well-known sport.

당연히 그럴 거야. 봅슬레이는 비인기 종목이니까.

Karen : So, did you find anything on bobsleigh?

음 그래, 그런데 봅슬레이에 관해서 뭐 더 찾은 것 있어?

Joe : Wait... Ok, here's some more information about bobsleigh. Oh! Here, there are so many pictures!

잠시만... 됐다, 여기에 봅슬레이에 대한 더 많은 정보가 있네. 오우! 여기에 사진들도 많이 있는데?

Karen : Let's enter "information."

'정보 보기'에 들어가 보자.

Joe : Look at this. It says the weight is 375kg for the two-man and 630kg for the four-man event. The 375kg must be the two-seater sled and the 630kg, the four-seater sled.

여길 봐. 여기 봅슬레이의 무게가 나와 있어. 음... 하나는 375kg이고 다른 하나는 630kg이구나. 내 생각에는 375kg이 2인 1조용 그리고 630kg는 4인 1조용 같아.

Karen : It is so heavy. I would've guessed it to be around 100 to 200kg. Here, it shows the velocity. Wow! It can go up to 120 to 140km. That's faster than a car!

정말 무겁구나. 난 100~200kg이라 생각했는데. 여기 봅슬레이 속도도 나와 있어. 우와! 봅슬레이는 120~140km까지 속도를 올릴 수가 있구나! 자동차보다 빠른데!

Joe : Let's look at the history of bobsleigh.

우리 간단한 봅슬레이의 역사도 조사해 볼까?

Karen : Yes. Let's see, here it is. Bobsleigh has two forms. There is a two person and a four person team for men, but there's only a two person team for women.

그래. 어디 보자…. 여기 있다. 봅슬레이는 두 가지의 형태가 있대. 2인 1조와 4인 1조. 여자의 경우에는 2인 1조만 있대.

Joe : There's only a two-man event for women! I never knew. I thought the women's event also included a four-man event.

여자들은 2인 1조만 있구나! 나도 이거 지금 알았어. 나는 여자들도 남자들처럼 4인 1조도 가능하다고 생각했거든.

Karen : It goes on. Bobsleigh was initially adopted in the 1924 Winter Olympics. But the women's event was adopted in 2002.

이게 끝이 아니야. 봅슬레이는 1924년 동계올림픽에서 처음으로 채택되었지만, 여자 경기는 2002년에 채택되었대.

Joe : It began in 1924? It has a long history.

1924년에 시작이 되었구나. 긴 역사를 가졌네.

Karen : Yes, but unfortunately it's still not a very popular game.

맞아. 그런데 안타깝게도 봅슬레이는 아직도 비인기 종목이야.

Joe : That's too bad. It's an exciting game to watch.

안타깝다. 신나는 경기인데.

The History

The word bobsleigh, or bobsledge, is a combination of the word 'bob', which was mainly used to describe the movement of bobsledders, and 'sled', a synonym of sledge. Sledge on snow or ice was generally used in northern European countries, where bobsleigh first appeared. The first competing event was held at St. Moritz at the Swiss Confederation in 1884. The track was at first a straight track, but as time passed, it was altered into a curved one. Also, the sled which was originally made of wood began to be made with metal.

In 1923, the Federation Internationale de Bobsleigh et de Tobaganning (FIBT) was established. In 1924, bobsleigh was initially adopted as an official sport that included only the men's four-man race; the two-man race was added in 1932. The women's event was accepted much later in the 1990s, then was officially adopted in the 2002 Winter Olympic games.

Korea became a member of the International Luge Federation in 1989, but formed the Korean Bobsleigh Skeleton Federation in 1992, and joined the International Bobsleigh and Skeleton Federation in 1999.

Top Athletes

Andre Lange was born on June 28, 1973 in Germany. Although now retired, he was a successful bobsledder. He holds four gold medals from Olympic competitions as well as various gold, silver, and bronze medals in the FIBT World Championships and World Cup events. He served as the bob pilot for his team in both the four-man and two-man events.

Andre Lange은 1973년 6월 28일 독일에서 태어났다. 현재 은퇴했으나 성공한 봅슬레이 선수다. 그는 4개의 올림픽 금메달을 획득했으며 FIBT 세계선수권대회와 월드컵에서 많은 금은동메달을 획득한 선수다. 그는 4인과 2인 종목에 모두 참가하며 조종사로 활약했다.

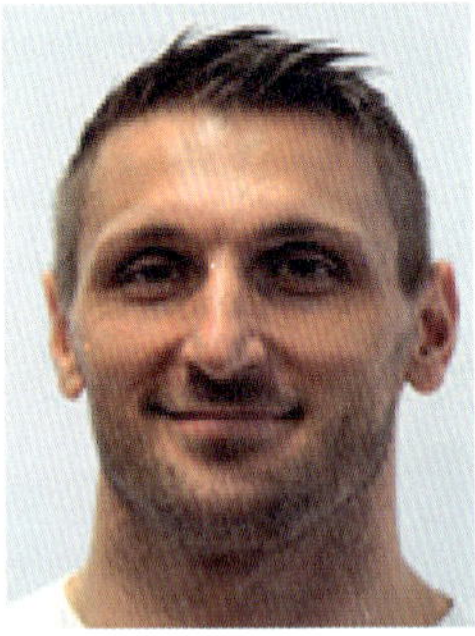

Kevin Kuske, a once sprinter athlete, was born on January 4, 1979 in Germany. Having won four gold medals in the Winter Olympics, alongside Andre Lange, this bobsledder earned medals in major competitions such as the FIBT World Championships.

달리기 선수로 선수 생활을 시작한 Kevin Kuske는 1979년 1월 4일 독일에서 태어났다. 그는 Andre Lange의 팀에서 함께 동계올림픽에서만 4개의 금메달을 받았으며 세계선수권대회와 같은 주요시합에서 많은 메달을 획득한 선수다.

Bernhard Germeshausen was born on August 21, 1951 in Germany. He was a bobsledder for the East German team prior to Germany's reunification. As an East German athlete he obtained three gold medals and one silver medal in the Winter Games.

Bernhard Germeshausen은 1951년 8월 21일 독일에서 태어났다. 그는 독일 통일 이전 동독의 대표로 선수 생활을 했다. 동독 대표선수로 동계올림픽에 참가하여 3개의 금메달과 1개의 은메달을 획득했다.

* Photo from Wikipedia

"How did it all start?"

KEY WORDS & EXPRESSIONS

over the years: 세월이 지나면서
that's new: 새롭다
hard to manage: 관리하기 힘들다
that's what I was thinking: 나도 그 생각을 하고 있었다
goes on and on: 계속 지속되다, 더 많다
come up: 나타나다
bob pilot: 봅슬레이 조종사

Joe : Karen, did you do your homework?
카렌, 너 숙제 했어?

Karen : Not yet. Did you?
아니, 아직 못 했어. 넌 숙제 했어?

Joe : Of course. By the way, why didn't you do your homework?
당연하지. 그런데, 왜 숙제 못 했어?

Karen : I was visiting my grandmother's house. She was sick, so I had to take care of her.
나 할머니 댁에 있었어. 할머니께서 편찮으셔서 돌봐드렸거든.

Joe : Hope she gets well soon. Do you need any help with your homework?
힘내! 할머님은 괜찮아질 거야. 그럼 지금부터 내가 숙제 도와줄게.

Karen : Oh thanks, Joe. You're too kind, my friend!
정말 고마워, 조. 넌 최고야, 친구!

Joe : Ok. First, we need to research the history of bobsleigh. But we already know that, right?
좋아 그럼. 먼저, 우리가 봅슬레이의 역사에 대해서 조사를 해야 하는데 우린 이미 알고 있어, 그렇지?

Karen : Yes, but I think we need more information.
맞아, 그런데 난 우리가 좀 더 정보가 필요하다고 생각해.

Joe : Here's what I researched. The origin of the word bobsleigh.
그래서 내가 조사를 했지. 자, 여기 있어. 이건 봅슬레이의 어원이야.

Karen : That's it? Oh, this picture, this is the first bobsleigh track, right?
단순하네. 와, 이거 최초의 봅슬레이 사진 맞지?

Joe : That's right. Look at this part. This is the track they used to use. Look, it was originally straight. It obviously changed into a curved track over the years.
맞아. 이 부분도 봐봐. 이 부분은 트랙 부분인데, 트랙이 처음에는 그냥 직선이었다가 시간이 지나면서 곡선 트랙이 되었어.

Karen : Well, that's new. Let me see... This is the body of the sled, right?

트랙의 변화는 새로 알게 되었네. 어디 보자, 이거 봅슬레이 차체 부분 맞지?

Joe : Yes. It was made of wood.

응. 봅슬레이는 나무로 만들어졌었어.

Karen : That has also changed. It's metal now. I think the wood body was hard to manage because of all the moisture wood picks up. It could also rot as a result.

하지만 금속 재질로 바뀌었지. 내 생각인데 나무 재질은 관리하기가 어려웠을 거야. 왜냐하면 나무 재질에 수분이 조금이라도 있으면 썩을 수가 있으니까.

Joe : That's what I was thinking. Oh my, there's so much history on this. The foundation of the institutes, date of adoption, the athletes. It goes on and on.

나랑 같은 생각이구나. 그 밖에도 많은 봅슬레이 기관들의 설립 역사, 봅슬레이가 동계올림픽에 채택된 과정 및 선수들 같은 역사들도 있어.

Karen : Let's focus on the athletes.

선수들에 집중해보자.

Joe : There are three major athletes who come up. Andre Lange, Kevin Kuske, and Bernhard Germeshausen. Guess what, they were all born in East Germany, before the unification. Lange and Kuske participated in the 2002 Winter Olympics with Lange as the pilot.

주요 선수 3명이 있어. Andre Lange, Kevin Kuske 그리고 Bernhard Germeshausen. 이것 참 흥미로운데. 세 선수 모두 통일 이전 동독 지역에서 태어났어. 그리고 Lange와 Kuske는 2002 동계올림픽에서 함께 참가했어. 그때 Lange가 조종사 하고.

Karen : Germany must be so proud to have so many top athletes in this game.

톱 선수들이 많아서 독일은 뿌듯하겠다.

Joe : I bet.

그렇겠지.

Equipment and Gear

Sledding suits 유니폼

Athletes wear tight suits with good elasticity to help them fit tightly into the sled.

선수들은 봅슬레이 썰매 안에서 몸이 밀착되기 때문에 신축성이 좋고, 몸에 달라붙는 유니폼을 입는다.

Helmets 헬멧

Athletes wear helmets to protect their head and prevent blinding from light reflected from the snow or ice.

선수들은 선수들의 머리를 보호하기 위해서 헬멧을 착용하며, 헬멧은 눈이나 얼음으로부터 반사되는 빛으로부터의 눈부심을 막는 역할을 한다.

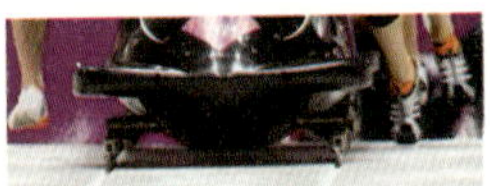

Start shoes 신발

Athletes use spiked shoes to increase friction when starting the push on ice.

선수들은 봅슬레이 경기에서 출발 시 얼음 위에서 마찰력을 필요로 하기 때문에 스파이크 신발을 신는다.

Sled 썰매

The sled is the most important equipment. The sled has specifications according to the number of people riding. The two-man has a maximum total weight of 390kg for men and 340kg for women. The four-man has a maximum total weight of 630kg.

썰매는 가장 중요한 장비이다. 타는 사람 수에 따른 제약이 있다. 2인조 썰매의 무게 규정은 최대 남자 390kg, 여자 340kg이며, 4인조 썰매는 630kg이다.

Parts of the Sled

- Cowling 덮개

  The cowling is made from metal or glass fiber.

  덮개는 금속 재질 혹은 유리섬유로 만들어진다.

	• Push handles 푸시 핸들 Push handles are used to push the bobsled. 푸시 핸들은 썰매를 밀 때 사용된다. • Steering system 조향 장치 The steering system is used to regulate direction. 조향 장치는 방향을 조절하는 데 사용된다. • Brakes 브레이크 Brakes are applied by using a lever in order to stop the sled. 브레이크는 썰매를 멈출 때 사용하며 레버를 이용한다.

* Photo from tutorialspoint.com

What is this contraption?

Joe : Hi, Karen. What are you doing, now?

안녕, 카렌. 지금 뭐 하고 있어?

Karen : Hi, Joe. I'm looking for some information on bobsleigh equipment. But it is so hard to find.

어, 안녕, 조. 난 지금 봅슬레이 장비에 대한 정보를 찾아보고 있어. 그런데 너무 찾기가 힘들어.

Joe : I see you are in a difficult situation. Ok, let me help you.

곤란해 보인다. 좋아, 내가 도와줄게.

Karen : You're a lifesaver, Joe!

고마워, 조!

Joe : Ok let's see. Look at this page. There's some basic information about bobsleigh equipment.

좋아, 어디 보자. 이 페이지 좀 봐봐. 여기에 봅슬레이 장비에 대한 기본적인 정보가 나와 있어.

Karen : Oh, the suit. It looks tight and that's because athletes need tight suits with a lot of elasticity.

오, 이건 유니폼이네. 달라붙게 생겼는데, 선수들은 신축성이 있는 옷이 필요해서 달라붙는 유니폼을 입는구나!

KEY WORDS & EXPRESSIONS

in a difficult situation: 어려운 환경에 처하다

lifesaver: 목숨을 구해준 사람

elasticity: 신축성

frictional force: 마찰력

tell the difference: 구분하다

count heads: 인원수를 세다

Joe : They also wear helmets to protect their head and prevent blinding from light reflected off the snow or ice.

게다가 선수들은 헬멧을 쓰는데, 이 헬멧은 머리 보호용이기도 하지만 얼음이나 눈에서 반사되는 빛을 막아주기도 하지.

Karen : Look at this. They use spiked shoes called start shoes. Let's see, oh here! When starting, they need frictional force. The spikes help increase friction so they can push the sled harder.

여길 봐봐. 선수들은 스타트 슈즈라고 하는 스파이크 신발을 사용해. 여기 있다! 선수들은 출발할 때 마찰력이 필요해. 신발에 장착된 스파이크가 마찰을 증대시키기 때문에 썰매를 더 힘 있게 밀 수 있는 거야.

Joe : Right, since the tracks are all ice. The shoes will stop you from slipping and let you run on it.

맞아, 트랙이 얼음으로 되었으니까 말이야. 이 신발을 신으면 미끄러지지 않고 달릴 수 있어.

Karen : What about the bobsleigh, or the sled?

썰매는?

Joe : There are two types of sleds.

썰매 두 가지가 있어.

Karen : I can't tell the difference.

어떻게 다른지 모르겠어.

Joe : That one's the two-man sled and this one is the four-man sled. The width of the two is the same, but the length is different. The two-man is 2.7 meters long and the four-man is 3.8 meters long.

하나는 2인용이고 또 다른 하나는 4인용이야. 두 썰매 모두 넓이는 같은데 길이가 달라. 2인용은 2.7m고 4인용은 3.8m야.

Karen : An easier way is to just count heads, I guess.

더 쉬운 방법은 인원수를 세는 거겠지?

해 석

An Introduction to the Game

봅슬레이는 좌우 방향조절이 가능한 썰매를 타고 얼음으로 만들어진 트랙을 달리는 경기이다. 봅슬레이는 '봅슬레지'로도 불리며, 봅슬레이의 무게는 2인승의 경우 최대 375kg의 제한이, 4인승의 경우에는 최대 630kg의 제한이 있다. 봅슬레이의 평균속도는 120~140km정도이며, 트랙의 총 길이는 1,500m이다.

봅슬레이 경기는 남자의 경우 2인 1조, 4인 1조의 두 개의 경기 종류가 있으며, 여자의 경우에는 2인 1조의 경기만 있다. 또한, 봅슬레이는 1924년 동계올림픽에서 최초로 정식 종목으로 채택이 되었으며, 2002년에는 여자 2인 경기가 채택되었다.

The History

봅슬레이 또는 봅슬레지의 어원은 썰매를 탄 선수들이 몸을 앞뒤로 끄덕거리는 모습을 묘사한 '봅(bob)'과 썰매를 의미하는 '슬레드(sled)'가 합쳐진 데서 시작되었다. 지구 북반부에 위치한 나라들 사이에서는 눈 또는 얼음 위에서 썰매를 타는 놀이가 일반적이었는데, 봅슬레이는 바로 이것으로부터 유래한 스포츠이다.

최초의 비공식 경기는 1884년 스위스 장크트모리츠에서 열렸다. 봅슬레이의 트랙도 시간이 지남에 따라 일직선에서 곡선 주로의 형태로 변하게 되었고, 나무로 만들어진 봅슬레이도 금속 재질로 바뀌었다. 1923년에는 국제봅슬레이연맹(FIBT)이 창설되었다. 1924년에는 최초로 동계올림픽 정식 종목으로 채택이 되었고, 남자 4인 경기가 선보였으며, 1932년에는 남자 2인 경기가 추가되었다. 여자 봅슬레이의 경우 시작은 1990년 초였으나, 정식 종목 채택을 받은 것은 2002년 동계올림픽 때였다. 한국의 경우, 1989년 국제루지연맹(FIL)에 가입하였으며, 1992년에는 대한 루지봅슬레이연맹을 창립, 1999년에는 국제봅슬레이연맹에 가입했다.

CROSS COUNTRY SKIING

크로스컨트리 스키

04

EVENTS

MEN'S EVENTS

15km men
4x10km relay men
50km men
15km+15km Skiathlon
Sprint 1.5km men
Team Sprint men

WOMEN'S EVENTS

10km women
30km women
4X5km relay women
7.5km+7.5km Skiathlon
Sprint 1.5km women
Team Sprint women

An Introduction to the Game

Cross-country skiing requires traveling on skis over snow-covered terrain, where skiers rely on their own locomotion rather than on ski lifts. Modern cross-country skiing shares self-locomotion as a core attribute with the original form of skiing, in which all skiing disciplines evolved from, including alpine skiing, ski jumping and telemark skiing. It is widely practiced as a sport and leisure activity; however it is still used as a means of transportation. Variants of cross-country skiing have been adapted to a wide range of terrain which spans from unimproved, sometimes mountainous terrain to groomed courses that are specifically designed for the

sport. Skiers propel themselves either by striding forward (classic style) or side-to-side in a skating motion (skate skiing), aided by the arms pushing on ski poles against the snow. It is practiced in regions with snow-covered landscapes, including Northern Europe, Canada, Russia and Alaska. Competitive cross-country skiing is a type of Nordic skiing sport. Cross-country skiing is also one of the two components in biathlon.

"What is Cross Country Skiing?"

KEY WORDS & EXPRESSIONS

glide: 활주

swing: 흔들다

Joe : Have you ever gone cross country skiing?
너 크로스컨트리 스키를 해본 적 있니?

Karen : Sure.
물론이지.

Joe : Do you think I could learn too?
나도 배울 수 있을까?

Karen : Of course. The basic techniques are pretty easy. I'll teach you.
그럼 당연하지. 기본 기술은 아주 쉬워. 내가 가르쳐줄게.

Joe : OK.
그래.

Karen : Are you ready?
준비됐니?

Joe : I think so. Now how am I supposed to move?
그런 것 같아. 이제 어떻게 몸을 움직이면 될까?

Karen : It's very simple. What you want to do is stretch every step you take to get the most glide. And you swing your arms to gain momentum.
매우 간단해. 네가 해야 할 일은 잘 미끄러질 수 있도록 한 걸음 한 걸음 보폭을 넓히는 거야. 그리고 힘을 얻기 위해 팔을 흔들어.

Joe : Wow, this is great!
와, 신난다!

Karen : Good! You're doing fine! You've got the idea.
좋아! 잘한다! 넌 이제 요령을 알았어.

The History

The origin of the words in the phrase 'snow skiing in new shoes' in Norwegian and English includes 'skid(skid)', 'skip', 'ski(skiff)', 'slide(slide)', and 'skate(skate)'. Skiing existed thousands of years ago in primitive times allowing those living in the Nordic and mountainous Altai Siberia regions, as well as those in the snow-covered hills of Scandinavia to utilize it for transport and to adjust to the harsh winter months. Skiing was also used in this region as a military tactic. Gradually, inhabitants from these areas grew to enjoy skiing as a sports activity.

Skiing originally developed from a means of transportation on heavily snowed areas of land. The type of terrain determines the different methods of skiing. Relatively gentle hills make up the Nordic areas, and therefore, street competitions and jumps developed in this area. Nordic skiing includes cross-country skiing marathon, the ski jump going down a steep path, and a combination of both in the Nordic combined.

Cross country skiing is one of the oldest sports of all time, in both the Summer and Winter Olympics. Cross country skiing was adopted as an official Olympic game in 1924 in Chamonix, France. Cross-country skiing requires stamina, a strong mentality, and a competitive spirit to endure the long course. Different rules and techniques, such as the classic and freestyle glides, are applied to specific events.

Top Athletes

Bjørn Dæhlie was born on June 19, 1967. He thrived as a cross country skier winning a total of 29 medals in the Olympics and World Championships combined over a period of eight years. He is retired and is now a successful businessman in Norway.

Bj ø rn Dæhlie는 1967년 6월 19일에 태어났다. 그는 크로스컨트리 스키 선수로 활약하며 8년 사이에 올림픽과 세계선수권대회에서 총 29개의 메달을 얻었다. 지금은 은퇴했으나 현재 노르웨이에서 성공한 비즈니스맨으로 산다.

Marit Bjoergen was born on March 21, 1980 in Norway. She is a female cross country skier and holder of six gold Olympic medals. She won three gold medals in the 2010 games and three gold medals in the 2014 games.

Marit Bjoergen은 1980년 3월 21일 노르웨이에서 태어났다. 그녀는 여성 크로스컨트리 스키 선수이자 올림픽 금메달 6개의 보유자다. 그녀는 2010년과 2014년 동계올림픽에서 각각 세 개의 금메달을 목에 걸었다.

Lyubov Yegorova was born on May 5, 1966 in Russia. As a female Olympic champion in cross country skiing, she won nine medals, including six gold medals and three silver medals, in the Winter Olympics. However, her many medals have been tainted after being disqualified in 1997 for testing positive for doping.

Lyubov Yegorova는 1966년 5월 5일 러시아에서 태어났다. 여성 크로스컨트리 스키 선수로서 올림픽에서 총 9개의 메달을 획득했으며 그중 6개는 금메달, 3개는 은메달이었다. 그러나 그녀는 1997년 도핑 검사를 통과하지 못해 실격처리되었다.

* Photo from Wikipedia&Sputnik Images&Getty Images

"How did it all start?"

> **KEY WORDS & EXPRESSIONS**
>
> oldest sports: 가장 오래된 종목
>
> date back to: 역사가 (시점) 까지 거슬러 올라가다
>
> get what you mean (know what you mean): 뜻을 이해하다
>
> early on: 초기에

Joe : Cross country skiing is one of the oldest sports in both the Summer and Winter Olympics combined.

크로스컨트리 스키는 하계와 동계올림픽 통틀어 가장 오래된 스포츠 중 하나야.

Karen : I know. It dates back about a thousand years.

글쎄 말이야. 천 년 전부터 존재했어.

Joe : Yes, but back then, it wasn't a sport. People were using skis in their daily lives to get across the snow.

그래, 그러나 그 당시에는 스포츠가 아니었지. 사람들이 눈 위에서 이동하기 위해 일상생활에서 스키를 사용하고 있었지.

Karen : Can you imagine what it was like for people who didn't have skis back then? They would've been isolated.

그 당시 그 사람들이 스키가 없었다고 상상해봐. 고립됐을 거야.

Joe : But how do you think people transformed it into a sport?

그런데 사람들이 어떻게 이것을 스포츠로 발전시켰을까?

Karen : I'm sure it's like many snow sports like the biathlon or alpine skiing. People just started having fun with the form of transportation. Maybe a few people started having races, which grew into small competitions, and then gradually into a sport.

눈 위에서 하는 다른 스포츠와 비슷할 것 같아. 예를 들어 바이애슬론이나 알파인 스키나. 사람들이 일상적인 교통수단으로 재미있게 변경시킨 거지. 몇 명이 시합을 하기 시작한 것이 점차 작은 시합으로 발전되고 나중에 스포츠 형태로까지 온 거지.

Joe : That's very general. But I get what you mean. I heard that cross country skiing was adopted as an official Olympic sport very early on in 1924 in France.

참 광범위한 설명이지만 그 뜻은 이해해. 크로스컨트리는 아주 일찍 1924년 프랑스에서 공식 올림픽 종목으로 채택되었다고 들었어.

Karen : Right. And it has some top women athletes as well. Other skiing sports don't mention many top women athletes, but this sport records two women out of the top three skiers.

맞아. 그리고 이 종목에서는 주요 선수 중 여성도 포함됐어. 다른 스키 관련 종목은 주요 선수로 여성이 흔하지 않지만, 이 종목에서는 주요 선수 3명 중 2명이나 여성 선수야.

Equipment and Gear

Skate Skis 스케이트 스키

Skate skis are short and firmer than classic skis. They have a smooth bottom like those used for downhill skiing. Skate skis are preferred for skating and doing technical skills.

클래식 스키보다 조금 짧고 단단하다. 다운힐 스키와 비슷하게 바닥이 매끄럽게 되어 있다. 이 종류는 스케이트나 기술적인 스키를 탈 때 선호된다.

Classic skis 클래식 스키

Classic skis are rather long with a different bottom pattern than skate skis. There are two types of classic skis, the waxable ski and the waxless ski.

스케이트 스키보다 조금 길고 바닥이 다른 패턴으로 되어 있다. 클래식 스키에는 바닥에 왁스를 바를 수 있는 waxable과 왁스를 바를 수 없는 waxless의 두 가지가 있다.

Roller skis 롤러 스키

Roller skis are on-road skis for training in the summer. They help to develop physical strength and keep a sense of skiing during off-seasons.

눈이 없는 여름철에 도로에서 타는 훈련용 스키이다. 스키 시즌이 아닐 때 체력을 기르고 스키 감각을 잃지 않기 위한 장비이다.

Skate poles 스케이트 폴

Skate skis use long poles. Skate poles come up between the nose and the lips.

긴 폴을 사용한다. 보통 입술과 코 사이에 오는 것이 적당하다.

	**Classic poles 클래식 폴** Classic skis use shorter poles, unlike those used in skate ski. Classic poles come up to the shoulders or right underneath the shoulder. 스케이트 스키보다 짧은 폴을 사용한다. 보통 어깨 근처 혹은 조금 밑에 오는 것이 적당하다.
	**Skate ski boots 스케이트 스키 부츠** Skate ski boots are long and the bottom is hard to increase support during techniques. 테크닉을 구사하는 동안 지지력을 높이도록 길고 바닥이 단단하게 되어있다.
	**Classic ski boots 클래식 스키 부츠** Classic ski boots are softer than skate ski boots. It is perfect for pushing and lifting the feet. 스케이트 스키 부츠보다 더 부드러워 발을 밀거나 드는 데 좋다.

What is this contraption?

Joe : I heard you were thinking of going skiing this weekend.
이번 주말에 스키를 타러 간다고 들었어.

KEY WORDS & EXPRESSIONS

hit the slopes: 스키 타다

Karen : Yes, I'm planning on going skiing on Saturday. Would you like to go skiing with me?
응, 토요일에 스키 타러 갈 계획이야. 나랑 같이 스키 타러 갈래?

Joe : No, I don't have any ski gear. Did you get your skiing equipment already?
아니, 나는 장비가 없어서 스키 타러 못 가. 너는 스키 장비들을 준비했니?

Karen : Of course. Before you hit the slopes, make sure you wear well-fitting clothing and use proper equipment. I bought skis, poles and boots a month ago. Let me see… Ah! Here it is.
물론이지. 스키를 타기 전에는 몸에 맞는 복장과 적절한 장비를 착용했는지 확인해야 해. 나는 스케이트 스키에 필요한 스키, 폴, 부츠를 한 달 전에 구입했지. 어디 보자, 여기 있다.

Joe : Let me see the equipment. Wow, this is expensive ski gear, complete with designer shades.

구경 좀 할게. 와, 이건 고급스런 디자인 색조로 마감된 값비싼 스키 장비잖아.

Karen : I decided to buy the top brand.

이왕에 사기로 했으면 좋은 걸로 사야지.

Joe : Well, where did you buy it? I don't think these boots will do for skate skiing. They are soft on the bottom. These boots are for classic ski.

그런데 그거 어디서 산 거니? 이 부츠는 스케이트 스키용 부츠가 아니야. 바닥이 부드러운걸. 이건 클래식 스키를 위한 부츠야.

Karen : Really? What am I going to do?

정말? 이를 어쩌지?

Joe : Fortunately, everything else is fine. Your skate skis are short and firm. And your skate pole is long. But these boots are for skate skis.

다행히, 다른 건 다 괜찮아. 네 스케이트 스키는 짧고 단단하고, 스케이트 폴은 길어. 스케이트 스키를 위한 것들이야.

SPORTS FACTS

CROSS COUNTRY SKIING

- First contested date in the Olympics :
  The 1st Olympic Winter Games in Chamonix 1924
- Nation of origin :
  Northern Norway
- Types of events :
  Interval start, Mass start, Skiathlon, Relay, Sprint
- Type of arena :
  A long course across plains and hills
- Race time :
  Timed according to each event
- Country with most medals :
  Norway

Athlete with most medals :
  Bjorn Daehlie (12 medals: 8 gold and 4 silver medals)

- Youngest athlete :
  Mariya Colaroseuka (16 years old)

해 석

An Introduction to the Game

크로스컨트리 스키는 스키를 타는 사람이 리프트보다도 그들 자신의 운동 능력에 의지하여 눈 덮인 지형을 스키로 달리는 것이다. 현대의 크로스컨트리 스키는 알파인 스키와 스키점프, 텔레마크 스키를 포함하고 있다. 이것은 스포츠 또는 여가 활동으로서 널리 행해졌지만, 어떤 사람들은 여전히 이것을 교통 수단으로서 사용한다. 변형된 크로스컨트리 스키는 다듬어지지 않은 산악지형과 때때로 스포츠를 위해 특별히 만들어진 코스가 있는 산이 많은 지형에 적합하도록 되어있다. 스키를 타는 사람들은 눈 위에서 스키 폴을 밀고 앞으로 나아가거나 좌우로 스케이팅을 하면서 앞으로 나아간다. 크로스컨트리 스키는 북유럽, 캐나다, 러시아 그리고 알래스카를 포함하여 눈 덮인 풍경이 펼쳐지는 지역에서 행해진다. 경쟁적인 크로스컨트리 스키는 노르딕 스키 스포츠 중의 하나이다. 크로스컨트리와 사격을 결합한 복합 스포츠 종목으로서 바이애슬론이 있다.

The History

스키의 어원은 '눈 위에서 신는 신발'을 뜻하는 노르웨이어와 영어의 '스키드(skid)', '스킵(skip)', '스키프(skiff)', '슬라이드(slide)', '스케이트(skate)' 등의 단어에서 찾아 볼 수 있다. 원시적 스키는 수천 년 전에 이미 고안되어 북유럽 · 시베리아 · 알타이의 산악지방에서 사용되었던 것으로 추정되며, 특히 북유럽 스칸디나비아반도의 눈 덮인 구릉지에서 일찍부터 겨울철 교통수단으로 발달하였다. 스키는 전쟁 수단으로 이용이 되다가 오락으로 즐기는 과정을 거쳐 스포츠의 형태로 자리를 잡게 되었다.

스키는 원래 눈이 많이 쌓인 곳에서 이동 수단으로 발전한 것인 만큼 지형에 따라 그 형태도 다른 방향으로 발전하였다. 비교적 완만한 구릉지대를 이루는 북유럽 지역에서는 거리경기와 점프를 겨루는 노르딕 스키가 발달하였다. 노르딕 스키는 설원의 마라톤이라 불리는 크로스컨트리 스키와 급경사면을 활강하다 도약하여 허공을 비행하는 스키점프, 그리고 이 두 가지를 합친 노르딕 복합으로 구분된다.

하계 및 동계올림픽 종목을 통틀어 가장 오랜 역사를 지닌 종목 가운데 하나인 크로스컨트리 스키는 1924년 프랑스의 샤모니에서 열린 제1회 동계올림픽 경기대회부터 노르딕 스키(크로스컨트리 · 스키점프 · 노르딕 복합)가 정식 종목으로 채택되었다.

평지와 언덕을 가로질러 긴 코스를 완주하는 경기로서 강인한 체력과 정신력을 갖추어야 하며, 세부 종목에 따라 클래식 주법과 프리스타일 주법의 활주법을 지정하는 것이 특징이다.

05 CURLING
컬링

EVENTS

MEN'S EVENTS
Curling men

WOMEN'S EVENTS
Curling women

An Introduction to the Game

Curling is a sport originating from Scotland. This sport is played on ice. Two teams play the game. One team consists of 4 players. Players direct the stone to approach a circle-shaped target called the house. Curling was adopted as an official sport in the 1998 Winter Olympics.

Talking about the Game

Joe : Karen, have you heard of curling?

컬링에 대해 들어본 적이 있니?

Karen : No, I haven't. What is curling?

없어. 컬링이 뭐야?

Joe : Curling is a kind of sport played on ice. It is one of the official sports events in the Winter Olympics.

컬링은 빙상스포츠의 일종이고 공식적인 올림픽 종목이야.

Karen : Oh, really? How many players are on a team?

정말? 한 팀에 선수는 몇 명이니?

Joe : A team consists of 4 players. Players use a ball, or stone. The player directs the stone to approach a target named house.

한 팀은 네 명의 선수로 구성되어 있어. 네 명의 선수는 스톤을 하우스라 불리는 원 모양의 표적으로 가깝게 가도록 만들어.

Karen : Anything else?

또 아는 것 없니?

Joe : Actually that is all I know about curling. Do you want to look for more information with me?

사실 내가 컬링에 대해 알고 있는 것은 그게 다야. 나와 함께 컬링에 대해 더 많은 정보를 찾아보지 않을래?

Karen : Sure. Let's look together.

그래. 우리 같이 찾아보자.

KEY WORDS & EXPRESSIONS

ice: 빙상

players: 선수

stone: 컬링 스톤

target: 목표

The History

Curling was invented in Scotland in the Middle Ages. Since Scotland's rivers froze every winter, Scotland was the perfect environment to play curling. Thus curling flourished from the 1600s to the 1900s. Curling began with a stone which players picked up from the river. They used this stone as the curling stone. At that time, there was no standardized size for the curling stone, making it impossible for the thrower to control the path and boundaries of the curling stone. Players basically depended on luck over skills. Curling was also called "the roaring game". This was because the sound of the sliding stone was similar to that of a roaring sound. But these days, it is also referred to as "chess on ice".

The name curling has its roots in the verb curl that describes the motion of the stone. Although the first form of curling appeared in Scotland, Canada is currently the strongest in the sport of curling. This may be because Canada has many immigrants from Scotland. However, it was the Scottish emigrants who introduced curling to other nations such as Switzerland and Sweden in the 1900s that propelled the sport to be played all across the globe.

The world's first ever curling competition was held in Scotland in the 1959 Scotch Cup, but it was limited to men. It became an official Olympic sport in 1998 and now includes both men's and women's events.

Top Athletes

Eva Lund was born on May 1, 1971 in Sweden. She is a two time gold medalist, winning in the 2006 and 2010 Winter Olympics. She has participated in many championships and boasts a range of medals. She is now retired.

Eva Lund는 1971년 스웨덴에서 태어났다. 2006년과 2010년 동계올림픽에서 2번 금메달을 획득했다. 또 다양한 경기에 참가하여 수많은 메달을 보유하고 있으나 현재 은퇴한 선수다.

Anna Le Moine was born on October 30, 1973. She led the Swedish team to victory in the 2006 Turin Winter Olympics. She also received a gold in the 2010 Vancouver Winter Olympics. She is still a member of the Swedish team.

Anna Le Moine은 1973년 10월 30일에 태어났다. 스웨덴 대표팀을 이끌어 2006년 토리노 동계올림픽에서 금메달을 얻었다. 2010년 밴쿠버 동계올림픽에서도 금메달을 획득했다. 현재 스웨덴 국가대표팀의 일원으로 활동한다.

Anette Norberg was born on November 12, 1966 in Sweden. Beginning her curling career at the age of ten, she has prized in the world championships and received numerous gold medals in the European championships. She has also, along with her team, received gold medals in both the 2006 Turin and 2010 Vancouver Olympics.

Anette Norberg는 1966년 11월 12일 스웨덴에서 태어났다. 10살이라는 어린 나이에 컬링을 시작하여 세계선수권대회에서 수많은 메달을 얻었으며 유럽리그 대회에서도 많은 금메달을 획득했다. 대표팀과 함께 2006년 토리노와 2010년 밴쿠버 올림픽에서도 금메달을 땄다.

* Photo from Wikipedia

"How did it all start?"

KEY WORDS & EXPRESSIONS

last: 지난/최근

in the lead: 앞장서다

consecutive (in a row): 연속

Scots (Scottish): 스코틀랜드 사람

Joe : Canada's curling team is so good! They won in both the women's and men's events in the last Sochi Olympics.

캐나다 컬링 팀 너무 잘한다! 소치에서 여성과 남성 팀 모두 금메달을 땄어.

Karen : But, in 2010 and in 2006 the Swedish team was definitely in the lead.

그러나 2010년과 2006년에는 스웨덴 팀이 앞섰어.

Joe : But that was only in the women's events. Canada's men's team won both those years. That makes three consecutive gold medals for Canada's men.

여자 팀만 이겼지. 사실 그해 남자 경기에서는 모두 캐나다가 우승했어. 캐나다 남자 팀은 3연속 금메달을 획득한 거야.

Karen : Really? Why are they so good at it? Do you think it started there?

정말? 왜 그렇게 잘할까? 그 나라에서 시작했을까?

Joe : I don't think so. I read somewhere that it started in Scotland around the Middle Ages with people rolling or gliding stones over frozen rivers.

아닌 것 같아. 어디서 읽었는데, 중세시대 스코틀랜드에서 시작한 스포츠야. 일부 사람들이 돌을 언 강 위에서 굴리기 시작한 거지.

Karen : So the Middle Ages weren't so gloomy after all.

중세시대가 그렇게 침울하지는 않았네.

Joe : Yes, but it was still a very unrefined and rough sport then. The ground was so rough that the stones gliding on the ice made roaring sounds. That's why people even called it "the roaring game".

그러나 그 당시는 아직 게임이 투박했지. 스톤이 지나가는 얼음이 너무 거칠어서 으르렁 하는 소리가 나서 사람들이 으르렁거리는 경기라고도 불렀다고 해.

Karen : But not anymore! It's "chess on ice" now.

이제는 그 이미지에서 벗어나 얼음 위의 바둑이라고 불리고 있지.

Joe : And it's Canada's area of strength, not the Scots.

그리고 이제는 스코틀랜드보다 캐나다의 주 종목이 됐지.

Karen : But the Scots did bring the game into Canada and other nations, like

Sweden and Switzerland, when they immigrated there.

그래도 스코틀랜드 사람들이 캐나다와 스웨덴과 스위스에 이민 가면서 소개했다고 볼 수 있지.

Joe : Thanks to the Scots, nations all over the world are enjoying this game.

스코틀랜드 사람들 덕분에 전 세계의 나라에서 이 게임을 즐길 수 있게 됐네.

Equipment and Gear

Curling sheet 컬링 시트

A curling sheet is a field of ice. The standard size recognized by the World Curling Federation is 45 to 46 meters long and 4.4 to 5 meters wide. The round target at the end of the sheet is called a "house" and is made up of three different sized circles that are either painted on the ice or marked in vinyl. The diameters of the rings from inside out are 4, 8, and 12 feet. The house is divided into 4 equal sections. The button is the middle of house where the center line and tee line intersect. Two hog lines are drawn 11 meters from and parallel to the backboard. The hack is drawn 12 feet behind each button. Usually in indoor rinks, the hack is installed on each end of the center line.

컬링 시트는 얼음 위에 만든 경기장이다. 길이는 45~46m, 너비는 4.4~5m이며 이 크기는 세계 컬링 규정에 의해 규격화되어 있다. 시트의 끝에는 원 모양의 하우스가 그려져 있다. 하우스는 세 개의 다른 크기의 원으로 만들어진다. 이 원들은 얼음 위에 칠해지거나 색깔을 입힌 비닐로 표시한다. 이 원들의 지름은 각 4, 8, 12피트이다. 하우스는 네 개로 나누어진다. 버튼은 하우스의 중심으로 센터라인과 티라인의 교차점이다. 두 개의 호그라인은 11m로 백보드와 평행하게 만들어진다. 해크는 각각의 버튼 12피트 뒤에 설치된다. 대체적으로 실내 링크에서 해크는 센터라인의 끝에 설치된다.

Stopwatch 스톱워치

Used to measure the speed of the stone when sweeping. It is usually attached to the clothes or a broom.

스위핑 할 때 스톤의 속도를 측정하기 위해 사용하며 옷이나 브룸에 부착한다.

Curling stone 컬링 스톤

The curling stone is a thick stone shaped in the form of a discus. It weighs between 17 to 20kg. The maximum circumference of the stone is 91cm, and is a minimum of 11cm in height. There is a handle on the top, which is fixed by bolts. The handle allows the curlers to grab the stone and spin it. The color of the stone is used to differentiate teams.

컬링 스톤은 원반 형태의 두꺼운 돌이며 무게는 17~20kg이다. 최대 둘레는 91cm, 최소 높이는 11cm이다. 위에는 손잡이가 있는데 볼트로 고정되어 있다. 그래서 핸들을 잡고 회전을 시킬 수 있다. 핸들은 팀을 구분하기 위해 색이 칠해져 있다.

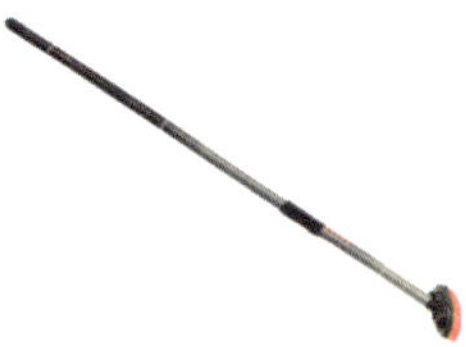

Curling broom 컬링 브룸

The curling broom, also called "a brush", is used to sweep the surface of the ice to set a course for the stone. Initially, the broom was made of corn strands and looked much like the broom used for cleaning. These days, the curling brush is made of fabric, pig or horse hair. The handles of the broom are made of fiberglass or carbon fiber, which is more durable than wood and is lighter, thus helping sweepers sweep quickly.

컬링 브룸은 스톤이 지나가는 얼음 위의 경로를 닦는 것이며 브러시라고도 불린다. 초기의 브룸은 옥수수 가지로 만들어졌었다. 또한 가정의 빗자루와도 비슷했다. 컬링 브러시는 섬유, 돼지 털, 말총으로 만들어진다. 요즘 브룸의 손잡이는 섬유유리나 탄소섬유로 만들어진다. 이 소재들은 나무보다 강하다. 또한 무게도 가볍고 스위퍼가 더 빨리 스위핑을 할 수 있게 한다.

Curling pants 컬링용 바지

Made with fabric to make throwing, stretching, or bending easier for the curlers.

선수들이 다리를 펴거나 구부리는 것을 쉽게 하도록 섬유로 만들어졌다.

Shoes 신발

Curling shoes are similar to ordinary sneakers, but have two different features for movement on ice; the slider shoe and the non-sliding shoe. The slider shoe feature helps curlers slide stably on the ice. Teflon sole bottoms are commonly used. Slider shoes are worn by throwers who throw the stone when they push the hack, or by the sweeper and skip for a faster slide and sweep. Curlers who don't throw wear grippers on their shoe, or wear non-sliding shoe. The non-sliding shoe have a special rubber sole to prevent sliding However, if Teflon or vinyl tape is attached, it can be used as a slider shoe.

컬링 신발은 다른 종목의 운동선수들이 사용하는 운동화와 비슷하다. 그렇지만 얼음 위에서 움직임을 돕기 위하여 두 개의 다른 특징을 가졌다. 한쪽은 슬라이더라 불리고 다른 한쪽은 논슬라이더라고 한다. 슬라이더는 선수가 빙판 위에서 안정적으로 미끄러지도록 한다. 일반적으로 테플론이 바닥 소재로 사용된다. 슬라이더를 신는 경우는 스로워들이 해크를 밀면서 스톤을 던질 때, 혹은 스위퍼나 스킵이 스위핑을 위해 얼음 위를 미끄러질 때나 시트 위에서 좀 더 빨리 이동하기 위해 신는다. 스로잉을 하지 않을 때에는 그리퍼를 덧붙이면 논슬라이더로 사용할 수 있다. 일반적인 운동화에 테플론이나 비닐테이프를 바닥에 붙이면 슬라이더로 사용할 수 있다. 논슬라이더는 잘 미끄러지지 않는 소재로 만든다. 바닥의 소재는 일반적인 운동화와 비슷하거나 특수한 고무재질로 만든다.

Curling gloves 컬링 글러브

Keep hands warm and help grab the broom comfortably.

손의 온도를 유지하고 브룸을 잡을 때 편하도록 한다.

* Photo from Wikipedia

What is this contraption?

Joe : Did you find the information on curling equipment?

컬링 장비에 대해 찾아봤니?

Karen : Yeah. I found seven kinds of curling equipment.

응. 7개의 장비를 찾았어.

Joe : Can you explain them to me?

나에게 설명해 줄래?

Karen : Sure. There is the curling sheet, stone, broom, shoes, pants, stopwatch and gloves. First, the curling sheet is installed on the ice and that is where curling is played. It is a standard size set by the World Curling Federation.

장비로는 컬링 시트, 컬링 스톤, 컬링 브룸, 신발, 컬링 바지, 스톱워치 그리고 컬링 장갑이 있어. 먼저 컬링 시트는 컬링을 하기 위해 빙상에 만든 것으로 규격은 세계컬링연맹 규정에 의해 규격화 되어 있어.

Joe : Can you explain in more detail?

좀 더 세부적으로 말해 줄래?

Karen : The length is 45 to 46 meters long, and it is 4.4 to 5 meters in width. Also there are three rings called the house.

길이는 45~46m, 너비는 4.4~5m야. 또한 하우스라고 불리는 세 개의 다른 원들이 있어.

Joe : What's the difference between the three rings?

세 개의 원에 차이점이 있어?

Karen : Well, each ring has a different diameter. The diameters are 4, 8, and 12 feet. In the middle of the house where the center line and tee line intersect, is the button. And two hog lines are drawn 11 meters from and parallel to the backboard. Last, there is the hack that is drawn 12 feet behind each button. Usually the hack is installed at the end of the center line in most

KEY WORDS & EXPRESSIONS

- equipment: 장비
- standard size: 규정된 규격
- World Curling Federation: 세계 컬링 연맹
- house: 컬링 표적
- rings: 컬링 표적의 부분
- button: 컬링 표적의 가장 중간 지점
- indoor rink: 실내 경기장
- discus: 원반
- circumference: 둘레
- tell them apart: 구분하다
- maintain temperature: 온도를 유지하다

indoor rinks.

물론이지. 각각 원의 지름은 4, 8, 12피트야. 버튼이라는 것이 있는데 하우스의 중심이고 센터라인과 티라인이 교차하는 곳이지. 또한 호그라인은 두 개의 선이 백보드로부터 11m 떨어진 위치에 백보드와 평행하게 표시되어 있어. 마지막으로 해크는 양 버튼의 12피트 뒤에 설치되어 있는데, 보통 실내 링크에서는 센터라인의 끝에 설치돼.

Joe : How about the stone and broom?

스톤과 브룸은?

Karen : The stone is shaped in the form of a discus and weighs 17 to 20kg. There is a handle on the top, which is fixed by bolts. The handle allows curlers to grab the stone and spin it. The stone's circumference can be a maximum of 91cm and the height can be a minimum of 11cm. The colors of the handles are used to tell the teams apart. Next, the broom is used for sweeping the ice surface to set the course of the stone. The end of the broom is called the brush. The curling brush is made of fabric, or pig and horse hair. These days the handles are made of fiberglass or carbon fiber, which is much stronger than wood. Also, it's light and helps the sweeper sweep fast.

스톤은 원반의 형태이고 17~20kg의 무게야. 위에 손잡이가 있고 볼트로 고정되어 있어. 그렇기에 손잡이를 잡아서 회전을 시킬 수 있어. 스톤의 최대 둘레는 91cm, 최소 높이는 11cm야. 보통 손잡이는 팀의 구별을 위해 색이 칠해져 있어. 그리고 브룸은 스톤이 얼음 위를 지나가는 경로를 닦는 도구이며 브룸의 끝은 브러시라고 해. 브룸은 직물, 돼지 털 혹은 말총으로 만들어지지. 요즘 브룸의 손잡이는 섬유유리나 탄소섬유로 만들어져. 이 재료들은 나무보다 강하고 무게도 가벼우며 스위퍼가 더 빠르게 스위핑할 수 있게 해줘.

Joe : I heard there are special curling shoes? What is so special about the shoes?

아까 컬링할 때 신발을 사용한다고 했지? 그 신발에는 무언가 특별한 것이 있어?

Karen : Yes. they have two different features that help movement on the ice.

맞아. 신발에는 얼음 위를 움직이기 위해 다른 두 가지 특징이 있어.

Joe : What feature?

그 특징이 뭐야?

Karen : There is the slider side that lets curlers slide stably on the ice. When the curler isn't throwing, they wear the gripper on the shoe. So the curler at this time uses a non-sliding shoe. But if Teflon or vinyl tape is added on the bottom, sliding is possible. Soles of non-sliding shoes are made of rubber material similar to sneakers.

컬러가 얼음 위를 안정적으로 미끄러지게 해주는 슬라이드라고 하는 신발 한 짝이 있어. 스로잉을 하지 않을 때는 그리퍼를 신발에 신지. 즉 컬러가 이때에는 논슬라이더라 불리는 신발을 사용하는 거야. 하지만 테플론이나 비닐테이프를 바닥에 붙이면 슬라이딩이 가능하게 돼. 논슬라이더의 바닥은 운동화와 유사한 고무 재질로 만들어져 있어.

Joe : Now there are three kinds of equipment left.

이제 세 개가 남았군.

Karen : The pants, stopwatch and gloves. Curling pants make the movement of the legs easy, allowing the thrower to bend or stretch.

컬링 바지, 스톱워치 그리고 컬링 장갑이 남았어. 컬링 바지는 스로워들이 다리를 굽혔다가 펼 수 있게 해줘.

Joe : How about the stopwatch?

스톱워치는?

Karen : The stopwatch is used to measure the speed of the stone. It is attached to clothes or a broom. Finally, the gloves help maintain the temperature of the hands. That way the hands can grab the broom more comfortably.

스톱워치는 스톤의 속도를 측정하기 위해 사용하지. 스톱워치는 옷이나 브룸 위에 부착해서 사용해. 마지막으로 컬링 장갑은 손의 온도를 유지하고 브룸을 잡을 때 좀 더 편하도록 해줘.

Joe : I see. Next time, I'll look into how to curling is played.

다음에는 컬링을 하는 방법에 대하여 조사해 올게.

SPORTS FACTS

Curling

- First contested date in the Olympics :
  1998 Nagano Winter Olympics
- Nation of origin :
  Scotland
- Types of events :
  Men's and women's
- Type of arena :
  Indoor ice rink
- Number of players :
  4 players per team
- Game time :
  73 minutes
- Country with most medals :
  Canada
- Athlete with most medals :
  Anette Norberg, Catherine Norberg, and Eva Lund

해 석

An Introduction to the Game

컬링은 스코틀랜드에서 시작된 빙상경기이다. 두 팀이 경기를 펼치는데 한 팀에 4명의 선수로 구성되어 있다. 선수들은 스톤을 하우스라고 불리는 원 모양의 표적으로 미끄러지게 한다. 현재 컬링은 동계올림픽 종목이며 1998년 정식으로 채택되었다.

The History

컬링은 중세 후반 스코틀랜드에서 발명되었다. 스코틀랜드는 겨울마다 하천이 완전히 결빙되기에 컬링을 위한 조건을 갖추고 있었다. 그렇기에 1600~1900년대에 컬링이 매우 번성했다. 초기 컬링은 강가의 자연석 중에서 바닥이 평평한 것을 골라 약간 다듬어 컬링스톤으로 사용했었다. 당시 스톤의 규격이 일정치 않고 거칠어 스로워(thrower)가 컬링 스톤을 컨트롤하는 데 한계가 있었고 기술이나 전략보다는 운에 의존하는 면이 컸었다고 한다. 과거에 컬링은 으르렁거리는 놀이(the roaring game)라고도 불렸다. 이것은 스톤이 페블(빙판 위의 미세한 얼음 알갱이) 위를 미끄러지며 내는 소리가 마치 으르렁거리는 소리와 비슷했기 때문이었다. 그렇지만 최근에는 컬링은 빙판 위의 체스라고 불린다.

컬링이라는 명칭은 스톤이 휘어져(curl) 나가는 모습을 설명하는 스코트어(및 영어)의 동사 curl에서 유래했다. 비록 스코틀랜드에서 처음 시작하였지만 오늘날 컬링이 가장 강한 나라는 캐나다이다. 캐나다는 스코틀랜드 출신 이주민들이 많았던 지역이다. 1900년대에 스위스와 스웨덴에도 스코틀랜드 출신에 의해 컬링이 보급되기 시작하여 전 세계에서 행해지게 되었다.

1959년 스코틀랜드에서 열린 Scotch Cup이 세계 첫 컬링대회였다. 그때는 남자 경기만 있었다. 1998년에 공식적인 올림픽 경기가 되었고 지금은 남자 경기와 여자 경기 모두 열린다.

FIGURE SKATING
피겨 스케이팅

06

EVENTS

MEN'S EVENTS	WOMEN'S EVENTS	MIXED EVENT
Individual men	Individual women	Ice dancing mixed Pairs mixed Mixed NOC Team mixed

An Introduction to the Game

Figure skating is a sport with individual, pair and mixed performances that displays the beauty of movement on ice. It first became a winter sport in the 1908 Olympics. There are five Olympic figure skating events including individual men, individual women, ice dancing mixed, mixed NOC team mixed, and pairs mixed. In the Olympics, skaters generally perform two programs (short and long) and depending on the discipline, they perform spins, jumps, moves in the field, lifts, throw jumps, death spirals, and other elements or moves.

This sport is also related to show business. After major competitions, the top skaters taking first to third place from each discipline and skaters from the host country perform freestyle programs in an exhibition gala to entertain their fans. It is different from ice shows, which is directed more towards retired professional skaters who perform in non-competitive programs.

Talking about the Game

Joe : Pyeongchang has been selected as the host country of the 2018 Winter Olympics.
평창이 2018 동계올림픽 개최국으로 선정되었구나.

Karen : Yes, Pyeongchang finally did it!
응. 평창이 마침내 해냈어!

Joe : I saw a promotional video clip for Pyeongchang. I was especially impressed with Yuna Kim.
평창 동계올림픽 홍보영상을 봤는데 특히나 김연아 선수가 나온 부분이 정말 인상 깊었어.

Karen : I agree. I think that Yuna Kim's part in this video clip was significant.
맞아. 이 홍보영상에서 김연아 선수의 공이 컸다고 생각해.

KEY WORDS & EXPRESSIONS

host country: 개최국
(you) did it: 해내다
familiar with: 익숙하다
grow an interest: 관심이 생기다
ice: 빙상
individual men: 남자 개인전
individual women: 여자 개인전
ice dancing: 아이스 댄싱(남녀 혼성)
pairs mixed: 페어 스케이팅(남녀 혼성)

Joe : Actually, I wasn't familiar with figure skating, but I've grown an interest in it because of her. I want to know more about figure skating.

사실 피겨 스케이팅에 대해 아는 게 전혀 없었는데 김연아 선수 때문에 요즘 들어 관심이 생겼어. 피겨 스케이팅에 대해 더 많이 알고 싶어.

Karen : If you want, I can tell you about figure skating.

원한다면, 피겨 스케이팅에 대해 설명해 줄 수 있지.

Joe : That sounds great!

그래주면 좋겠어!

Karen : Let me give you a brief explanation on figure skating. Figure skating is a sport involving individual, pair and group performances. It shows beautiful skating movements on the ice.

그럼 피겨 스케이팅에 대해 간략하게 설명할게. 피겨 스케이팅은 개인, 2인조, 그리고 집단이 피겨 스케이트를 신고 빙상을 활주하며 율동의 아름다움을 연기하는 경기야.

KEY WORDS & EXPRESSIONS

- jumps: 점프(공중에 뛰는 동작)
- spins: 스핀(한 축으로 회전)
- step sequence: 스텝 시퀀스(발 동작)
- spirals: 스파이럴(회전하면서 연속으로 동작을 연계하는 기술)
- throw jumps: 스로우 점프(남성 선수가 여성 선수가 점프할 수 있도록 던지는 동작)
- lifts: 리프트(들어올리는 동작)
- pair spins: 페어 스핀(두 선수가 같은 축으로 회전하는 동작)
- death spirals: 데드 스파이럴(남녀가 손을 잡고 남성 선수 축으로 여성 선수가 회전)
- intricate footwork: 정교하고 복잡한 발 기술

Joe : I see. When skaters perform on the ice, it looks really beautiful. By the way, are there different kinds of figure skating?

그렇군. 선수들이 빙상에서 연기를 할 때 정말 아름다워 보여. 그런데 피겨 스케이팅에도 종류가 있겠지?

Karen : Yes. There are five Olympic events. The individual men, individual women, ice dancing mixed, mixed NOC team mixed, and pairs mixed.

응. 올림픽 종목으로는 남자 싱글 스케이팅, 여자 싱글 스케이팅, 아이스 댄싱, 혼합(mixed NOC team mixed), 페어 스케이팅 5가지가 있어.

Joe : Can you tell me a little bit more about some of the Olympic events?

각 올림픽 종목들에 대해서 좀 더 설명해 줄 수 있어?

Karen : Of course! The single or individual event consists of competitions for men and women. Skaters perform jumps, spins, step sequences, spirals, and other elements in their programs. Pair skating is a team competition.

A woman and man make up one team. Skaters perform techniques that only pairs can do, such as **throw jumps**, **lifts**, **pair spins**, **death spirals**. Ice dancing is also a team competition, but it differs from pair skating. Skaters focus on performing **intricate footwork** to the music while closely holding onto their partners.

물론이지! 싱글은 남자 경기와 여자 경기로 구성되어 있어. 선수들은 점프, 스핀, 스텝 시퀀스, 스파이럴 그리고 다른 요소들을 연기해. 페어 스케이팅은 여자와 남자로 구성된 팀 경기야. 선수들은 드로우 점프, 리프트, 페어 스핀, 데스 스파이럴 등 페어에서만 가능한 요소들을 연기해. 아이스 댄싱 또한 팀 경기인데 페어 스케이팅과는 차이를 보여. 선수들은 파트너를 가까이 잡고 음악에 맞추어 복잡한 발 기술을 연기하는 데 중점을 둬.

Joe : Wow. There are so many elements involved. It is very interesting.

와. 정말 다양한 요소들이 있구나. 정말 흥미롭다.

Karen : Next time, I'll tell you more interesting stuff.

다음엔 더 흥미로운 내용들을 알려줄게.

Joe : Good!

좋아!

The History

Figure skating originated in the mid-19th century. In the beginning, figure skating involved techniques such as drawing fixed shapes without any errors. Unlike modern figure skating, it was very stiff and mechanical. In the mid-1860s, American skater Jackson Haines who is considered the "father of modern figure skating" encompassed artistic movements taken from ballet. This newly included element of freedom and artistic expression became the model for modern figure skating.

The International Skating Union was founded in 1892. The first European Championships were held in 1891, and the first World Championships were held in

1896. But these events were only for men. In 1902, British woman and skater Madge Syers competed in the World competition for the first time, where she received a silver medal. The ISU banned women from competing with men and made an independent ladies' singles discipline in 1906. Pair skating was introduced at the 1908 World Championships. Figure skating was held in the 1908 Summer Olympics for the first time and has been a main discipline in the Winter Olympics since 1924.

Top Athletes

Gillis Grafstrom was born on June 7, 1893 in Sweden. He is marked as an innovator in the history of figure skating, creating techniques that include spiral, change sit spin and flying sit spin. Such ability was acknowledged with his three successive gold medals and one silver in the Olympics. This record puts him on top of the list of figure skaters with the most Olympic medals.

Gillis Grasfstrom은 1893년 6월 7일 스웨덴에서 태어났다. 그는 피겨 스케이팅 역사에 혁신적인 기술개발로 기여했다. Grafstrom의 기술 중에는 스파이럴, 체인지 싯스핀 그리고 플라잉 싯스핀이 포함된다. 그의 능력은 3연속 올림픽 금메달과 1개의 은메달로 증명되었다. 메달 수로만 봐도 그는 올림픽 메달을 가장 많이 얻은 피겨 선수로 꼽힌다.

Irina Rodnina was born on September 12, 1949 in Russia. Her parents pushed her into the ice rink to improve her health because she suffered from chronic pneumonia. She not only regained her health, but gained a career in figure skating. She became a successful pair figure skater, winning three Olympic gold medals and eleven European titles. Upon retiring, she resumed to stay in the sport by coaching pairs in Russia.

Irina Rodnina는 1949년 9월 12일에 러시아에서 태어났다. 폐렴에 시달리는 Irina는 건강을 회복하기 위해 부모님의 권유로 스케이트장을 찾게 됐다. 그녀는 건강도 얻고 피겨 스케이트 선수로 거듭날 수 있는 기회가 됐다. 성공한 페어 스케이팅 선수로 3연속 금메달을 얻었고 유럽에서는 11개의 우승을 차지했다. 은퇴 후에도 피겨 현장을 떠나지 않고 러시아 팀의 코치로 활동하였다.

Sonja Henie, born on April 8, 1912, was from an affluent Norwegian family. She was introduced to a variety of sports at an early age, but took up figure skating professionally, competing at the age of 11 in the 1924 Chamonix Winter Games. Although she placed last in her first Olympic competition, she grew to record three gold medals in the individual women's event. Her popularity and fame began to grow, becoming a sports star. After her competitive career she went into the movie industry, where her fame grew ever greater, making her a celebrity.

Sonja Henie는 1912년 4월 8일 유복한 노르웨이 가정에서 태어났다. 어렸을 때부터 다양한 스포츠를 경험하였지만 피겨 스케이트에 집중하면서 1924년에 열한 살의 나이에 샤모니 동계올림픽에 참가하였다. 첫 올림픽 경험에 가장 낮은 등급을 받았으나 곧 여성 개인전에서 3개의 금메달을 얻게 될 만큼 성장했다. 그리고 그녀의 인기가 높아지면서 스포츠 스타로 탄생하게 됐다. 스케이트 선수 생활을 마무리하면서 그녀는 영화계에 들어가 그녀의 유명세를 더욱 키웠다.

* Photo from Wikipedia

"How did it all start?"

KEY WORDS & EXPRESSIONS
look into: 살펴보다, 조사하다
in its infancy: 초창기에
the father of: 무엇을 시작한 원조
none other than: 다름 아닌 바로
on her own: 혼자서

Joe : Let's look into the history of figure skating today.

오늘은 피겨 스케이트의 역사와 선수에 대해 얘기해 볼게.

Karen : That sounds interesting!

그거 재미있겠는데!

Joe : Figure skating originated in the mid-19th century. Unlike modern figure skating that is free and expressive, figure skating in its infancy was too stiff and mechanical.

피겨 스케이트는 19세기 중반에 시작되었어. 자유롭고 표현력 있는 현대 피겨 스케이팅과 달리 초기의 피겨 스케이트는 매우 딱딱하고 기계적이었다고 해.

Karen : Then how did modern figure skating start?

그렇다면 현대 피겨 스케이팅은 어떻게 만들어졌지?

Joe : In the mid-1860s Jackson Haines incorporated artistic movements based on ballet. That became the foundation for modern figure skating.

1860년대 중반에 잭슨 하인즈가 발레에 기반을 둔 예술적인 동작들을 고안해내었고 이것이 현대 피겨 스케이팅의 기반이 되었어.

Karen : Who is Jackson Haines?

잭슨 하인즈는 어떤 사람이지?

Joe : He is an American ballet dancer and figure skater. He is considered to be the "father of modern figure skating".

그는 미국의 발레댄서이자 피겨 스케이팅 선수로서 현대 피겨 스케이팅의 아버지로 생각되는 사람이야.

Karen : He seems like an incredible man!

대단한 사람이군!

Joe : Right. There's another person I want to talk about. That other great person is none other than Yuna Kim.

맞아. 이제 또 한 명의 대단한 사람인 김연아 선수에 대해 얘기해볼게.

Karen : I've been looking forward to the story about Yuna Kim!

김연아 선수에 대한 이야기를 기대하고 있었어!

Joe : Yuna Kim is a South Korean figure skater. She received many gold medals in the 2005 **Junior Grand Prix Final champion**, the 2006 **World Junior champion**, the **2009**, **2013** World champion, the 2009 **Four Continents champion**, and is a three-time (2006–2007, 2007–2008, 2009–2010) **Grand Prix Final champion.** And she is the 2010 Olympic champion.

김연아는 한국의 피겨 스케이트 선수야. 그녀는 2005년 주니어 그랑프리 파이널, 2006년 주니어 세계선수권대회, 2009년과 2013년 세계선수권대회, 2009년 4대륙 선수권대회, 그리고 시니어 그랑프리 파이널에서 3번 연속하여 많은 금메달을 석권했어. 그리고 마침내 그녀는 2010년 올림픽 금메달리스트가 되었지.

Karen : Amazing! I think she is a genius!

놀라워! 그녀는 천재 같아!

Joe : I agree 100%! Actually Korea wasn't famous for figure skating so it was difficult for skaters to receive support from the government. But despite it all, she succeeded completely on her own.

완전 동의해! 사실 한국은 피겨 스케이팅이 유명하지 않았기 때문에 선수들은 정부로부터 많은 지원을 받을 수 없었어. 이런 열악한 상황임에도 불구하고 그녀는 그녀의 노력만으로 성공을 이루어냈어.

Karen : She's a star, but she's so modest and compassionate. I heard she makes lots of donations for the needy. She really is an amazing person!

게다가 그녀는 겸손하고 어려운 사람들을 위해 많은 기부를 하지. 그녀는 정말 멋진 사람이야!

Equipment and Gear

Skates 스케이트

Footwear skaters wear to move on the ice and perform techniques.

Parts of the skate include:

- Boot: top part of the skates that is made of stiff, strong leather and custom made to fit the skater's foot.
- Boot tongue: made to give the boot flexibility during movement.
- Heel: having evolved from regular wearable boots, the heel differs in height according to the type of event.
- Blade: attached to the bottom of the boot, the blade is sharp and slightly curved with a hollow. The hollow is a groove that runs down the middle of the blade and adds speed and control to the skater's movements.
- Toe pick: The front part of the blade that looks like sharp teeth. The toe pick acts like brakes and is used during jumps and spins.

스케이트는 얼음 위에서 움직임과 기술을 가능하게 해주는 신발이다.

스케이트는 다음과 같은 부분들로 이뤄졌다:

- 부츠: 스케이트의 가장 윗부분으로 단단하고 강한 가죽으로 만들어졌으며 선수의 발에 맞게 주문 제작된다.
- 부츠텅: 부츠의 혀 부분은 부츠에 유연함을 주기 위해 만들어졌다.
- 굽: 일반 부츠에서 개발된 스케이트 신발은 굽이 있으며 그 높이는 종목에 따라 다르다.
- 날: 부츠 아래에 장착된 날은 매우 날카롭고 휘어졌으며 '할로우'라고 불리는 홈이 있다. 할로우는 날의 중심에 파인 홈이며 움직임에 스피드와 컨트롤을 향상시키는 역할을 한다.
- 토픽: 날에서 가장 앞부분에 있는 날카로운 이빨 모양을 토픽이라고 한다. 토픽은 브레이크 역할도 하며 점프나 스핀을 할 때 사용된다.

Hard plastic skate guards 스케이트 날 보호대

Guards used to protect the blades when not on the ice.

빙상이 아닌 곳에서 스케이트 날을 보호하기 위하여 날에 끼우는 장치.

	**Figure skating costume 피겨 스케이트 복장** Figure skating costume guidelines have been set for safety reasons, restricting excessive accessories and theatrical-like costumes. Clothes required for women skaters are unitards with skirts attached and leggings or tights worn underneath. Since 2004, women skaters are allowed to wear trousers during competitions. However, men must wear trousers because tights are restricted. 피겨 스케이트 복장은 안전을 위해 규정됐으며 지나친 액세서리나 분장을 금한다. 여성 스케이트 선수는 스커트가 있는 유니타드와 레깅스 또는 타이츠를 허용한다. 2004년부터 여성 스케이트 선수도 경기에서 바지를 입는 것을 허용했다. 남자 선수들은 바지를 착용해야 하며 타이츠는 금지됐다.

What is this contraption?

Joe : Today's topic is figure skating equipment.
오늘은 피겨 스케이팅의 장비에 대해서 설명해볼게.

Karen : That's easy. Skates!
뭔지 알 것 같아. 스케이트지!

Joe : You're right. Skates used in figure skating are specifically made for the sport. See, this jagged teeth in front of the blade is the toe pick. Have a look!
맞아. 피겨 스케이트에는 날 앞부분에 삐죽삐죽한 이 모양의 토픽이 있어. 이걸 봐!

Karen : Wow, it looks dangerous.
와, 위험해 보여.

Joe : Yes, but it is an important part of the skates. Skaters use it to perform jumps. And because it acts like brakes, it is not used during strokes or spins. The toe pick can cause a loss in momentum or movement away from the

KEY WORDS & EXPRESSIONS

jagged teeth: 뾰족한 이빨 모양
toe pick: 토픽(스케이트 날의 앞 부분)
groove: 홈
edge of the blade: 스케이트의 날
score is deducted: 점수가 차감되다
pull off: 해내다
custom-made: 주문 제작
braces: 보호대
off the ice: 빙판에서 내려온 상태
skate guards: 스케이트 날 보호대
dulling the blades: 날이 둔해지다

center of a spin.

응. 하지만 토픽은 중요한 부분이야. 스케이트 선수들은 점프를 연기할 때 토픽을 이용해. 그러나 활주와 스핀을 연기할 땐 사용해서는 안 돼. 왜냐하면 가속도가 손실되거나 스핀의 중심에서 벗어날 수 있게 되기 때문이지.

Karen : How interesting.

흥미로운데.

Joe : The skates also have a **groove** on the bottom of the blade that creates two sides to the edge, the inside and outside.

그리고 스케이트에는 날의 바닥 부분에 홈이 있는데 이 홈으로 인해 두 부분, 인사이드 에지와 아웃사이드 에지가 형성돼.

Karen : Two sides? I didn't know there were sides to the blade!

두 부분? 그건 몰랐는걸. 난 그저 1개의 날인 줄만 알았어.

Joe : When skaters perform, they have to use only one **edge of the blade**. If they use both at the same time, their **score is deducted.**

선수들이 기술을 연기할 때 날의 하나의 에지만 사용해야 해. 만일 두 에지를 동시에 사용한다면 낮은 기술 점수를 받게 될 수 있어.

Karen : If you think about it, it isn't just a beautiful sport, it is difficult. I admire figure skaters for that.

와, 선수들이 존경스럽다. 단순히 아름다운 것만이 아닌 정말 어려운 스포츠였구나.

Joe : I know. To **pull off** the techniques they have special protection.

나도 그렇게 생각해. 기술을 하기 위해 보호장비가 있어.

Karen : That's good!

그래야지!

Joe : The boots are all **custom-made** for the skaters so that their feet get the best protection. They are made of really strong leather and have extra **braces** to prevent ankle injuries. Also, when **off the ice**, skaters put those hard plastic skate guards on their blades so they can walk around. They prevent dust and other particles from getting into the blade or **dulling the blades.**

선수용 부츠는 선수 발을 보호하기 위해 각 발에 맞게 주문 제작해. 그리고 단단한 가죽으로 만들고 안에 발목보호대를 추가적으로 넣지. 빙판에서 내려오면 선수는 스케이트 단단한 플라스틱 날 보호대를 착용하는데, 착용하면 걷기도 편하고 먼지와 다른 이물질이 날에 끼는 것과 날이 둔해지는 것을 막아줘.

SPORTS FACTS

FIGURE SKATING

- First contested date in the Olympics :
  1908 London Olympics
- Nation of origin :
  England
- Types of events :
  Men's individual / Women's individual Mixed: ice dancing / pairs / mixed NOC
- Type of arena :
  Indoor ice skating rink
- Country with most medals :
  Russia
- Athlete with most medals :
  Gillis Grafstrom and Evgeni Plushenko
- Youngest athlete :
  Yulia Lipnitskaya

해 석

An Introduction to the Game

피겨 스케이팅(영어: figure skating, 문화어: 휘어)은 개인, 2인조, 집단이 피겨 스케이트를 신고 빙상을 활주하며 율동의 아름다움을 연기하는 경기이다. 1908년에 올림픽에서 첫 번째 동계 경기가 되었으며 남자 싱글 스케이팅, 여자 싱글 스케이팅, 페어 스케이팅, 혼합 NOC, 아이스 댄싱의 다섯 가지 올림픽 종목으로 구성되어 있다. 선수들은 올림픽에서 짧고 긴 두 가지 프로그램을 연기하게 되는데 종목에 따라 스핀, 점프, 활주, 리프트, 스로우 점프, 데스 스파이럴, 다른 여러 기술이나 움직임 등 다양한 기술을 사용한다. 또한 피겨 스케이팅은 쇼비니지스와 관계가 있다. 주요 경기가 끝난 후 일반적으로 각 종목에서 1위~3위를 차지한 상위권 선수들과 개최국 선수들이 갈라쇼에서 형식에 구애받지 않고 프로그램을 연기하며 팬들과 즐긴다. 이는 선수들이 선수 시절과 선수 시절이 끝난 후에도 경기를 하지 않고 공연만 펼치는 아이스쇼와는 다르다.

The History

피겨 스케이팅은 19세기 중반에 시작되었다. 초기의 피겨 스케이팅은 어떠한 오차도 없이 정해진 형태의 도형을 그리는 것으로서 현대의 피겨 스케이팅과 달리 너무 딱딱하고 기계적이었다. 1860년대 중반에 현대 피겨 스케이팅의 아버지라 불리는 미국의 스케이터인 잭슨 하인즈가 발레에 기반을 둔 예술적인 동작들을 고안해내었고 이것이 더 자유롭고 표현력 있는 현대 피겨 스케이팅의 기반이 되었다. 1892년에 국제빙상연맹이 결성되었으며 1891년에 첫 번째 유럽 피겨 선수권대회가, 1896년에 첫 번째 세계 피겨 선수권대회가 개최되었다. 그러나 이러한 대회들은 오직 남자 선수들만 출전할 수 있었다. 1902년에 영국의 여성 스케이터인 마지 시어스가 처음으로 세계선수권대회에 출전하여 은메달을 획득했다. 이에 ISU는 여성이 남성과 경쟁하는 것을 금지하고 1906년에 독립된 여자 싱글 종목을 만들었다. 페어 스케이팅은 1908년에 세계선수권대회에서 소개되었다. 피겨 스케이팅은 1908년 하계올림픽에서 처음으로 올림픽 경기로서 개최되었고, 1924년에 동계올림픽이 창설된 이래로 동계올림픽의 주요 종목이 되었다.

07 FREESTYLE SKIING
프리스타일 스키

EVENTS

MEN'S EVENTS	WOMEN'S EVENTS
Aerials men	Aerials women
Moguls men	Moguls women
Ski Cross men	Ski Cross women
Halfpipe men	Halfpipe women
Slopestyle men	Slopestyle women

An Introduction to the Game

Freestyle skiing is a competition in which participants ride freely according to one's own style. Skiers can perform various maneuvers and stunts. It has various types of events such as mogul skiing, ballet (arc) skiing, aerial skiing, slope style, ski cross and half-pipe. Most freestyle skiers can jump over 20m.

Talking about the Game

Joe : Karen, where are you going?

카렌, 어디 가니?

Karen : Hi, I am going to the ski slope to watch the freestyle ski game.

안녕. 나는 프리스타일 스키 경기를 보러 경기장에 가고 있어.

Joe : Freestyle skiing? Do you mean the game where skiers spin in the air while skiing?

프리스타일 스키? 스키 타며 공중에서 도는 그 경기 말하는 거니?

Karen : Yes. It is very interesting watching the skiers show off their skills. Would you like to come with me?

응, 맞아. 선수들이 다양한 기술을 보여주는 것이 정말 흥미롭더라고. 너도 같이 갈래?

Joe : Let's go!

그래! 가자.

KEY WORDS & EXPRESSIONS

ski slope: 스키장

show off: 자랑하다

The History

Freestyle skiing is a recent skiing style that began in the 1920s and 1960s with the younger generations who wanted to deviate from traditional skiing and freely express themselves. It was practiced in countries such as Norway, Italy, Austria, and eventually the United States where it became increasingly popular. The new "hot dogging" style, as it began to be called because of the various tricks, took a more dynamic form than traditional skiing. For example, freestyle skiing includes back flips, aerial twists, turns and so on.

The competition in the form of a combination of traditional skiing and dynamic techniques was held for the first time in 1966 in New Hampshire, USA. In 1979 freestyle was accepted by the International Ski Federation (FIS), which enhanced the regulations to promote the safety of the athletes in this field. Freestyle finally made its debut in the Winter Olympics in the 1988 Calgary Games for men and women in the events of the mogul, aerial and ballet.

Sarah Burke, born on September 3, 1982 in Canada was a freestyle skier. She was a pioneer in the superpipe event. She won four gold medals in the Winter X Games. Unfortunately, in 2012, she suffered a crash during practice, causing deep cerebral hemorrhage. Surgery was to no avail and she died 10 days following the accident. Sarah, signing up as an organ donator, helped others in need of healthy organs.

Sarah Burke는 1982년 9월 3일에 캐나다에서 태어난 프리스타일 스키 선수이다. 그녀는 superpipe 이벤트의 선구자였다. 그녀는 Winter X 게임에서 4개의 금메달을 땄다. 불행하게도 2012년에 연습 도중 충돌사고를 당했고 이로 인해 뇌출혈이 심해 수술했지만 사고 후 10일 만에 숨을 거두었다. 장기기증에 서약을 했었던 그녀는 건강한 장기를 필요로 하는 많은 사람들을 돕고 떠났다.

Alexandre Bilodeau was born on September 8, 1987 in Canada. His first Olympic victory was in the mogul, in his home country of Canada in 2010. Despite his young age, Bilodeau has many titles, as the first Canadian to win a gold medal in Canada, the first to defend his gold medal in the following Olympic Games, and he is the Canadian with the most World Cup medals.

Alexandre Bilodequ는 1987년 9월 8일 캐나다에서 태어났다. 그의 첫 번째 올림픽 메달은 모글 종목이었으며 그의 모국인 캐나다에서 열린 2010년 동계올림픽에서 획득했다. 어린 나이에도 불구하고 Bilodeau는 최초의 캐나다 선수 출신으로 캐나다에서 열린 동계올림픽에서 금메달을 얻은 선수이자 올림픽 게임 연속으로 자신의 종목에서 금메달을 받은 선수이며 캐나다 선수 중 월드컵 메달을 가장 많이 획득한 선수다.

Kari Traa was born on January 28, 1974 in Norway. She has won three Olympic medals, a gold in the 2002 Salt Lake City Olympics, a silver in the 2006 Turin, and a bronze in the 1998 Nagano Olympics.

Kari Traa는 1974년 1월 28일 노르웨이에서 태어났다. 그녀는 3개의 올림픽 메달을 획득했다. 2002년 솔트레이크 올림픽에서 금메달, 2006년 토리노에서는 은메달, 1998년 나가노 올림픽에서는 동메달을 얻었다.

* Photo from Wikipedia

"How did it all start?"

KEY WORDS & EXPRESSIONS

too bad: 안타깝다

hot dogging: 묘기를 부리다

Joe : Hi, Karen What are you doing?

안녕 카렌, 너 뭐하고 있니?

Karen : I'm looking at this picture.

난 사진을 보고 있어.

Joe : Who is she?

그 여자가 누군데?

Karen : She is Sarah Burke. She's a freestyle skier from Canada.

그녀는 사라 버크야. 그녀는 캐나다 프리스타일 스키 선수야.

Joe : She's beautiful!

진짜 예쁘다.

Karen : Yeah, she is. It's too bad she had such a short athletic career and life. She injured her head during a practice and wasn't able to recover from it. She died only ten days later.

예쁘지. 그런데 너무 짧은 선수 생활을 한 게 안타까워. 연습 중 사고로 머리를 다치면서 회복이 안 됐어. 10일 후 바로 생을 끝냈지.

Joe : Freestyle skiers are always at risk because their techniques are so dangerous.

이 종목의 선수들은 항상 위험에 놓여 있지. 기술이 보기만 해도 위험하잖아.

Karen : But the International Ski Federation drew up more limiting restrictions and rules to regulate dangerous techniques and protect athletes when they recognized it as a discipline.

그러나 국제스키연맹이 프리스타일 스키를 종목으로 인정하면서 위험 요소가 큰 기술을 통제하고 선수들을 보호하기 위해 제한적인 규정과 규칙을 만들었어.

Joe : That's true, and yet even with those regulations, freestyle proves to be dangerous.

그렇지만, 규칙이 존재함에도 불구하고 프리스타일은 위험해.

Karen : I know, but the somersaults, aerials, jumps and all those tricks are so amazing to watch.

나도 그렇게 생각해. 그렇지만 공중제비, 공중몸비틀기, 점프와 다양한 기술들은 보기에 너무 신기해.

Joe : That's called "**hot dogging**". The first freestylers were probably people who were looking for something fresh and new instead of the classic skiing method. Maybe that's why the techniques started getting trickier and harder.

그런 기술 부리는 것을 hot dogging이라고 불러. 최초 프리스타일 스키 선수들은 기존 스키 방식보다 새롭고 신선한 스키 방식을 고집하지 않았을까? 그래서 기술들이 더욱 어렵고 교묘해진 것 같아.

Equipment and Gear

Twin-tip skis 트윈팁 스키

Mogul skiing skis are firm at the front and rear tip. The length of the skis are limited at 190cm for men and 180cm for women.

모글 스키의 장비는 앞부분과 뒷부분의 재질이 단단하다. 스키의 길이는 남자 190cm, 여자 180cm로 제한한다.

Poles 스키 폴

Poles are a tool that helps maintain balance when skiing. It looks like a long stick and there are straps to hold onto and rest the hands.

스키를 탈 때 균형을 유지할 수 있게 도와주는 도구이다. 긴 막대기처럼 생겼으며 손에 낄 수 있는 끈이 달려 있다.

	**Binding 스키 바인딩** This is a device that connects the ski boots and skis. When skiing, it helps securely connect the boots and skis while minimizing impact on a fall. 스키 부츠와 스키를 연결하는 장치이다. 스키를 탈 때, 견고하게 연결하여 탈 수 있도록 도와주고, 낙하 충격을 최소화시키는 것을 도와준다.
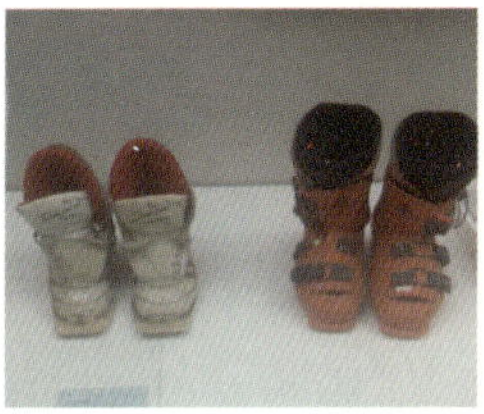	**Boots 부츠** They are footwear for skiing and are used together with the bindings. 스키를 탈 때 신는 신발이다. 바인딩을 이용해서 스키와 연결하여 신는다.

What is this contraption?

Joe : Karen, did you buy new ski boots?

카렌, 새로운 스키 부츠 샀니?

Karen : Yes, I did. Yesterday I went to the store to buy skiing equipment.

응. 맞아. 나는 어제 스키 용품을 사러 가게에 갔었어.

Joe : Really? I'm planning to go skiing frequently this winter. That's why I have to buy new skis today.

진짜? 나도 올 겨울에 스키장에 자주 갈 계획이야. 그래서 오늘 스키 용품을 새로 사려고 해.

Karen : What type of skiing do you want to do?

어떤 스키를 타고 싶은데?

Joe : I love freestyle skiing. So I'm going to buy twin- tip skis.

나는 프리스타일 스키가 좋아. 그래서 트윈팁 스키를 살 거야.

Karen : Twin-tip skis? What are those?

트윈팁 스키? 그게 뭐야?

KEY WORDS & EXPRESSIONS

planning to go : 갈 계획이다
this winter : 올 겨울
have to : 꼭, 반드시
twin-tip ski : 트윈팁 스키
binding : 바인딩
last time : 지난번
check : 확인하다
safety first : 안전 우선

Joe : They're the ones with a solid material in the tip and tail.

앞뒤의 재질이 단단한 스키를 말하는 거야.

Karen : Wow, then it's faster and safer on turns?

우와, 그러면 회전하는 데 더 빠르고 안전하겠네.

Joe : That's right. Skiers love it.

맞아. 그래서 스키 타는 사람들이 이 스키를 좋아한대.

Karen : Are you going to buy other equipment?

너는 다른 장비도 살 거니?

Joe : Yes, I am. My bindings broke the last time I went skiing.

응. 저번에 스키를 타다가 바인딩이 망가진 거 같아.

Karen : You must always check your bindings before skiing. It's so important.

바인딩은 스키를 타기 전 꼭 확인해보아야 해. 그만큼 중요한 장비야.

Joe : That's right. I didn't know they were broken till a week ago. I was skiing and fell in the snow.

맞아. 저번에도 망가진 것을 모르고 탔다가 미끄러졌어.

Karen : Oh, did you get hurt?

오, 다치지 않았니?

Joe : My boots suddenly separated from my skis. So I fell in.

갑자기 스키가 부츠랑 떨어져서 중심을 잃고 넘어졌어.

Karen : Safety first! Always be careful.

안전이 우선이야! 항상 조심해.

SPORTS FACTS

Freestyle Skiing

- First contested date in the Olympics :
  1992(Moguls), 1994(Aerials)
- Nation of origin :
  Norway
- Types of events :
  Aerials, Moguls, Ski Cross, Halfpipe, Slopestyle
- Type of arena :
  Outdoor Freestyle skiing stadium
- Country with most medals :
  Canada (9 medals : 4 gold, 4 silver, 1 bronze)
- Athlete with most medals :
  Alex Bilodeau
- Youngest athlete :
  Dara Howell

해 석

An Introduction to the Game

참가자들이 자신의 스타일대로 자유롭게 스키를 타는 대회이다. 스키를 타는 동안 선수들은 다양한 동작과 묘기를 수행할 수 있다. 주요 종목에는 모글 스키, 발레(아크로) 스키, 에어리얼 스키, 슬로프 스타일, 스키 크로스와 하프 파이프 등 다양한 유형이 있다. 보통 프리스타일 스키 선수들은 20m 높이를 뛴다.

The History

프리스타일 스키는 1920년대와 1960년대에 전통적 스키에서 벗어나고 싶어하는 청년들이 스키를 변형해서 타면서 시작되었다. 프리스타일 스키는 노르웨이, 이탈리아, 오스트리아 등에서 행해졌고 궁극적으로 미국에서 크게 유행하게 되었다. 다양한 기술들로 인해 그렇게 불리게 된 hot dogging 스타일은 전통 스키보다 더 역동적이다. 예를 들어 프리스타일 스키는 뒤공중제비, 공중비틀기, 회전 등의 기술을 보여준다.

1966년에 미국 뉴햄프셔 주 바틀릿의 아티타시에서 전통적인 스키에 화려한 기술을 첨가한 형태의 경기가 처음 열렸다. 그리고 1979년 프리스타일 스키는 국제스키연맹(FIS)에서 인정받으면서 선수들을 보호하기 위한 게임 규정이 확립됐다. 이 종목은 마침내 1988년 캘거리 동계올림픽에서 최초로 올림픽 경기로 개최되었고 이때 여자와 남자 모글, 에어리얼과 발레 종목이 모두 열렸다.

08 ICE HOCKEY
아이스하키

EVENTS

MEN'S EVENTS
Ice hockey men

WOMEN'S EVENTS
Ice hockey women

An Introduction to the Game

Ice hockey is a sport played by two teams of six trying to score a goal against the opposing team. Players play with a stick and a puck, or a small discus made of rubber. Ice hockey began at McGill University in Montreal, Canada in 1875. J.Crichton and other students divided themselves into two teams and played on a frozen river.

Ice hockey was adopted as one of the first games in the 7th Winter Olympics held in Antwerp, Belgium before it was divided into the Summer and Winter Games. Today, all 61 countries belong to the IIHF (International Ice Hockey Federation).

Canada is indispensable when talking about ice hockey. In a survey held during the Vancouver Olympics, most Canadians responded that they did not mind losing in other games, yet wanted to win at ice hockey.

Talking about the Game

Joe : The Winter Olympics is coming soon, which sport are you excited about?

이제 곧 동계올림픽 시즌인데 넌 어떤 종목이 제일 기대되니?

Karen : Ice hockey!

아이스하키!

Joe : You mean hitting marbles, or more like hitting stones and brooms?

돌이랑 빗자루 가지고 알까기 하는 거?

Karen : That's curling. Hockey is more like soccer played with a stick.

그건 컬링이고, 아이스하키는 스틱으로 하는 축구와 비슷하지.

Joe : Which country is the best?

그건 어느 나라가 제일 잘해?

Karen : Canada is definitely the best. And their fans are zealous. If Canada loses to any other country, I'm sure there's going to be a riot.

캐나다가 가장 잘하지. 그리고, 팬들도 광팬이야. 만약 다른 나라에 진다면 아마도 폭동이 일어날 거야.

Joe : Why do you like that sport?

그 스포츠가 왜 좋니?

Karen : It is the roughest sport on ice. So thrilling!

빙판에서 하는 스포츠 중에 제일 격렬하잖아. 스릴이 넘쳐서 좋아!

Joe : How can a sport with a few players hitting a little rubber discus be rough and thrilling?

선수 몇 명이 작은 고무원판 가지고 골 넣는 게 그렇게 격렬해?

Karen : Are you serious? You need to watch the game.

맙소사, 그냥 경기를 한번 봐.

KEY WORDS & EXPRESSIONS

hitting marbles: 구슬치기

stick: 하키용 스틱

rough sport: 격렬한 스포츠

rubber discus: 고무 원반(hockey puck)

are you serious: 정말이야, 진심이야, 믿을 수 없어, 설마(놀라움의 표현)

The History

Ice hockey developed with the introduction of an Irish and Scottish game played on ice, called "bandy". Scottish and Irish immigrants, as well as British soldiers introduced it to Canadians.

In 1885 in Montreal, Canada, the first national hockey team was organized. At that time, an amateur hockey association set a limit of seven players for each team. Then from the twentieth century, athletes were required to wear shin guards and chest protectors for goalkeepers. Furthermore, ice rinks began to be constructed on the entire eastern area in Canada. The building of infrastructure, equipment, and regulations allowed ice hockey to make advances in Canada. The sport was then introduced to Europe, where fervent responses resulted in an agreement by those countries to gather their organizations to found the International Ice Hockey Federation, which held its first meeting in May of 1908 in Paris.

The European Championships for ice hockey began in 1910, and the World Championship and International Conference began in 1920. It was adopted as one of the first games in the Winter Olympics at the 7th Olympic Games held in Antwerp, Belgium before the Olympics was divided into the Summer and Winter games. Since its first Winter Olympic games in 1924, ice hockey has taken the center stage as a popular winter sport.

Sidney Crosby (Canada's National Team Member)

At the 2014 Sochi Olympics, this player led his team to win with a fascinating goal. He is now a captain of the NHL Pittsburgh Penguins and also a representative center of the team. He was born on August 7, 1987. His first draft was in 2005 and he let people know of his real worth by the fact that he was one of the most highly regarded draft picks throughout the history of hockey. He holds outstanding records such as the youngest player to get 100 points in one season (18 years, 253 days), the youngest player to get 200 career points (19 years and 207 days), the youngest winner of the Art Ross Trophy and Lester B. Pearson Award, the youngest player named as the First All-Star Team, the youngest NHL captain to win the Stanley Cup (21 years, 10 months, and 5 days), and so on. Sidney Crosby has been lauded as one of the greatest hockey players in his time. His jersey number is 87 because his birthday is on August 7, 1987.

캐나다 대표 공격수 '시드니 크로스비'

2014 소치 올림픽에서 그림 같은 골을 넣으며 캐나다 우승에 일조한 이 선수는 현재 NHL피츠버그 펭귄의 주장으로 NHL을 대표하는 센터이다. 그는 1987년 8월 7일에 태어났다. 그의 첫 정규 리그 데뷔는 2005년에 이루어졌다. 첫 드래프트부터 가장 높은 드래프트 순위로 간주되면서 그 진가를 알렸으며 그 이후 가장 어린 나이에 한 시즌에서 100점의 기록, 가장 어린 나이에 통산 200점 달성, 가장 어린 나이로 ART와 LBP Award에서 우승, 첫 번째 올스타 팀에 뽑힌 가장 어린 선수, 가장 어린 NHL 캡틴으로서 Stanley Cup에서 우승 등 이 밖에도 많은 걸출한 기록을 가지고 있는 선수로 현재 가장 뛰어난 선수라고 칭송받고 있다. 그의 등 번호는 87번인데 그 이유는 그가 1987년 8월 7일생이기 때문이다.

Alexander Ovechkin (The Treasure of Russia)

He is currently a winger and captain of the NHL Washington Capitals. He earned the Hart Memorial Trophy and also became MVP in the 2013 season. His parents were both athletes; his father, a professional football player and his mother, an Olympic gold medalist in women's basketball. He was a big fan of hockey in his childhood. Whenever there was a hockey game on TV, he would just stop to watch it. From his teens to his thirties, he has devoted his life to ice hockey. Having come into the spotlight recently, he has a fancy record boasting the first winner of the Art Ross Trophy, Maurice Richard Trophy, Lester B. Pearson Award and Hart Memorial. He received all four in a single season and was the only player named the NHL First All-Star Team in each of his first five seasons. He also scored the most goals as a left-winger in one season (2007–08), 65 goals. He has 10 medals from several public conferences. He and the superstar of Canada, Sidney Crosby, are rivals who were drafted around the same time. They share similar records, for example receiving the MVP award while Sidney was No.2 and being No. 2 when Sidney was awarded the MVP. Alexander Ovechkin is a "Treasure of Russia" who has been loved since his 2004 draft.

러시아의 보물 '알렉산더 오베츠킨'

그는 현재 NHL Washington Capitals의 윙이자 주장으로 작년 2013년 NHL 시즌에서 Hart Memorial Trophy를 받으며 MVP에 등극했다. 그의 부모님은 프로 축구 선수, 여자 농구 올림픽 금메달리스트의 운동선수들이었다. 그는 어렸을 때부터 TV에서 하키 게임이 나오면 가지고 놀던 장난감도 버려놓고 하키 게임에 집중할 정도로 하키 팬이었다. 이렇게 그는 10세부터 30세까지 인생을 하키로 보내게 된다. 어렸을 때부터 두각을 나타낸 만큼 그 기록도 화려한데, 우선 한 시즌에서 ART, MRT, ABP Award, HMT을 모두 석권한 첫 번째 선수, 그의 첫 5개의 시즌마다 첫 번째 올스타 팀에 뽑힌 단 한 선수, 왼쪽 윙어로서 (2007-08) 한 시즌에 가장 많은 골인 65골을 넣은 선수 등의 기록을 가지고 있으며, 가지고 있는 공식 대회에서의 메달만 10개이다. 그와 캐나다의 슈퍼스타 시드니 크로스비는 비슷한 시기에 NHL에 입성한 라이벌이다. 때문에 기록도 여러 가지 면에서 비슷한데 그가 MVP에 등극했을 때는 시드니가 2위, 그리고 시드니가 MVP에 등극했을 때는 그가 2위였다. 그는 2004년 드래프트부터 지금까지 꾸준히 사랑받고 있는 러시아의 보물이다.

* Photo from Wikipedia

"How did it all start?"

Joe : Did you see last night's game? It was awesome!

지난밤 경기 봤어? 끝내줬는데!

Karen : I know. You mean the game that Sidney played? I'm so happy for his victory! He is such a wonderful player. He's this year's MVP right?

알아, 시드니 크로스비 경기 말하는 거지? 이겨서 너무 기뻐! 그는 정말 훌륭한 선수야. 올해에도 MVP였지?

Joe : What? Alexander was the MVP last year. I'm such a big fan of his. It's too bad he didn't get the MVP. Well, Sidney was fabulous last night anyways. It seemed like he was injured in the game, wasn't he?

올해에도라니, 작년엔 알렉산더가 MVP였거든? 난 알렉산더 팬인데, 올해 MVP 못 타서 너무 아쉬웠어. 그래도 어제 경기에서 시드니는 멋졌어! 어제 경기에서 좀 다친 것 같던데?

Karen : Thank goodness he was wearing those guards. If he wasn't wearing them, he could've been hurt worse than that.

보호구를 차고 있어서 망정이지, 아니었으면 더 크게 다쳤을 거야.

Joe : When did ice hockey players start wearing guards?

그러게, 그런데 보호구는 언제부터 착용하기 시작한 거야?

Karen : Since the 20th century. Ice hockey players started wearing shin guards

KEY WORDS & EXPRESSIONS

happy for: 때문에 기뻐하다
to be hurt: 다치다, 부상을 입다
if S 과거~S would 동사원형 –: 만약 ~하다면 ~했을 텐데
start to: 을 시작하다
shin guard: 정강이 보호대
chest protector: 가슴 보호대
win(receive) fervent response: 열렬한 환호를 받다, 호응을 받다
International Ice Hockey Fédération: 국제하키연맹(IIHF)
adopted as: 무엇으로 채택되다
Formal subject(event): 공식 종목

and chest protectors.

20세기부터 가슴 보호대와 정강이 보호대를 착용하도록 했다고 들었어.

Joe : From the 20th? And since when did ice hockey become so popular?

20세기부터? 하키는 언제부터 이렇게 인기가 많아진 건데?

Karen : It was received fervently when introduced to Europe in the 1900's. And the International Ice Hockey Fédération was founded through a joint effort of many countries. They held their first meeting in Paris, France in May, 1908.

1900년대 유럽에 소개되고 나서부터 많은 호응이 있었대. 그때 많은 나라의 협력 덕에 1908년 5월 프랑스 파리에서 제1회 국제아이스하키연맹이 결성되었지.

Joe : Wow. It's been quite a long time. Do you know when ice hockey was adopted as a formal Olympic event?

와, 꽤 오래됐네? 올림픽에는 언제부터 정식 종목으로 채택된 건지 알아?

Karen : Nope, I don't know.

아니, 그건 모르겠다.

Joe : It was adopted in the 7th Olympics! After the Olympics was divided into the Winter and Summer Olympics.

제7회 올림픽 경기부터야! 동계랑 하계올림픽이 분리된 이후에.

Karen : What? Adopted as a formal event in such an early state of ice hockey? It must have been a super popular sport then.

그래? 정말 인기 많은 운동이었나 보다. 초창기부터 정식 종목으로 채택되다니.

Joe : I'm proud to be an ice hockey fan!

내가 아이스하키 팬이라는 게 자랑스럽다니까!

Karen : Me too! I'll cheer for Alexander's game next week. He will probably score many goals! Because he is a player who scores a lot even as a left winger.

나도! 다음 주에 있을 알렉산더 경기는 내가 응원해줄게! 아마 많은 득점을 할 거야! 그는 왼쪽 윙어임에도 불구하고 골을 많이 넣는 선수잖아.

Joe : I hope so. I can't wait to see that game!

나도 그러길 바라. 어서 빨리 경기를 보고 싶어!

Equipment and Gear

	**Puck** 퍽 (아이스하키 공) A type of disc used in ice hockey to score a goal. It is in the shape of a discus and is made of rubber. 골을 넣기 위해 아이스하키에서 쓰는 일종의 '공'으로 고무로 만들어져 있다.
	**Skates** 스케이트 This equipment allows movement on ice. Ice hockey skates are thicker and more solid than skates used in other sports. 선수들로 하여금 얼음에서 움직일 수 있도록 하는 장비로, 다른 스포츠의 스케이트들보다 날이 더 두껍고 견고하다.
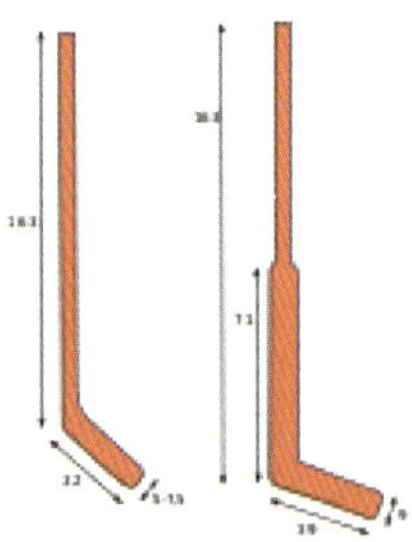	**Stick** 하키 스틱 The stick which is typically 150-200cm long is a bar used to handle the puck. It is divided into two parts, the grip and the blade. The blacle used to contact the puck is 25 to 40cm long. The goaltender's stick is wider and slightly curved. 스틱은 보통 150-200cm이고 퍽을 다루는 데 사용된다. 그립과 블레이드로 구분될 수 있다. 퍽을 직접 접촉하는 블레이드는 25-40cm 길이이다. 골키퍼가 사용하는 스틱은 폭이 더 넓다.
	**Helmets** 헬멧 Players wear helmets to protect their heads. 선수들의 머리를 보호하기 위해 사용된다.
	**Guards** 보호구 Guards protect the player's neck, chest, elbow and shins. They are classified into two types; the shoulder pad and the shin guard. Equipment for the goaltender is heavier; usually more than 6kg and running up to 15kg to 20kg in total weight. The goaltender also wears protective gloves. 보호구는 목, 가슴, 어깨, 팔꿈치, 정강이를 보호한다. 크게 어깨 패드와 정강이 패드로 구분한다. 골키퍼의 장비는 6kg 이상으로 무거우며 보통 무게가 15kg-20kg정도 되는 중장비이다. (골키퍼는 눈 보호용 고글 역시 착용한다.)

What is this contraption?

Joe : You said that you went shopping with your father. What did you buy?

저번에 아빠랑 쇼핑 갔다고 했었지. 뭐 샀어?

Karen : I'm learning how to play ice hockey these days, so I went to the sportswear department. My coach told me that I needed to get set to practice.

내가 요새 아이스하키를 배우잖아, 그래서 스포츠웨어 매장에 갔었어. 우리 코치님이 이것저것 갖출 필요가 있다고 하셔서.

Joe : You mean equipment for ice hockey? Like what?

아이스하키 장비들 말하는 거야? 이를테면 어떤 거?

KEY WORDS & EXPRESSIONS

these days: 요새

Sportswear department: 스포츠 의류 매장

Get set: 갖추다. 준비하다

Like what?: 예를 들면?, 이를테면?

Shin guard: 정강이 보호대

or something: (뭐뭐) 따위, … 등등

Puck: 아이스하키 전용 구

Goaltender: 아이스하키 골키퍼

Karen : Generally, most of the equipment are guards for protecting my body. Such as a helmet, chest guard, shin guard, gloves…

일반적으로 대부분의 장비는 내 몸을 보호하기 위한 보호구들이야. 예를 들어 헬멧이나, 가슴 보호대, 정강이 보호대, 글러브…

Joe : Wow, that sounds really cool. What about other equipment? Don't you need a pair of skates or something?

와! 멋지다. 다른 장비들은? 스케이트나 뭐 그런 거 필요하지 않아?

Karen : Oh, I also bought a stick to handle the puck. The puck is a ball we use. I wanted to buy a puck but my father said I wouldn't need it personally.

아, 퍽 다루는 데 쓰는 스틱도 샀어. 퍽은 우리가 쓰는 공이야. 퍽도 사고 싶었는데, 아빠가 개인적으로는 필요 없을 거라 하셨어.

Joe : You must have spent a lot of money on the stick, guards, and skates. Is there a difference between the goalkeeper's gear and the player's gear?

돈 정말 많이 썼겠다. 보호장비며, 스틱, 스케이트까지. 골키퍼랑 일반 선수들이랑 장비에 차이가 있어?

Karen : Yes. The goalkeeper's equipment is much heavier and they wear goggles for their eyes! By the way, we don't say goalkeeper, it's a goaltender.

그럼. 골키퍼 장비가 훨씬 무거워. 그리고 눈을 위한 고글도 있어! 그나저나, 우리는 골키퍼라고 하지 않고, Goaltender라고 해.

Joe : How about skates? Are they the same ones that are used in figure skating?

스케이트는 어때? 피겨 스케이트에서 쓰는 것과 같아?

Karen : No! Ice hockey skate blades are thicker and firmer. But nowadays, many corporations are making very light and smooth skates.

아니! 아이스하키 스케이트 날은 더 무겁고 견고해. 하지만 요새 많은 기업들이 더 가볍고, 부드러운 스케이트를 만들고 있지.

Joe : I see. Can I go to your house to see them today?

그렇구나. 오늘 너희 집에 장비들 보러 갈 수 있을까?

SPORTS FACTS

ICE HOCKEY

- First contested date in the Olympics :
  1924 Chamonix Winter Olympics
- Nation of origin :
  Canada
- Types of events :
  male event / female event
- Type of arena :
  Indoor ice rink
- Number of players :
  Six players per team
- Game time :
  1 period=20 min, Total 1hour
- Country with most medals :
  Canada
- Athlete with most medals :
  Hayley Wickenheiser

해 석

An Introduction to the Game

빙상에서 스케이트를 착용한 6명으로 구성된 두 팀이 상대팀의 골대에 골을 넣는 게임이다. 선수들은 소형의 고무원반인 퍽을 스틱으로 치면서 경기한다.

캐나다 몬트리올(Montreal) 맥 길 대학의 J. 크라이턴을 비롯한 학생들이 1875년 결빙한 강에서 편을 갈라 경기를 한 것이 최초이다. 올림픽이 동계와 하계로 나누어지기 직전에 벨기에의 안트베르펜에서 열린 제7회 올림픽경기대회에서 처음 정식 종목으로 채택되었다. 현재 61개의 국가가 국제아이스하키연맹(IIHF)에 가입되어 있다.

아이스하키 하면 빼놓을 수 없는 국가가 바로 캐나다인데, 아이스하키 경기가 있는 날이면 매상이 40~60% 정도 증가한다고 한다. 2010 동계올림픽 때 설문조사로는 다른 경기는 다 져도 아이스하키만은 우승하라는 답변이 대부분이었다고 한다.

The History

아일랜드와 스코티시의 국기와 비슷한 밴디라는 경기가 스코틀랜드와 아일랜드의 이주민들 및 영국의 군인들에 의해 캐나다로 전해지면서 발전하였다.

최초로 전국적인 하키단체가 설립된 것은 1885년 몬트리올 캐나다이다. 이때 아마추어 하키협회가 설립되었고, 여기서 각 팀의 선수를 7명으로 제한하였다. 20세기부터 선수들은 정강이 보호대를, 골키퍼는 가슴 보호대를 착용하기 시작하였다. 또한 아이스하키 링크가 캐나다 동부 전역에 지어지게 된다. 이렇게 아이스하키는 캐나다를 중심으로 발전한다. 이 경기가 유럽에 소개되자 여러 나라에서 많은 호응이 있었고, 그 나라들에서 국제단체를 조직하자는 의견에 따라 1908년 5월 파리(Paris)에서 열린 제1회 회합에서 IIHF(International Ice Hockey Fé dé ration: 국제아이스하키연맹)가 결성된다.

1910년에는 유럽선수권대회, 1920년에는 세계선수권대회 및 국제대회를 개최하기 시작하였으며, 올림픽이 동계와 하계로 나누어지기 직전에 벨기에의 안트베르펜에서 열린 제7회 올림픽 경기대회에서 처음으로 정식 종목에 채택되었다. 그리고 1924년 하계올림픽과 분리되어 열린 제1회 동계올림픽 경기대회 이후 인기 있는 동계 스포츠 종목으로 각광받고 있다.

09

LUGE
루지

EVENTS

MEN'S EVENTS	WOMEN'S EVENTS	MIXED EVENT
Singles men	Singles women	Doubles Mixed Team Relay

An Introduction to the Game

Luge was adopted during the 9th Congress in Innsbruck, Austria in 1964 as an official Winter Olympic sport. In luge, the athlete lies flat on their backs on a sled and slides down a 1,000m track. The track course has many curves, which increases the rider's speed. It's on these curves where the player must maximize their speed.

There are three events, the men's singles, the women's singles, and doubles. At the 2014 Sochi Winter Olympics, they added a team relay event. The individual events consist of four slides over the course of two days. The winner is determined by a combined time score of four fastest times. The doubles luge event consists of two slides during a one day period, where the winner is decided by combining the two fastest times.

Talking about the Game

Joe : Karen. Do you know what a luge is?

카렌. 루지가 뭔지 알아?

Karen : Luge? Is it some kind of food?

루지? 글쎄, 음식 종류인가?

Joe : No, it's a sport. My brother just got drafted by the Korean national luge team.

아니, 스포츠야. 내 형이 루지 한국 국가대표로 선발됐어.

Karen : Oh! Really? Congratulations! By the way, what kind of sport is it?

오! 정말? 축하해! 그런데 어떤 종류의 게임이야?

Joe : Hm... It's a sledding sport. The player lies flat on their backs on a sled and goes down a 1,000m track. It's kind of like bobsleigh.

음… 썰매 경기야. 선수가 평평한 썰매에 등을 대고 누워서 약 1,000m 트랙을 내려가는 경기야. 봅슬레이와 비슷해.

Karen : Sounds interesting.

재미있겠다.

The History

The luge is actually the sled used in the sport, which is made of wood. The beginning of this sport dates back to the 16th century, when wooden sleds were used in the Alps in Switzerland. It is also known that an owner of a Swiss hotel built the very first luge track, in order to provide some activity for guests wanting to have a little fun. Although it has its roots in Switzerland, Austria played a great role in developing this leisure activity into a sporting event. Also, luge became a popular and eventually a traditional winter sport in Austria, Germany, and Poland.

The first competition was held in 1883 by travel agents in Switzerland. However, it was adopted into the Olympics much later in 1964. The sport is dominated by German athletes who excel in luge. Just between 1964 and 1988, the German team took home 15 gold medals. Italy and Austria follow, making the three countries the nations with the most Olympic medals in the luge event.

Top Athletes

Felix Loch was born on July 24, 1989 in Germany. He debuted as a luger in 1995 and was accepted onto Germany's national team in 2006. He has received many medals in the FIL World Luge Championships. However, his 2008 victory at 18 made him the youngest world champion and the youngest Olympic gold medalist in the history of men's luge.

Felix Loch는 1989년 7월 24일 독일에서 태어났다. 그는 루지 선수로 1995년에 첫 경기를 치르고 2006년에 독일 국가 대표팀에 선발됐다. 그는 세계루지선수권대회에서 많은 메달을 획득했다. 하지만 2008년, 18살이라는 어린 나이에 얻은 승리가 그를 가장 어린 세계 챔피언으로 만들어줬으며 그는 남자 루지 역사상 가장 어린 올림픽 금메달 선수다.

Armin Zoggeler was born on January 4, 1974. He is an Italian luger. He has a total of six Olympic medals, proving him to be a successful luger. He began the sport at a very young age, winning his first medal in the World Cup at the age of 14 and starting off as a member of the Italian national team at 19. His success as a luger is amazing considering Italy's lack of a luge track until the 2006 Turin Winter Olympics.

Armin Zoggeler는 1974년 1월 4일에 태어났다. 그는 이탈리아 출신 루지 선수다. 그는 총 6개의 올림픽 메달을 획득하여 성공한 루지 선수임을 증명했다. 루지를 어린 나이에 시작하여 첫 메달을 14살에 월드컵에서 얻었고 국가대표팀으로 19살에 합류했다. 그가 성공적인 루지 선수로 발전한 것은 놀라운 일이다. 특히 2006년 토리노 동계올림픽 이전까지 이탈리아에 루지 트랙이 없었기 때문이다.

Georg Hackl was born on September 9, 1966. He is a German national athlete in the luge event. He has participated in five Winter Olympics, placing in all five, with three gold medals and two silver medals. He was an active athlete and is now an active luge coach for the German team.

Georg Hackl은 1966년 9월 9일에 태어났고, 독일의 루지 국가대표팀 선수다. 그는 동계올림픽을 5번 참여하면서 매번 메달을 획득했으며 금메달 3개와 은메달 2개를 받았다. 그는 적극적인 선수였으며 현재 선수로서는 은퇴했으나 독일 루지 대표팀의 코치로 활약 중이다.

* Photo from Wikipedia

"How did it all start?"

Joe : Do you know which sport Germany is strongest in?

독일이 어떤 스포츠를 잘하는지 알아?

Karen : Germany is good at football.

독일은 축구를 잘하지.

Joe : Germany is also good at luge. Almost all Winter Olympic medalists in luge are German.

독일은 루지도 잘해. 대부분의 동계올림픽 메달리스트들은 독일 선수야.

Karen : Is it because it started in Germany?

독일에서 루지가 시작해서 그런가?

Joe : No, luge is actually rooted in 16th century Switzerland. The first luge track and competition was also made and held in Switzerland. A hotel owner made the luge track and the first competition was held by travel agents. Isn't that odd?

루지는 16세기 스위스에서 시작됐어. 최초의 루지 트랙도 그곳에서 만들어지고 최초의 대회도 스위스에서 개최됐어. 그런데, 루지 트랙을 만든 사람이 바로 호텔 주인이었고 대회 주최자들은 여행사들이었다고 해. 이상하지?

Karen : Maybe they were really desperate in attracting visitors.

여행객들을 끌어모으는 데 급했나 봐.

KEY WORDS & EXPRESSIONS

be rooted in: –에 뿌리를 두고 있다

don't know about: 무엇은 잘 모르겠지만

stand out: 두드러지다

Joe : I don't know about the visitors, but it must have been fun because it became a popular and traditional winter sport. That's why it spread to countries like Italy, Austria and Germany.

여행객들에 관해서는 모르겠지만 무척 재미있었을 것 같아. 순식간에 대중적인 게임이 되면서 곧 전통적인 겨울 스포츠로 등장했으니까. 그랬기 때문에 주변 국가들, 특히 이탈리아, 오스트리아와 독일로 건너갔지.

Karen : And from those three countries, Germany currently stands out, right?

그리고 그 세 나라 중 독일이 월등해, 그렇지?

Joe : Germany has a total of 15 gold medals counting those won from 1964 to 1988. But Italy and Austria are also good. Italy also has a really famous luger, Armin Zoggeler.

독일은 1964년에서 1988년 사이에 참석한 올림픽에서만 15개의 금메달을 획득했어. 그런데 이탈리아와 오스트리아도 잘해. 이탈리아에는 그 유명한 선수 Armin Zoggeler도 있잖아.

Karen : But Germany has Felix Loch, the youngest Olympic gold medalist in the history of men's luge.

그러나 독일에는 남자 루지 종목에서 최연소 올림픽 금메달리스트인 Felix Loch가 있지.

Equipment and Gear

	**Sled 썰매** Luge sleds are different from general sleds used for sledding. There are no brakes or steering systems. It is solely controlled by the rider's foot position. 활주를 위한 썰매로 일반적인 썰매와는 다르다. 브레이크와 특별한 조향 장치가 없고 선수의 발의 위치로만 조종한다.
	**Racing suit 루지 수트** The suit is made in order to minimize air resistance. 공기의 저항을 최소화하기 위해 만들어졌다.

	**Helmet 헬멧** There is a special luge helmet that has been certified by the International Luge Federation. There is a clear windscreen in the front of the helmet to prevent wind from getting into the eyes. 국제루지연맹에서 공인한 루지 경기 전용 헬멧만 사용할 수 있다. 전면부에 바람을 막기 위한 투명한 바람막이가 있다.
	**Gloves 글러브** The special gloves are studded with spikes to add speed when starting. 출발할 때 속력을 내기 위한 스파이크가 박혀있는 특수한 장갑이다.
	**Shoes 슈즈** The luge shoes are shaped to reduce air resistance. 공기의 저항을 덜 받기 위한 루지 전용 신발이다.

What is this contraption?

Joe : Welcome to Alpensia Resort. Our resort is now opening for the luge experience event. Come and experience the fun.

알펜시아 리조트에 온걸 환영해. 우리 리조트는 지금 루지 체험 행사 중이야. 이용해봐.

Karen : Luge? That sounds like fun! Is the equipment free of charge?

루지? 재밌겠네! 장비는 다 무료로 주니?

Joe : Sure, of course! We lend luge sleds and gloves for free.

물론이지! 루지 전용 장갑과 썰매를 대여해주고 있어.

KEY WORDS & EXPRESSIONS

now opening: 최초로 열다
free of charge: 무료
try it out: 시도하다
steering systems: 조정 장치
foot position: 발 받침, 발 위치
spikes: 뾰족한 것, 스파이크
studded with: 박혔다, 장식되다
get it caught in: 어디에 걸리다

Karen : Can I wear any type of clothing?

옷은 아무거나 입고 타도 돼?

Joe : Yes, you can. There are special suits that athletes wear to shorten their time record. But you can just wear comfortable clothes.

응, 괜찮아. 선수용 수트가 있지만 단지 기록 단축을 위한 것이니 편한 옷을 입고 타면 돼.

Karen : OK right. I'll try it out.

그렇군. 그럼 한번 해볼게.

Joe : The sled has no brakes or steering systems. It is controlled only by the foot position and your weight.

썰매는 브레이크와 특별한 조향 장치가 없고 발의 위치와 몸의 무게중심으로 썰매를 조종할 수 있어.

Karen : What are these spikes on the gloves?

장갑에 있는 스파이크는 뭐야?

Joe : The special gloves are studded with spikes to increase speed when starting. Be careful not to get it caught in your clothes.

썰매가 출발할 때 속력을 내기 위한 스파이크가 박혀있는 특수한 장갑이야. 옷에 걸리지 않게 조심해.

Karen : Thank you.

고마워.

Joe : Enjoy.

즐거운 시간 되렴.

SPORTS FACTS

Luge

- First contested date in the Olympics :
  1964 Innsbruck Winter Games
- Nation of origin :
  Switzerland
- Types of events :
  Men's singles, Women's singles, Doubles, Team Relay
- Type of arena :
  Luge track
- Country with most medals :
  Germany
- Athlete with most medals :
  Georg Hackl

해 석

An Introduction to the Game

루지는 동계올림픽의 정식 종목으로 1964년 오스트리아의 인스브루크에서 열린 제 9회 대회부터 채택되었다. 평평한 썰매에 등을 대고 누워 약 1,000m가 되는 얼음 트랙을 내려가는 경기이다. 코스에 많은 커브 구간들이 있어 커브구간에서 최대한 속력을 줄이지 않고 내려가는 것이 관건이다.

경기종목으로는 남자 싱글, 여자 싱글, 2인 경기가 있다. 그리고 2014년 소치 동계올림픽부터 팀 릴레이경기가 새로 추가되었다. 개인경기는 이틀 동안 4번의 기회로 구성되어 있고 기록을 합산하여 제일 빨리 들어온 선수가 우승자이다. 2인 경기는 하루 동안 2번의 기회로 구성되어 있다.

The History

루지는 나무로 만든 썰매를 말한다. 19세기부터 스위스, 오스트리아 등 알프스 산지의 나무썰매타기 놀이로 시작되어 스포츠경기로 발전하였다. 오스트리아에서는 겨울철 전통 스포츠였고 독일과 폴란드에서도 유행하였다. 1883년 스위스에서 관광업자들이 개최하여 첫 국제대회가 열렸다.

루지는 독일이 전통적으로 강세다. 독일이 뛰어난 선수를 가장 많이 배출하였고 그 뒤로 이탈리아, 오스트리아가 뒤를 잇는다. 올림픽에서도 이 세 나라가 대부분 메달을 차지했다.

10 NORDIC COMBINED

노르딕 복합

EVENTS

MEN'S EVENTS

Sprint K120 men
Individual, ski jumping K90 (70m) men
Team 4X5km men

An Introduction to the Game

Nordic combined is a type of Nordic skiing that combines ski jumping with cross-country skiing. The first tournament began with the adoption of the sport in the 1924 Winter Olympics. In 2010 at the 21st Winter Olympic Games, the game was divided into three events. In this event the scores from both the cross-country and ski jump are summed up and the athlete with the highest overall score wins the game, regardless of individual ranking.

Talking about the Game

Joe : Hi, how have you been?

안녕, 잘 지냈어?

Karen : I've been good. I'm doing fine. I'm glad to see you again!

매우 잘 지냈지! 다시 만나게 되어 반가워.

Joe : I'm glad to hear that. Have you heard about Nordic combined?

다행이다. 노르딕 복합 경기에 대해서 들어봤니?

Karen : Nordic combined? No, I haven't. What is it?

노르딕 복합 경기? 한 번도 들어본 적이 없어. 그게 뭐야?

Joe : Actually, I just found out about this sport. So I looked into it.

사실 나도 이번에 처음 알았어. 그래서 조사를 해봤지.

Karen : Can you explain it to me?

나한테 설명해 줄래?

Joe : Nordic combined includes both ski jumping and cross-country skiing.

노르딕 복합 경기는 크로스컨트리 스키와 스키점프를 함께 치르는 경기야!

Karen : Oh! I've heard about it before. I wish I could actually watch it!

아! 내가 알고 있는 경기 종목이야! 직접 보고 싶다!

Joe : Let's go see the game right now!

그렇다면 우리 노르딕 복합 경기를 보러 지금 당장 가보자!

Karen : Really? Sounds great.

정말? 좋아.

The History

Nordic combined is a Nordic skiing sport developed in Northern Europe, including countries like Scandinavia and the Norway provinces. The word ski is known to have its origins in the Old Norse word "skid," which means wood split into long pieces. The sport is a combination of cross country skiing and ski jumping. The scores from both areas are combined for a total score that is applied in the ranking decision. Like many skiing sports, the Nordic combined also has a practical history. Since the cold northern countries were covered with snow, many inhabitants used skis when hunting for food, gathering wood for fire, or for transportation.

This game developed from such a humble background until 1892, when the first official competition for the Nordic combined was held in Oslo during a ski festival. This festival is known to have attracted even the King Olav V of Norway, who also competed in this ski festival in the 1920s. The players who participated in the ski festival in Norway during the 19th century grew as skiers contesting in both cross-country skiing and ski jumping. The sport has been with the Olympics since the adoption of the men's individual event in the 1924 Winter Olympics in Chamonix, France.

Top Athletes

Samppa Lajunen was born on April 23, 1979. He is an athlete on the Finnish team. He won five Olympic medals that includes three golds, all won at the 2002 Salt Lake City Winter Olympics, and two silver medals at Nagano. He retired at the age of 24, cutting his athletic career short to continue his graduate studies in Economics and Business Administration.

Samppa Lajunen은 1979년 4월 23일에 태어났다. 그는 핀란드 대표선수로 활동하였다. 선수로서 5개의 올림픽메달을 획득했으며 2002년 솔트레이크시티 동계올림픽에서 획득한 금메달 3개와 나가노에서 획득한 은메달 2개를 자랑한다. 그러나 그는 대학원에서 경제학과 경영학을 공부하기 위해 선수 생활을 24살이라는 이른 나이에 은퇴했다.

Felix Gottwald was born on January 13, 1976 in Austria. He first competed in the Olympics at the age of 18 in 1994; however, his first Olympic medal came in the 2002 Salt Lake City Olympics where he received bronzes in the 7.5 km sprint, 15km individual, and the 4X5 km team event. However, it was the 2006 Turin Olympics that showered him with two gold medals.

Felix Gottwald는 1976년 1월 13일 오스트리아에서 태어났다. 그는 1994년 18살에 첫 올림픽 경기를 치렀다. 그러나 최초의 올림픽 메달은 2002년 솔트레이크시티 동계올림픽에서 받았으며 이때 7.5km 스프린트, 15km 개인, 그리고 4x5km 팀 종목에서 모두 동메달을 획득했다. 하지만 2006년 토리노 올림픽이 그에게 2개의 금메달을 안겨주었다.

Ulrich Wehling was born on July 8, 1952. As a German skier he won three gold medals in three consecutive Olympic Games. After retiring as an athlete, he took on a new role as a director for the Nordic combined in the FIS(International Ski Federation), participating under this title at the 2006 Turin Winter Olympics and the FIS Nordic World Ski Championships in 2007.

Ulrich Wehling은 1952년 7월 8일에 태어났다. 독일 스키 선수로서 3연속 올림픽 금메달을 획득했다. 선수 생활을 끝내고 은퇴 후 그는 FIS 국제스키연맹 노르딕 복합 경기 부문 책임자로 활동하면서 2006년 토리노 동계올림픽과 2007년 국제스키연맹의 노르딕 스키 경기에서 활약했다.

* Photo from Wikipedia

"How did it all start?"

Joe : We have some time before the game starts.

경기가 시작하려면 아직 시간이 남았어.

Karen : Then why don't you look into the history of Nordic combined before the game?

그럼 우리 경기 시작 전에 노르딕 복합 경기의 역사에 대해서 알아보는 게 어때?

Joe : I looked up several facts.

내가 몇 가지 찾아보았어!

Karen : Can you explain it to me?

나한테 설명해 줄 수 있겠니?

Joe : The Nordic combined competition is a type of Nordic skiing developed in Northern Europe, including countries like Scandinavia and Norway. This sport combines the scores of cross-country ski and ski jump in determing the rank.

노르딕 복합 경기는 노르웨이를 비롯한 북유럽 스칸디나비아 지방에서 발달한 노르딕 스키의 한 종목이야. 거리 경기인 크로스컨트리 스키와 비약 경기인 스키점프를 함께 치러 두 점수를 합산하여 순위를 정하는 경기지.

This game began in the 19th century with a Norwegian ski festival where the best athletes came to compete and show off their overall cross country skiing and ski jumping abilities. The first official game was held in 1892 in Oslo. Since the first competition in the 1924 Winter Olympics in Chamonix, France; the men's individual event was adopted as an official sport. The Nordic combined team competition was added during the 15th congress in 1988.

이 경기는 19세기 노르웨이에서 열린 스키축제에 참가한 선수들이 크로스컨트리 스키와 스키점프의 기량을 종합적으로 겨루어 최고의 선수를 가린 데서 유래했어. 1892년 오슬로에서 처음으로 정식 경기가 열렸고, 동계올림픽에서는 1924년 프랑스의 샤모니에서 열린 제1회 대회부터 남자 개인전이 정식 종목으로 채택되었다고 해. 그리고 1988년 제15회 대회부터 단체전이 추가되었어.

Karen : After listening to the history, I am more interested than ever about

KEY WORDS & EXPRESSIONS

look up: 무엇을 조사하다, 찾다

familiar with: 무엇에 대해 익숙하다, 잘 알고 있다

successful athlete: 성공한 선수

Nordic combined.

오! 역사를 알고 나니까 더 흥미가 생긴다.

Joe : Do you know any famous players of Nordic combined?

혹시 노르딕 복합 경기에서 유명한 선수를 알고 있니?

Karen : No, I'm not familiar with any. Do you have a favorite athlete?

아니, 선수들에 대해서는 잘 몰라. 너는 좋아하는 선수가 있니?

Joe : I know the most famous Nordic combined athlete.

나는 노르딕 복합 경기의 가장 유명한 선수를 알고 있어.

Karen : Who is it?

그게 누군데?

Joe : Georg Thoma!

게오르그 토마야!

Karen : What do you know about him?

자세히 설명해 줄 수 있어?

Joe : Georg Thoma was born on August 20, 1937 in Hinterzarten. He is a former German Nordic combined skier. He won two Winter Olympic medals in the Nordic combined with a gold in 1960 and a bronze in 1964.

힌테르차르텐에서 1937년 8월 20일에 태어난 게오르그 토마는 전 독일 노르딕 복합 스키 선수야. 그는 두 번의 동계올림픽에서 1960년에는 금메달을, 1964년에는 동메달을 받았어.

Thoma also won the gold in the individual event at the 1966 FIS Nordic World Ski Championships in Oslo. Thoma's strength in the Nordic combined was jumping. He was a three time German champion in ski jumping in 1960, 1961, and 1963.

토마스는 오슬로에서 1966년 FIS 노르딕 스키 세계선수권대회에서 개인 이벤트에서 금메달을 수상했어. 노르딕 복합에서 토마스의 강점은 점프였는데 그는1960년, 1961년, 1963년 스키점프에서 세 번 독일 챔피언이었대.

Karen : What a successful athlete! Hey the game's going to start soon!

대단한 선수야! 이제 곧 경기가 시작하겠다!

Joe : Come on. Let's watch it!

얼른 보러 가자!

Equipment and Gear

Bindings 바인딩

Bindings are mounted parallel to the run-direction. They are used only at the toe of ski boots.

진행방향과 수평이 되도록 받침대로 설치된다. 스키 부츠의 앞부분만 고정한다.

Boots 부츠

Boots are fixed to the ski with a binding. Boots are constantly under pressure in skating techniques. Nordic combined boots are more flexible and are cut lower in the front to allow skiers to bend their ankles.

발가락을 지지하기 위해서 바인딩과 함께 스키에 고정된다. 끊임없이 압력을 받는다. 스케이팅 기술을 펼칠 때 이 종목에서 사용되는 스키 부츠는 일반 부츠에 비해 유연하고 앞부분이 낮아 선수들이 발목을 쉽게 구부릴 수 있게 해준다.

Helmets 헬멧

Helmets prevent head injuries.

충격으로부터 머리를 보호한다.

Goggles 고글

In the snow, goggles protect the eyes from reflected sunlight.

고글은 눈이 쌓인 곳에서 태양 빛이 반사되어 눈을 자극하는 것을 방지한다.

Poles 폴

They are long and straight sticks that allow skiers to push against the snow.

스키 타는 사람이 눈을 헤치고 나아갈 수 있게 하는 길고 곧은 장비이다.

Suit 스키복

A suit is similar to a runner's training clothing, yet it is made to fit the body of the skier.

육상 선수들의 연습용 옷과 비슷하나 몸의 모양에 맞춘다.

Jumping skis

Cross country skis

Skis 스키

Jumping skis are manufactured especially for use on ski jumping hills. The curvature and shape are restricted by certain geometric features.

스키점프의 스키는 스키점프힐에서 사용할 수 있도록 특별히 제조된다. 그것의 굴곡이나 모양은 기하학적인 특징의 제한을 받는다.

Cross country skis are smaller and lighter than the skis used in alpine skiing. They are long and have curved ends with slight bumps in the waist. They are 2 meters long.

크로스컨트리 스키는 알파인 스키에서 사용되는 스키보다 더 좁고 가볍다. 길고 끝부분에 굴곡이 있으며 중간에서 약간 위로 향한다. 2m 정도이다.

What is this contraption?

Joe : I think ski clothes all look the same.
스키 선수들은 옷이 다 비슷한 거 같아.

Karen : You're right! The suits are all skin tight.
정말 그렇네! 옷이 몸에 딱 달라붙어 있어.

Joe : After watching the ski competition, I started getting interested in the equipment they use.
스키 대회를 보고 나서 스키 선수들이 사용하는 장비가 궁금해졌어!

KEY WORDS & EXPRESSIONS

all look the same: 똑같이 보인다
keen: 예리한, 날카로운
jumping hills: 점프 기술을 하는 언덕
curvature: 굴곡
geometric: 기하학적인
waist: 스키의 중간 부분
push against: 무엇에 대고 밀다

Karen : I know! The skis differ depending on the type of skiing sport.
그래 맞아! 특히 스키 종목별로 스키 모양이 다른 거 같아.

Joe : You are really keen! The Nordic combined uses two types of skis.
너 정말 예리하다! 노르딕 복합 경기에서 스키는 두 가지로 나누어져 있어.

Karen : How are they different?
어떻게 달라?

Joe : First of all, jumping skis are manufactured especially for use on the jumping hills. Their curvature and shape are restricted by certain geometric features.

우선 스키점프의 스키는 스키점프힐에서 사용할 수 있도록 특별히 제조되어 있어. 그것의 굴곡이나 모양은 기하학적인 특징의 제한을 받지.

Karen : Wow! That's amazing. How about the other type of skis?

우와! 신기하다. 그럼 나머지는 어떤데?

Joe : Cross country skis are smaller and lighter than the skis used in alpine skiing. They are long and have curved tips with a slight bump in the waist. They are about 2 meters long.

크로스컨트리 스키는 알파인 스키에서 사용되는 스키보다 더 좁고 가벼워. 길고 끝부분에 굴곡이 있으며 중간에서 약간 위로 향하고 있어. 길이는 2m 정도야.

Karen : Ah! The two are really different! Is there any other equipment?

아! 두 가지가 정말 다르구나! 다른 장비에는 뭐가 있어?

Joe : There are helmets and goggles!

헬멧이랑 고글도 있어!

Karen : Helmets prevent the head from injury. And the goggles protect the eyes!

헬멧은 머리를 다치지 않게 보호해주는 역할을 해. 고글은 눈을 보호하지.

Joe : You're right! Especially, the goggles. Skiers need them to protect their eyes from sunlight reflected off the snow.

맞아! 특히 스키 선수들은 눈에 반사되는 태양빛으로부터 눈을 보호하기 위해 고글을 써야 해.

Karen : They are really necessary equipment for skiers!

스키 선수들에게 정말 필요한 장비로구나!

Joe : Do you know what that skier is holding on to?

저 선수가 손에 쥐고 있는 게 뭔지 아니?

Karen : What is it?

저게 뭐야?

Joe : It is a pole! It is a long and straight stick. It allows skiers to push hard against the snow.

폴이라는 거야. 폴은 길고 일직선이야. 스키를 타는 사람이 힘껏 누르며 눈을 헤치고 나아가게 해줘.

Karen : There is so much equipment for skiing!

스키를 타는 데 필요한 장비가 굉장히 많구나!

SPORTS FACTS

NORDIC COMBINED

- First contested date in the Olympics :
  1924 Chamonix Winter Olympics
- Nation of origin :
  Norway
- Types of events :
  Men's events in sprint K120, individual/ski jumping K90, Team/4X5 km
- Type of arena :
  Outdoor Nordic Combined Stadium
- Country with most medals :
  Norway
- Athlete with most medals :
  Birger Ruud
- Youngest athlete :
  Eric Frenzel

해 석

An Introduction to the Game

노르딕 복합은 노르딕 스키의 한 종목으로서 크로스컨트리 스키와 스키점프를 함께 치르는 경기이다. 1924년 제1회 동계올림픽 경기대회부터 정식 종목으로 채택되었다. 2010년 제21회 동계올림픽 대회에서는 3개의 세부 종목으로 나누어 경기를 치렀다. 이 종목에서는 크로스컨트리와 스키점프를 합산하여 높은 총점을 가진 선수가 개별 대회의 순위와 상관없이 우승하게 된다.

The History

노르딕 복합 경기는 노르웨이를 비롯한 북유럽 스칸디나비아 지방에서 발달한 노르딕 스키의 한 종목이다. 영어 ski는 고대 스칸디나비아 단어인 skid에서 그 어원을 두고 있다. skid는 긴 나무 조각이라는 뜻을 지니고 있다. 이 스포츠는 거리 경기인 크로스컨트리 스키와 비약 경기인 스키점프를 함께 치러 두 점수를 합산하여 순위를 정하는 경기이다. 그리고 많은 스키 종목들과 같이 노르딕 복합 경기도 매우 실용적인 역사에서부터 출발한다. 북부의 추운 국가에서는 눈이 많이 내려 그 지방 주민들은 음식을 얻거나 나무를 하고 이동을 하기 위해 스키를 사용했다.

이 경기는 19세기 노르웨이에서 열린 스키축제에 참가한 선수들이 크로스컨트리 스키와 스키점프의 기량을 종합적으로 겨루어 최고의 선수를 가린 데서 유래하였다. 1892년 오슬로에서 처음으로 정식 경기가 열렸다. 스키축제는 유명하여 오슬로 왕 올라브 5세도 경기에 참여했다고 알려져 있다. 동계올림픽에서는 1924년 프랑스의 샤모니에서 열린 제1회 대회부터 남자 개인전이 정식 종목으로 채택되었다. 그리고 1988년 제15회 대회부터 단체전이 추가되었다.

11 SHORT TRACK SPEED SKATING
쇼트트랙 스피드 스케이팅

EVENTS

MEN'S EVENTS	WOMEN'S EVENTS
500m men	500m women
1,000m men	1,000m women
1,500m men	1,500m women
5,000m relay men	3,000m relay women

An Introduction to the Game

Short track speed skating is a classic Winter Olympic event. Short track events are held at an indoor stadium, so it is called indoor short track speed skating. Players compete against other countries in an ice rink. This stadium's circumference is 111.12m which is shorter than the long track used for speed skating. Also, short track speed skating requires more than two skaters to start the competition. Short track speed skating is divided into men and women's events. First, the men have four events: 500m men, 1,000m men, 1,500m men and 5,000m relay men. Women also have four events. The 500m women, 1,000m women, 1,500m women, which are the same as the men's. However, women's relay is only 3,000m. It is 2,000m shorter than the men's relay event.

Talking about the Game

KEY WORDS & EXPRESSIONS

have much interest in: (무엇에) 관심/흥미를 갖는다

talking about: (무엇을 강조하는 뜻으로 사용)

like yourself: 당신과 같은

is that all?: (that's it) 그것이 다다

hold on: 잠깐

ice rink: 빙상경기장

go get a bite (to eat): 식사하러 가자

Joe : I love winter sports! Especially short track speed skating. How about you Karen?

난 동계스포츠가 정말 좋아! 특히 쇼트트랙이 제일이지. 넌 어떠니?

Karen : Hm... Actually, I don't have much interest in the Winter Olympics, so I don't know anything about skating.

음... 사실 난 동계올림픽에 관심이 없어. 그래서 스케이팅은 잘 몰라.

Joe : I'm talking about short track speed skating not just any skating. Come on, don't you want to know about short track speed skating? Please say yes!

쇼트트랙 스피드 스케이팅이야! 그냥 스케이팅이 아니라구. 난 쇼트트랙에 대해 잘 알아. 알고 싶지 않니? 그렇다고 해!

Karen : Sure, I really want to know. Please tell me Professor Joe.

그래, 좋아. 난 정말로 알고 싶어요. 제발 가르쳐 주세요, 교수님.

Joe : Don't be sarcastic! You should know about at least one winter sport. It's common sense, buddy. Let me see, many people, like yourself, call this sport short track or skating. But it's wrong! It is called short track speed skating! Okay?

비꼬진 말고! 몇몇 동계스포츠에 대해선 어느 정도 알고 있어야 돼. 이건 상식이야. 보자, 몇몇 사람들은 너처럼 이것을 쇼트트랙이나 스케이팅이라고 부르지. 그건 잘못된 거야. 정확한 명칭은 쇼트트랙 스피드 스케이팅이야!

Karen : Okay, I got it. Is that all, professor?

알았어. 그게 다예요, 교수님?

Joe : Hold on. Short track speed skating needs four to six people to race. You've probably seen many people on the rink on TV.

기다려봐. 쇼트트랙은 넷에서 여섯 명 정도가 경기를 해. 아마도 넌 TV에서 본 적이 있을 거야.

Karen : Yeah, I remember. By the way Joe, how big is the ice rink?

맞아, 기억난다. 근데 그 경기장이 얼마나 커?

Joe : Great attitude! The short track speed skating rink is almost is 111.12m.

좋은 태도야! 쇼트트랙 링크는 거의 111.12m 정도야.

Karen : You are such a genius! How did you memorize all that?

넌 정말 천재야! 그런 걸 어떻게 다 기억해?

Joe : It's easy. Also, short track speed skating is also called an "indoor short track speed skating" because it's played indoors.

기본이지. 또 쇼트트랙은 인도어 쇼트트랙 스피드 스케이팅이라고 불려. 왜냐면 안에서 경기를 치르니깐.

Karen : Indoor speed, what? It's too long and I'm hungry. Why don't we get some food, please?

인도어 뭐... 에이 너무 길다. 나 배고파. 우리 밥 좀 먹으러 가는 게 어때? 제발.

Joe : Ok. But, just one more important thing.

알았어. 내가 마지막으로 중요한걸 하나 설명할 기회를 줘.

Karen : I give up! Ok! What is it?

포기했다! 뭔데?

Joe : Thank you. This sport has four events for men and women. There are three events that are the same in both men and women; the 500m, 1,000m, and 1,500m. But the relay events are different. Men's relay is 5,000m and the women's is 3,000m. Wasn't that brief? Let's go get a bite!

고마워. 쇼트트랙은 각 성별마다 4개의 종목이 있어. 남녀 3가지 종목은 500m, 1,000m 그리고 1,500m로 같아. 그런데 계주 경기는 다르게 되어 있어. 남자 계주 종목은 5,000m이고 여자 계주는 3,000m야. 여기까지가 간략한 설명이야, 친구! 이제 밥 먹으러 가자!

Karen : Awesome! I love you!

멋져! 사랑해!

The History

Short track speed skating originated in Canada in North America. In the 1988 Calgary Winter Olympics, short track speed skating was chosen as a demonstration sport. Short track speed skating was finally selected as a formal discipline in the 1992 Winter Olympics in Albertville, France. Also, short track speed skating was adopted in the Asian Winter Games in Sapporo, Japan. Korea's short track team participated in the 1986 Asian Winter Olympics for the first time. After Japan's Winter Games, interest in short track speed skating grew in Korea. Since then, Korea has become a top nation in short track speed skating. Short track speed skating has become an indispensable Olympic event in Korea.

Top Athletes

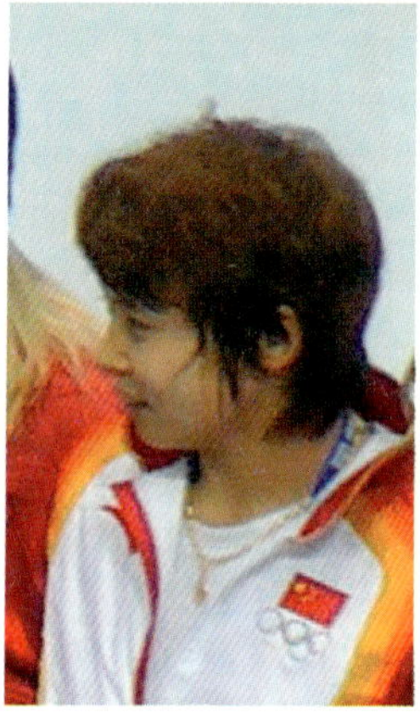

Wang Meng was born on April 10, 1985 in China. She participated in two Winter Olympics, the 2006 Turin and the 2010 Vancouver games, placing for medals in both Olympics. She was decorated with three gold medals in the Vancouver Olympics and one gold, silver, and bronze medal in the Turin Olympics. She was unable to participate in the 2014 Sochi Games due to injury, but still remains the women's short track queen.

Wang Meng은 1985년 4월 10일 중국에서 태어났다. 그녀는 2006년 토리노와 2010년 밴쿠버 올림픽에 참여했으며, 두 올림픽 모두에서 메달을 획득했다. 밴쿠버에서는 3개의 올림픽 메달을 얻었고 토리노에서는 금은동 메달 한 개씩을 얻었다. 부상으로 인해 2014년 소치 올림픽에 참여하지 못했으나 최고의 여성 쇼트트랙 선수로 뽑힌다.

Victor Ahn was born on November 23, 1985 in Korea. He began his short track career in his native country of South Korea. He also competed for the Korean national team, winning three Olympic gold medals at the 2006 Turin Olympics. He unfortunately left the Korean Team after a political conflict arose within the Korea Skating Union then immigrated to Russia. Skating for the Russian national team, he competed in the 2014 Sochi Olympics and won three gold medals in the 500m, 1,000m, and the 5,000m relay and a bronze in the 1,500m race. He boasts the title of being the first short track skater to win medals in every short track event.

Victor Ahn(안현수)은 1985년 11월 23일 한국에서 태어났다. 안현수는 한국에서 쇼트트랙 선수 생활을 시작했으며 한국 대표팀 선수로서 2006년 토리노 올림픽에서 3개의 금메달을 획득했다. 그러나 대한빙상경기연맹에 정치적 문제가 발생하여 대표팀을 떠났다. 그 이후 안현수는 러시아로 이민을 가서 러시아 대표팀에서 선수 생활을 이어갔다. 러시아 선수로 그는 2014년 소치 동계올림픽에 참여한 결과 500m, 1,000m, 5,000m 계주에서 금메달을 받고 1,500m에서는 동메달을 획득했다. 2014년 성과 이후 안현수는 쇼트트랙 역사상 처음으로 모든 종목에서 메달을 획득한 선수로 우뚝 섰다.

Lee Kyung Chun was born on January 6, 1976 in South Korea. She won the 3,000m relay and the 1,000m race in the Lillehammer Winter Olympics in 1994. Her next Olympics at Nagano added two more golds and one bronze to her medal collection, making her one of seven women to win more than four or more gold medals in the Winter Olympics.

전이경은 1976년 1월 6일 한국에서 태어났다. 그녀는 1994년 릴레함메르 올림픽에서 3,000m 계주와 1,000m 경기를 모두 이겼다. 다음 나가노 올림픽에서는 금메달 2개와 동메달 1개를 얻었다. 이로 인해 그녀는 동계올림픽에서 금메달 4개 이상 획득한 여성 쇼트트랙 선수 중 1명이 됐다.

* Photo from Wikipedia & naver.com

"How did it all start?"

> **KEY WORDS & EXPRESSIONS**
>
> yes and no (in some ways and not another): 그렇기도 하고 안 그렇기도 하다
>
> naturalized citizen: 귀화시민
>
> top class: 최고의
>
> no worries: 걱정하지 마, 걱정 없다

Joe : Wow, look at that! He is so fast! He won the race!

우와, 저거 봐! 저 사람 진짜 빠르다! 그가 우승했어!

Karen : Where? Oh, I know him. He is very famous. Don't you know him?

어디? 아, 나 저 남자 알아. 엄청 유명한 사람이야. 넌 저 남자가 누군지 몰라?

Joe : Well, not really. Who is he?

음... 난 잘 모르겠는데. 누군데?

Karen : He is Viktor Ahn.

빅토르 안이라고 하는 사람이야.

Joe : Is he Russian?

러시아 사람이야?

Karen : Yes and no. Actually he was Korean but is now a naturalized citizen of Russia.

음... 맞아! 사실 한국인이었는데 러시아로 귀화했지.

Joe : Oh, I get it. Anyway, he is very talented at short track.

아, 무슨 말인지 알겠다. 그나저나 저 남자 쇼트트랙에 엄청난 재능이 있네.

Karen : He is a top international athlete in the short track speed skating events. In the 2014 Sochi Winter Olympics, he was awarded three gold medals at the 500m, 1,000m, and 5,000m relay. Also, he was awarded the first overall prize in the 2014 ISU Short Track World Championship.

그는 쇼트트랙 종목에서는 세계 최정상 선수야. 2014 소치 동계올림픽에서 500m, 1,000m, 그리고 5,000m 계주에서 금메달 세 개를 획득했어. 또, 2014 ISU 세계선수권대회에서는 종합 1위를 차지했지.

Joe : Amazing! He is a top class athlete!

놀랍다! 그는 세계 최고의 선수구나!

Karen : The Korean team is very unfortunate to have lost such a great athlete.

훌륭한 선수가 다른 나라로 귀화했다는 사실이 안타깝네.

Joe : No worries. Korea is still a leading country in short track speed skating. It's interesting how the sport began in the west, namely Canada, and spread to Asian countries, like Korea and Japan.

걱정 마. 한국이 아직 쇼트트랙에서 선두적인 나라야. 이 종목이 서양 나라인 캐나다에서 시작해서 한국과 일본과 같은 아시아 국가들에게까지 전파됐다는 것이 신기하기만 하지.

Equipment and Gear

Skates 스케이트

Skates used in short track speed skating have two sharp blades that are curved and placed to the left of the boot so as to prevent skaters from touching the ice during turns. The boot is made with heavy material to give the skater stability and support for the ankle.

쇼트트랙 스피드 스케이트에서 사용되는 스케이트는 두 개의 날카로운 날이 달렸다. 선수가 턴을 할 때 얼음에 닿지 않도록 날은 휘어져 있으며 부츠 바닥 왼쪽에 장착됐다. 부츠 또한 무거운 소재로 만들어 안전성을 높이고 발목을 보호해준다.

Helmet 헬멧

A helmet protects the head from injuries and accidents during a race.

경기 중 일어날 수 있는 사고로부터 머리를 보호하기 위한 장비이다.

Goggles 고글

Goggles are glasses made of solid plastic glass to protect the eyes from ice chips and wind. Although most skaters prefer to use goggles during a race, it is not mandatory.

단단한 플라스틱 유리로 이루어진 안경이고 얼음 파편과 바람으로부터 눈을 보호한다. 필수 장비는 아니지만, 대다수의 선수들이 착용한다.

Gloves 글러브

Gloves are worn to protect the hands during curves, as well as from the blades of skates.

글러브는 코너링에 도움을 주며 스케이트 날로부터 손을 보호해준다.

	**Skin-tight suit 복장** The suit worn in this sport is tightly fitted to reduce wind resistance. 선수들의 유니폼이며 바람저항을 줄여준다.
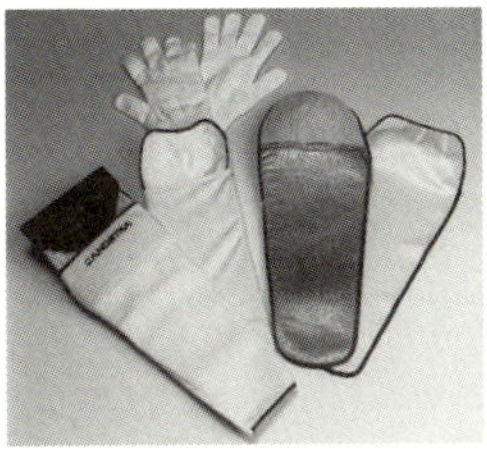	**Protective wears 보호장비** Shin, neck and knee guards protect skaters from contact with skate blades. 정강이, 목 그리고 무릎 보호대는 스케이트 날과의 접촉으로부터 보호해준다.

What is this contraption?

Joe : Hey Karen, do you know what kind of equipment is used in short track?
이봐 카렌, 쇼트트랙에 어떤 장비가 쓰이는지 아니?

Karen : Well... I'm not quite sure. Can you explain it to me?
음... 잘 모르겠어. 설명해줄래?

Joe : Sure! First, skates. Skates are...
물론! 우선 스케이트야. 스케이트는...

Karen : Oh, Joe. I know what skates are. They are the shoes the skaters wear. Aren't they? Tell me about the other equipment.
조. 스케이트는 나도 알아. 스케이트는 신발이잖아.
그렇지? 나는 다른 쇼트트랙 장비에 대해 알고 싶어.

KEY WORDS & EXPRESSIONS

not quite sure: 확실하지 않다
quite: 아주, 정말
fit the needs of: 필요에, 상황에 맞는
let' say: 예를 들어
is that all: 그것이 전부인가
not an option: 선택의 여지가 없다, 필수다
pretty: 꽤나, 정말
wind resistance: 바람의 저항
a must: 필수다

Joe : Okay. But the skates used in short track is different from other skates. Skates used in each sport are made to fit the needs of that sport. So these skates have longer and sharper blades than, let's say, figure skating. There are also two blades that are curved and set on the left side of the boot so that the skaters don't come in contact with the ice on curves. Another common piece of equipment is the helmet. They must wear helmets to protect their heads.

알았어. 그러나 쇼트트랙에서 사용되는 스케이트는 달라. 그 종목에 맞게 스케이트도 다르게 만들어졌지. 이 종목에서 사용되는 스케이트는 날이 피겨 스케이트와 같은 종목에 비해 더 길고 더 날카롭지. 그리고 날이 두 개인데, 약간 휘어졌고 신발의 왼쪽에 장착됐어. 이렇게 해야 선수가 커브에서 얼음과 접촉을 피할 수 있으니까. 또 흔히 사용되는 장비는 헬멧이야. 선수들은 헬멧을 꼭 착용해야 돼. 머리를 보호해 주기 때문이야.

Karen : Ok, is that all?

그래. 그게 다야?

Joe : Also, players wear goggles. It helps protect their eyes. I have a pair. Let me show you. Here.

그리고 선수들은 고글도 쓰지. 고글은 눈을 보호해줘. 내가 하나 가지고 있어. 보여줄게. 이거야.

Karen : Oh! I think they are fashionable. Ha ha. Anything else?

아! 멋진 거 같다. 하하. 다른건 없어?

Joe : Hmm… Skaters also wear protective shin, neck and knee guards.

음… 선수들은 보호장비들을 착용해. 정강이 보호대나 목, 무릎 보호대 같은 것들 말이야.

Karen : That sounds reasonable. They will need those guards to protect them from cuts and injuries from the blades of the skaters in front of them. The skaters skate so close to each other, so safety is not an option

말이 된다. 앞에 있는 선수의 스케이트 날로부터 다치는 것을 예방하기 위해서 그런 보호장비가 꼭 필요할 것 같아. 너무 가까이 스케이트를 타니까 안전은 필수인 것 같아.

Joe : Yeah. Karen did you see their suits? They are pretty tight, right?

그렇지. 카렌 너 선수들 복장을 본 적 있니? 약간 달라붙는거 말이야.

Karen : Oh I saw that. Is it a special suit?

응. 본 적 있어. 뭐 특별한 거라도 있니?

Joe : Of course! The suit is fitted tightly to reduce wind resistance. That way, skaters can skate faster. And another really important piece of equipment are their gloves. Skaters use their hands to keep their balance during curves, so they have to wear gloves to protect their hands when they touch the ice.

물론이지! 그 복장이 바람저항을 줄여서 선수들이 더 빨라질 수 있게 해줘. 또 중요한 장비는 바로 글러브야. 선수들은 커브를 돌 때 균형을 유지하기 위해 손으로 얼음을 만지는데, 이때 손을 보호하기 위해 글러브를 착용하는 거야.

Karen : There's a lot more than I thought.

아하! 쇼트트랙은 많은 장비가 필요하구나.

Joe : Yeah, and they are all a must!

그렇지. 장비들은 필수적이야.

SPORTS FACTS

SHORT TRACK SPEED SKATING

- First contested date in the Olympics :
  1992 Albertville Winter Olympics
- Nation of origin :
  Canada
- Types of events :
  Men: 500m, 1,000m, 1,500m, 5,000m relay
  Women: 500m, 1,000m, 1,500m, 3,000m relay Women
- Type of arena :
  Ice rink
- Number of players :
  500m, 1,000m race : 4 players
  1,500m, 3,000m 5,000m race : 6 to 8 players
- Athlete with most medals :
  Victor Ahn (Russia)
- Youngest athlete :
  Ariana Fontana

해 석

An Introduction to the Game

쇼트트랙 스피드 스케이팅은 대표적인 동계올림픽 종목이다. 쇼트트랙 종목은 실내의 경기장에서 진행되기 때문에 '인도어 쇼트트랙 스피드 스케이팅'이라고도 불린다. 선수들은 다른 국적의 선수들과 아이스 링크에서 경쟁한다. 이 경기장의 둘레는 111.12m인데 이는 롱 트랙 스피드 스케이팅보다는 짧다. 또한 롱 트랙 스피드 스케이팅은 한 경기에 두 명의 선수가 필요한 반면, 쇼트트랙 스피드 스케이팅은 두 명 이상의 선수들로 공개경기가 진행된다. 쇼트트랙 스피드 스케이팅은 남성, 여성 종목으로 나뉜다. 첫 번째로 남성 종목은 네 가지 종목이 있는데, 각각 500m, 1,000m, 1,500m, 그리고 5,000m 계주 경기가 있다. 다음으로 여성 종목 또한 네 가지 종목이 있다. 500m, 1,000m, 1,500m 종목은 남성 종목과 같다. 하지만 여성 계주 종목은 3,000m이다. 이는 남성 계주 종목보다 2,000m가 더 짧다.

The History

쇼트트랙 스피드 스케이팅은 북미의 캐나다에서 발생하였다. 1988년 캐나다 켈거리에서 쇼트트랙 스피드 스케이팅은 시범 종목으로 선택되었다. 마침내 1992년 프랑스 동계올림픽에서 쇼트트랙 스피드 스케이팅은 정식 종목으로 선택되었다. 또한 쇼트트랙 스피드 스케이팅은 일본 삿포로에서 열린 동계아시안게임에서 이미 채택되었다. 한국 쇼트트랙 팀은 1986년 일본 동계올림픽에서 처음 참가했다. 일본에서 개최한 아시아 동계올림픽 이후 한국에서의 쇼트트랙에 대한 관심은 증가되었다. 지금까지 한국은 쇼트트랙 종목에서 좋은 성과를 냈다. 한국에서 쇼트트랙 스피드 스케이팅은 빼놓을 수 없는 올림픽 종목이 되었다.

12 SKELETON
스켈레톤

EVENTS

MEN'S EVENTS
Individual men

WOMEN'S EVENTS
Individual women

An Introduction to the Game

Skeleton is a winter sledding sport where the athlete lies face down on a sled and rides down an ice track. The athlete experiences gravitational forces up to 5G and reaches speeds over 135 km/h. It originated from a sled for carrying possessions in North America. Skeleton was held in St. Moritz, Switzerland in 1928 for the first time, and was added to the Olympic program in the 2002 Winter Olympics.

Talking about the Game

Joe : What are you watching on TV?

TV에서 뭐 보고 있어?

Karen : I'm watching the Pyeongchang Winter Olympics.

지금 평창 동계올림픽 시청 중이야!

Joe : Oh, I know what that is. Isn't that bobsleigh?

아, 저 종목 알아. 봅슬레이 맞지?

Karen : No, it's like bobsleigh, but it's called skeleton.

봅슬레이와 유사하지만 스켈레톤이라고 불러.

Joe : Skeleton? What's that? Does it use some kind of stones?

스켈레톤이라고? 그게 뭐야? 돌 같은 것을 사용하는 거야?

Karen : Skeleton is a sliding sport. The athlete sleds facing down an ice track.

스켈레톤은 썰매를 엎드려 타서 얼음 트랙을 타고 내려오는 경기야.

Joe : That sounds really thrilling! Let me watch it with you.

재미있겠다. 같이 보자.

The History

The skeleton sled is a type of toboggan. The skeleton originated from the practical transport method of North American Indians who used sleds to transport possessions during the winter. However, the sled started to be used in races in 1882 when Davos and Klosters, British and American holidaymakers, funded the building of the first toboggan track. In 1884, after opening the game in Saint Moritz, Switzerland, it settled as a sport. The first championship was held in Austria in 1906. In 1923, FIBT(International Federation of Bobsleigh and Skeleton) was created to conduct bobsleigh and skeleton games.

The skeleton was initially adopted as an official sport in the 1928 Saint Moritz Winter Olympics, but it dropped at the next Olympics. It reappeared in 1948, but was again dropped due to the high level of danger and speed. It was in the 2002 Salt

Lake City Winter Olympics that both the men's and women's events were finally added to stay.

Top Athletes

Alexander Tretiakov was born on April 19, 1985. He is a Russian skeleton racer and the first Russian skeleton racer to win a gold medal. The prized gold medal was received in the 2014 Sochi Olympics when he outran the strongest contender Martins Dukurs. He also participated in the 2010 Vancouver Winter Olympics where he took the bronze medal.

Alexander Tretiakov는 1985년 4월 19일에 태어났다. 그는 러시아의 스켈레톤 선수이자 최초의 러시아 스켈레톤 금메달리스트다. 금메달은 2014년 소치 올림픽에서 Martins Dukurs라는 강한 도전자를 이긴 결과였다. 그는 2010 밴쿠버 동계올림픽에도 참가했으며 이때 동메달을 얻었다.

Jon Montgomery was born on May 6, 1979. Montgomery first began his skeleton career with a meager start when competing in the World Cup tours. It was in 2008 in Cesena, Italy where he won his first World Cup. He then went on to qualify for the 2010 Vancouver Winter Olympics and came home with a gold medal.

Jon Montgomery는 1979년 5월 6일에 태어났다. Montgomery는 월드컵 대회 참가로 스켈레톤 선수 생활을 시작했으나, 미흡했다. 2008년이 되어서야 그는 생애 첫 메달을 월드컵에서 획득하게 됐다. 이후 2010 밴쿠버 동계올림픽에 참가하여 올림픽 금메달을 목에 걸게 됐다.

Amy Williams was born on September 29, 1982. She is a skeleton racer for the British national team. She entered the 2010 Vancouver Winter Olympics and won a gold medal, becoming the first British athlete to win the gold in an individual event in the Winter Olympics in thirty years.

Amy Williams는 1982년 9월 29일에 태어났다. 그녀는 영국 스켈레톤 국가대표 선수다. 2010년 밴쿠버 동계올림픽에서 금메달을 획득하면서 30년만에 동계올림픽 개인 종목에서 금메달을 딴 최초의 영국 선수가 됐다.

* Photo from Wikipedia

"How did it all start?"

Joe : It is really fun watching the skeleton event!

스켈레톤 경기 정말 재미있다!

Karen : It is fun to watch but the force of gravity the racers experience is enormous.

보이는 건 재미있어 보이지만 실제로 선수가 받는 중력은 어마어마해.

Joe : Really?

정말?

Karen : Yes. They experience 5g force at 130km per hour coming down the ice track.

선수들은 엄청난 중력을 경험하게 되며 빙상 트랙에서 시속 130km의 빠른 속도로 질주해.

Joe : Oh my goodness! It is a dangerous sport.

보기보다 위험한 운동이네.

Karen : That's why the adoption of the skeleton as a formal Olympic sport was dropped twice until its final adoption in the 2002 Games. When it was finally given the go, both the men's and women's events were added.

그래서 올림픽 정식 종목으로 채택되는 데 두 차례의 번복이 있었지. 그러다가 2002년 동계올림픽 때

KEY WORDS & EXPRESSIONS

force of gravity (gravitational force): 중력의 힘

drop (reversed/turned over): 번복되다

give the go ahead (go ahead): 허용되다, 허락받다

toboggan: 썰매의 종류

pull (it) off: 해내다

pay off: 성공하다

정식 종목으로 채택되고, 남녀 종목 모두 추가되었어.

Joe : When did skeleton become a sporting event?

스켈레톤은 언제부터 스포츠 경기가 된 거야?

Karen : North American Indians used the sled to transport things during the winter months. But it was the British and Americans who built the toboggan track in 1882 that got it started as a sport.

원래는 북아메리카 인디언들이 겨울철에 사냥물을 옮기기 위한 수단으로 썰매를 이용했어. 그러다가 영국인들과 미국인들이 1882년 썰매 트랙을 만들면서 진정한 스포츠로 발전한 거야.

Joe : So that's how skeleton started.

스켈레톤이 그렇게 시작했구나.

Karen : Who won the gold medal in last night's skeleton event?

어제 우리가 봤던 스켈레톤 경기에서 누가 금메달을 땄어?

Joe : Lizzy Yarnold from England.

영국의 리지 야놀드 선수.

Karen : That player is amazing.

응. 그 선수 정말 대단한 선수인 것 같아.

Joe : Why?

왜?

Karen : I heard she didn't have any money to buy equipment so she had to earn it by working at an insurance company, while training at the same time.

가난한 형편 때문에 장비 살 돈이 없어서 보험회사에서 아르바이트를 하면서 운동을 했대!

Joe : That takes a lot of passion and hard work to pull off.

진정한 열정과 노력이 있어야만 가능한 일이지.

Karen : But it paid off in the end. She won the gold medal. How amazing.

그렇지? 그런 상황에서 금메달을 따다니. 정말 대단해.

Equipment and Gear

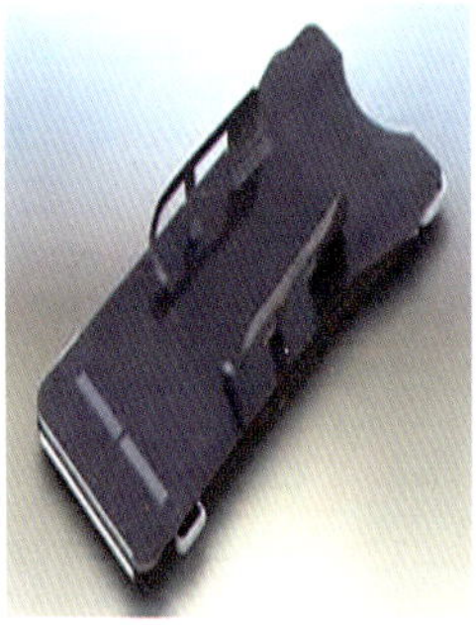

Skeleton 스켈레톤

A standard skeleton is 80 to 120cm in length, 8 to 20cm in height, and the distance between the blades are 34 to 38cm far. The sled is made up of a rear bumper, movable runner, front bumper, and seats.

스켈레톤의 규격은 길이 80~120cm, 높이 8~20cm, 양쪽 날 사이의 거리는 34~38cm로 규정되어 있다. 썰매는 뒤 범퍼, 이동식 러너, 앞 범퍼, 좌석으로 구성되어 있다.

Rear bumper 뒤범퍼

The back part of the sled that absorbs damage and protects the athlete when they touch the track's wall.

썰매 뒤쪽에 부착된 측면 부분. 충격을 흡수하여 선수가 트랙의 벽에 접촉되는 경우에 선수를 보호하기 위한 것이다.

Movable runner 이동식 러너

This is the iron blade attached under the sled. It can be controlled to make slight changes in the sled's contact with the surface of the ice.

썰매 바닥에 부착되어 있는 조절 가능한 강철 날. 곡선으로 되어 있어 얼음 면과 접촉을 바꿀 수 있도록 약간 조절하기 위한 것이다.

Front bumper 앞 범퍼

Front part of the sled that absorbs damage and provides protection on contact with the track's wall.

썰매의 앞쪽에 부착된 측면 부분. 충격을 흡수하여 선수가 트랙의 벽에 접촉되는 경우에 선수를 보호하기 위한 것이다.

Seat 좌석

A part of the sled where the player lies down.

선수가 엎드리는 부분이다.

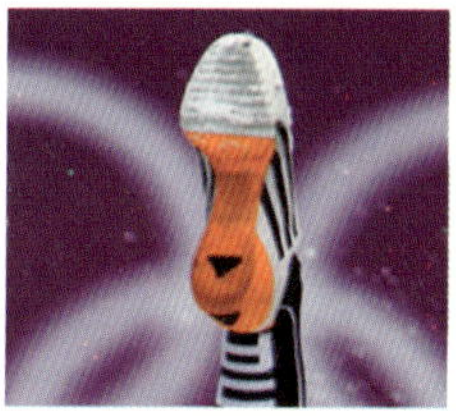	**Cleated shoes** 미끄럼 방지 신발 Shoes that have small cleats on the sole. They raise the frictional force when the athletes start on the ice. 밑창에 작은 징이 붙어 있는 신발. 출발할 때 얼음 위에서 마찰력을 높여주기 위한 것이다.
	**Chin guard** 턱 보호대 The hard part attached to the helmet that helps protect the player's chin when hitting the ice. 헬멧에 부착된 딱딱한 부분. 얼음에 부딪칠 때 턱을 보호하기 위한 것이다.
	**Crash helmet** 크래시 헬멧 The crash helmet protects the athlete's head. 머리를 보호하기 위한 것이다.

What is this contraption?

Joe : Remember the skeleton game we watched at the Pyeongchang Winter Olympics yesterday? I researched it on the internet, and it is more dangerous than I thought.

어제 평창 올림픽 경기에서 본 스켈레톤 말이야. 인터넷으로 검색해 봤는데 생각했던 것보다 위험한 운동이더라.

Karen : Like bobsleigh and luge, skeleton also uses a sled. But it is very thrilling and also very dangerous.

봅슬레이, 루지와 같이 스켈레톤도 썰매를 사용해. 그러나 3종목 가운데 가장 스릴감을 경험할 수 있지만 그만큼 굉장히 위험한 운동이지.

KEY WORDS & EXPRESSIONS

more dangerous than I thought: 생각보다 더 위험하다
protection: 보호 장비
runner: 스켈레톤 선수
high speed sport: 고속도를 내는 운동
absorb shock: 충격을 흡수하다
sled itself: 썰매 자체
under: 미만

Joe : What kind of equipment does skeleton have?

스켈레톤의 장비에는 어떤 것들이 있니?

Karen : Skeleton requires a sled, helmet, elbow pads, and shoes.

스켈레톤의 장비에는 썰매와 헬멧, 팔꿈치 보호대와 신발이 있어.

Joe : What? A helmet and elbow pads are the only protection for runners?

뭐? 그럼 선수를 보호할 수 있는 장비는 고작 헬멧과 팔꿈치 보호대뿐이야?

Karen : Yes. No other equipment is allowed when riding the skeleton. Runners just control the sled with their shoulders and legs.

응. 스켈레톤을 탈 때에도 다른 장치를 부착하는 것은 금지되어 있기 때문에 어깨와 다리를 이용해서 만 썰매를 조종할 수 있어.

Joe : It is a high speed sport, but they don't have much protection. That's why skeleton is a dangerous sport.

빠른 속도로 내려오는 운동인데 보호장비가 별로 없다니. 그래서 스켈레톤이 위험한 종목이구나!

Karen : Yes. The sled parts include the rear bumper, front bumper, movable runner, and the seat.

응. 썰매는 뒤 범퍼와 앞 범퍼, 이동식 러너와 좌석으로 구성되어 있어.

Joe : The sled is not just a simple sled.

스켈레톤 썰매가 단순한 썰매가 아니었구나.

Karen : Bumpers protect and absorb shock if the sled touches the wall. And the seat is where the runner lies down.

범퍼들은 벽에 부딪혔을 경우 충격을 흡수하여 선수를 보호하기 위한 것들이고, 좌석은 선수가 엎드리는 부분이야.

Joe : What is a movable runner?

이동식 러너는 뭔데?

Karen : It refers to the iron blade under the sled.

썰매 아래에 부착되어 있는 강철 날을 뜻해.

Joe : I see. They don't have other regulations for the equipment?

그렇구나. 장비에 대해 다른 규정은 없어?

Karen : They have rules for weight. The maximum weight is 115kg for men and 92kg for women. That includes the sled and runner's weight. The sled itself is 33kg for men and 29kg for women. Also, if the total weight is under 115kg for men and 92kg for women, then the sled's weight is increased to 43kg for men and 35kg for women.

무게에 대한 규정이 있어. 썰매와 선수의 체중을 합해 남자는 115kg, 여자는 92kg을 초과해서는 안 돼. 썰매 자체의 무게로 남자는 33kg, 여자는 29kg 이하로 규정하지. 또한 합계 무게가 남자 115kg, 여자 92kg 미만일 경우에는 썰매의 무게가 남자는 43kg, 여자는 35kg 이내로 늘어나.

Joe : Those are specific limits. Skeleton is getting more interesting with this new information.

의외로 까다로운 규칙이 있었구나. 스켈레톤은 알면 알수록 흥미로운 것 같아.

Karen : Right. Then do you want to find some more information on skeleton?

맞아. 그럼 우리 스켈레톤에 대해서 좀 더 자료를 찾아볼까?

Joe : Of course!

좋아!

SPORTS FACTS

Skeleton

- First contested date in the Olympics :
  1928 and 1948, but dropped until 2002 Salt Lake City Winter Olympics
- Nation of origin :
  Great Britain and America
- Types of events :
  Men and Women's individual
- Type of arena :
  Frozen outdoor tracks
- Sled weight regulations :
  Men : 115 kg
  Women : 92 kg
- Country with most medals :
  United States (8 medals : 3 gold, 4 silver, 1 bronze)
- Male Olympic Champion :
  Alexander Tretiakov (Russia)
- Female Olympic Champion :
  Lizzy Yarnold (Great Britain)

해 석

An Introduction to the Game

스켈레톤은 머리를 아래로 하여 썰매를 타고 얼음 트랙을 타는 겨울 스포츠이다. 선수는 5갈[G]의 중력을 받고 135km/h의 속도감을 경험한다. 이것은 북아메리카에서 짐을 옮기기 위한 썰매에서 유래되었다. 스켈레톤은 1928년 생 모리츠에서 처음 개최되었고, 2002년 동계올림픽 때 올림픽 종목으로 채택되었다.

The History

터보건(toboggan)의 한 종류인 스켈레톤은 스켈레톤 슬레딩(skeleton sledding)이라고도 한다. 스켈레톤은 북아메리카 인디언들이 겨울에 짐을 운반하기 위하여 썰매를 이용하던 것에서 유래되었다. 1882년 다보스와 클로스터스 사이에 썰매 코스가 설치되었고, 1884년 생모리츠에서 처음으로 경기가 열린 뒤 스포츠 종목으로 자리 잡게 되었으며, 1906년 오스트리아에서 첫 선수권대회가 개최되었다. 1923년부터 국제봅슬레이 스켈레톤연맹(FIBT)이 창설되어 봅슬레이와 스켈레톤 경기를 주관하고 있다.

동계올림픽에서는 1928년 스위스 생모리츠에서 정식 종목으로 채택되었으나 다음 대회부터 중단되었다가 1948년 생모리츠에서 두 번째로 열린 동계올림픽 경기대회에서 다시 정식 종목으로 경기가 열렸다. 그러나 고속 질주로 인한 위험성 때문에 또 중단되었다가 2002년 솔트레이크시티 동계올림픽에서 다시 정식 종목으로 추가되었다. 원 래는 남자 종목만 경기를 치렀으나, 2002년부터 여자 종목도 추가되었다.

13 SKI JUMPING
스키점프

EVENTS

MEN'S EVENTS
K120 individual (90m) men
K90 individual (70m) men
K120 team (90m) men

WOMEN'S EVENTS
K90 individual (70m) women

An Introduction to the Game

Ski jumping is a sport where jumpers fly into the empty sky in a straight line from the hill after skiing down an artificial slope. Ski jumpers go through four stages every run; the in-run, take-off, flight and landing. It has been a part of the Winter Olympics since the first Winter Olympics in Chamonix, France. The Olympic ski jumping competition consists of four events. They are the men's k-95 normal hill, men's k-125 large hill, men's team event on the large hill and women's k-95 normal hill. The women's k-95 normal hill was added to the Olympic ski jumping competition in the 2014 Sochi Winter Olympics.

Talking about the Game

KEY WORDS & EXPRESSIONS

jumper: 스키점프 선수

slope: 활주로

upper body: 상반신

takeoff position: 이륙 자세

landing: 착지

take up much of: 많이 차지하다

Joe : Have you ever seen the movie *Take Off*?

너 '국가대표'라는 영화 본 적 있니?

Karen : No, what is it about?

아니, 무슨 내용인데?

Joe : It's about five men who challenge themselves to participate in the Olympic ski jumping competition.

다섯 명의 남자가 올림픽 스키점프 경기에 도전한다는 내용이야.

Karen : Ski jumping? Do you know how to ski jump?

스키점프? 너는 스키점프 어떻게 하는지 아니?

Joe : A jumper skis down a long slope by bending their upper body. When the jumper reaches the takeoff position, they fly into the air by obtaining a driving force while stretching the knees and body into a straight position. After flight, they land.

활강할 때 선수는 상체를 구부린 채로 활강해. 도약지점에 도달한 후에 그의 다리와 몸을 직선으로 펴면서 추진력을 얻어 도약하면서 활강하고 마지막으로 착지해.

Karen : Oh, I see. Did they win a medal in the movie?

아, 알겠다. 영화에서 그들은 메달을 따니?

Joe : No, they didn't because one of them failed the landing. Landing is very important in ski jumping. Landing takes up much of the score.

아니, 못 따. 다섯 선수 중 한 명이 착지하는 데 실패했어. 스키점프에서 착지는 매우 중요해. 착지가 점수 비중이 제일 높아.

Karen : That's too bad. By the way, which Olympics did they participate in?

안타깝다. 그런데 그들은 어떤 올림픽에 출전했니?

Joe : It was the Nagano Winter Olympics in 1998.

1998년에 열린 나가노 올림픽이었어.

Karen : When was ski jump chosen as an official winter Olympic sport?

스키점프는 언제 동계올림픽 정식 종목으로 채택되었니?

Joe : It has been a part of the Winter Olympics since the first Winter Olympics in

1924 in Chamonix, France.

스키점프는 1924년 샤모니 프랑스 동계올림픽을 계기로 동계올림픽에 채택되었어.

The History

Ski jumping originated from a type of recreation. Then, it gradually transformed into a sport. It took shape as a competitive sport in the late 19th century. In 1862, ski jumping held its first competition in Norway. Ski jumping was adopted as a Winter Olympic sport in 1924 in Chamonix, France. Through the development of the sport, many jumpers contributed in forming and refining techniques to bring the sport into its current state. The very first pioneers were Thulin Thamas and Sigmund Ruud. They created the Kongsberger Technique, a new jumping technique requiring the jumper to bend their upper body at the hips. Andreas Daescher was another jumper who refined the jumping technique by holding his arms backwards closely to his body while leaning forward.

Simon Ammann is a key ski jumper. He was born in May of 1981 and is a two-time Olympic medalist of the men's individual normal hill event. The 2002 Salt Lake City Winter Olympics and 2010 Vancouver Olympics awarded him medals in this event, making it the first time for a ski jumper to win four medals in the Winter Olympics. A more recent uprising ski jumper is Kamil Stoch. He was born on May 25, 1987. He received two Olympic medals in the men's individual normal and large hill event at the 2014 Sochi Olympics.

Top Athletes

Matti Nykanen was born on July 17, 1963 in Finland. He is most noted for his three gold medals in the 1988 Calgary Winter Olympics, but he also won a silver and a gold medal in the 1984 Sarajevo Games. He is so famous in his homeland of Finland that he even has a stamp depicting his image.

Matti Nykanen은 1963년 7월 17일 핀란드에서 태어났다. 그는 1988년 칼거리 동계올림픽에서 획득한 금메달 3개로 가장 유명하다. 그러나 그는 1984년 사라예보에서도 은메달과 금메달을 얻었다. 핀란드에서 Nykanen을 묘사하는 우표를 만들 정도로 유명하다.

Simon Ammann was born on June 25, 1981 in Switzerland. He entered the competing world at the age of 16, going on to the Nagano Olympics in 1998. He did not win medals in either the world championships or the Olympics until 2002 in Salt Lake City, where he achieved two gold victories in the 70m men's individual and 90m men's individual event. He suffered injuries but made another entry in the 2010 Vancouver games to win a second round of two gold medals.

Simon Ammann은 1981년 6월 25일 스위스에서 태어났다. 16살에 스키점프 선수 생활을 시작하고 1998년 나가노 올림픽에 참가했다. 그렇지만 그는 세계선수권대회나 올림픽에서 메달을 얻지 못하다가 2002년 솔트레이크시티 올림픽에서 70m와 90m 남자 개인전에서 금메달 2개를 획득했다. 한때 부상을 겪었으나 2010년 밴쿠버 올림픽에서 또다시 2개의 금메달을 획득했다.

Thomas Morgenstern was born on October 30, 1986. He was an Austrian ski jumper who won a total of twelve gold medals in both the world championships and the Olympics. He participated in the 2006 Turin, 2010 Vancouver, and the 2014 Sochi Games and then retired in September of 2014.

Thomas Morgenstern은 1986년 10월 30일에 태어났다. 그는 오스트리아 스키점프 선수이며 세계선수권대회와 올림픽을 합쳐 총 12개의 금메달을 획득했다. 그는 2006 토리노, 2010 밴쿠버, 그리고 2014 소치 올림픽에 참가한 후 2014년 9월에 은퇴를 했다.

* Photo from Wikipedia

"How did it all start?"

Joe : Wow, he is cool. Who is he?

우와, 잘생겼다. 이 사람은 누구니?

Karen : Simon Ammann. He is a ski jumper.

시몬 암만. 스키점프 선수지.

Joe : Is he popular?

유명하니?

Karen : Of course! He is the first ski jumper to win four medals at the Winter Olympics.

그럼! 동계올림픽 통산 4관왕을 달성한 최초의 선수야.

Joe : Does he have a nickname like "the figure queen" Yuna Kim.

그는 피겨 여왕 김연아처럼 별명을 가지고 있니?

Karen : He has been nicknamed the "wall of Ammann" because it's really hard for other ski jumpers to break his record.

그는 "암만의 벽"이라는 별명을 가지고 있어. 왜냐하면 다른 선수들이 그의 기록을 깨기 매우 어렵기 때문이야.

Joe : Which country does he play for?

어느 국가 대표선수야?

KEY WORDS & EXPRESSIONS

break a record: 기록을 깨다
play for: (어느 팀/국가)에서 뛴다
make tweaks: 변화를 시키다, 수정을 하다

Karen : He's from Norway, where ski jumping originated.

그는 노르웨이 출신이야. 노르웨이는 스키점프가 유래한 곳이기도 해.

Joe : Then, the first ski jumper must have also been a Norwegian?

그럼 첫 스키점프 선수도 노르웨이 출신이니?

Karen : That's right. His name is Olaf Rye. He was a soldier for both Norway and Denmark. He has a record of flying 9.5m.

맞아. 노르웨이와 덴마크의 군인인 올라프 리예가 첫 스키점프 선수로 알려져 있어. 그는 9.5m를 날았다고 해.

Joe : The way they lean forward in almost a horizontal line is probably the reason why they are able to fly so far.

저렇게 수평선이 될 정도로 몸을 기울이기 때문에 멀리 날 수 있는 것 같다.

Karen : But the technique wasn't always like this. After 1924, when the sport was added to the Winter Olympics, many jumpers made tweaks to the technique. Andreas Daescher was the first to put his arms backwards closely to his body. Before him, the technique was to put the arms in a forward position.

그런데 점프 기술이 많이 변했어. 1924년 동계올림픽에 추가된 이후로 많은 선수들이 기술을 변화시켰어. 예를 들어 Andreas Daescher가 팔을 뒤로 뻗어 몸에 붙이는 기술을 선보인 최초의 선수였지. 그 이전에는 팔을 앞으로 놓는 자세로 선수들이 점프를 했어.

Equipment and Gear

	**Jumping skis 스키** Jumping skis are used for skiing downhill and landing. 스키는 활강과 착지에 쓰인다.
	**Boots 부츠** Boots support the jumper's body when skiing downhill and landing. 부츠는 스키점프 선수가 활강하고 착지할 때 선수의 몸을 받쳐준다.

	**Bindings 바인딩** Bindings are used to attach the boots to the jumping skis. 바인딩은 부츠를 스키에 장착해주는 장치로 사용된다.
	Connection cord 커넥션 코드 (부츠 뒷 부분을 스키에 연결해주는 줄) Connection cords connect the boots and jumping skis during flight. 커넥션 코드는 스키점프 비행 때 부츠와 스키를 연결해준다.
	**Ski jumping suit 스키복** The suit protects a ski jumper against the cold weather. 추운 날씨로부터 스키점프 선수를 보호해준다.
	**Helmet 헬멧** To protect jumper from getting hurt on the head. 스키점프 선수가 머리를 다치지 않도록 보호한다.
	**Ski jumping tower 스키점프대** Where the jump is done(ski downhill, leap, fly and land). 활강, 도약, 활공, 착지 등 경기를 벌이는 곳이다.

What is this contraption?

Joe : Where is this?
여기가 어디니?

Karen : This is the Alpensia ski jump tower
여기는 알펜시아 스키점프대야.

Joe : What's this part of the tower for?
이 타워 부분은 뭐하는 곳이니?

Karen : The tower consists of a start platform,

KEY WORDS & EXPRESSIONS

start platform: 출발 지점
in run: 점프대의 활강 경사면
take off table: 평평한 이륙 지점
norm point: 결승과 시작의 경계선
critical point: 벌점이 가해지는 지점
jury point: 될 수 있는 최대 거리
out run: 넓은 정지 지점

in-run and take-off table.

이곳은 스타트 플랫폼, 인런, 이륙판으로 이루어져 있어.

Joe : What does the in-run do?

인런이 무엇이니?

Karen : In-run has a 35~40' slope. This slope raises the speed of a jumper so they can fly.

인런은 35~40'로 경사졌는데 이 경사는 스키점프 선수가 활공하는 데 필요한 속도를 내게 해.

Joe : What's this landing area for?

이 착륙 지역은 뭐하는 곳이니?

Karen : This area has a norm point, critical point, jury point, and out run.

이곳은 규정점, 크리티컬 포인트, 심판 포인트 그리고 아웃런으로 이루어져 있는 곳이야.

Joe : What is the jury point?

심판 포인트가 뭐니?

Karen : It's the maximum distance a jumper can safely fly within.

그건 스키점프 선수가 안전하게 활공할 수 있는 최대 거리를 나타내는 한계선이야.

Joe : What is the critical point?

크리티컬 포인트는 무엇이니?

Karen : If a jumper lands over this point, they lose points.

만약 스키점프 선수가 이 포인트를 넘어서 착지하면 감점이 돼.

Joe : What is the norm point?

규정점은 뭐니?

Karen : It's the boundary of the beginning of the finish line.

그건 결승점의 시작을 나타내는 경계선이야.

Joe : What's this small structure beside the ski jump tower for?

스키점프대 옆의 작은 건축물은 뭐하는 것이니?

Karen : That area is for coaches and judges.

코치석과 심판석이야.

Joe : This structure is located in a high place.

건물이 높은 곳에 위치해있구나.

Karen : From there they can observe the jumper's flying position better.

스키점프 선수의 활강 자세를 자세히 볼 수 있도록 하기 위해서지.

SPORTS FACTS

Ski Jumping

- First contested date in the Olympics :
  1924 Chamonix Montblanc Winter Olympics
- Nation of origin :
  Norway
- Types of events :
  Men : individual (90m / 70m), team (90m)
  Women : individual (70m)
- Type of arena :
  Ski jumping hill (outdoor)
- Male Olympic Champion :
  Simon Ammann (Switzerland)
- Ski Jumpers with maximum score of 20 :
  (Only five jumpers in the world)
  Anton Innauer (Austria)
  Kazuyoshi Funaki (Japan)
  Sven Hannawald (Germany)
  Hideharu Miyahira (Japan)
  Wolfgang Loitzl (Austria)

해 석

An Introduction to the Game

스키점프란 스키를 타고 인공으로 만들어진 급경사면을 활강하여 내려오다 도약대로부터 직선으로 허공을 날아 착지하는 스키 경기이다. 노르딕 스키의 한 종목이며, 활강, 도약(점프), 비행, 착지의 4가지 기술로 구성된다. 스키점프는 샤모니 프랑스 동계올림픽을 계기로 동계올림픽과 함께한 종목이다. 스키점프의 올림픽 경기 종목에는 남자 k-95 노머힐, 남자 k-125 라지힐, 라지힐에서 열리는 남자 단체전 그리고 2014년 소치 올림픽 때부터 추가된 여자 k-95 노머힐 경기로 4가지 종목으로 구성되어 있다.

The History

스키점프는 놀이에서부터 기원하여 점차 스포츠의 형태를 갖추게 되었다. 19세기 후반에 겨울 스포츠의 한 종목으로 자리 잡게 되었다. 스키점프는 1862년 노르웨이에서 처음으로 경쟁 스포츠 경기로 열렸다. 스키점프는 1924년 프랑스에 위치한 샤모니에서 열린 제1회 동계올림픽 때부터 정식 종목으로서 채택되었다. 많은 선수들이 기술을 창조하고 개선하여 지금의 모습으로 스키점프가 발전하였다. 최초의 스키점프 선수들 중 Thulin Thamas와 Sigmund Ruud가 상반신을 굽혀서 점프하는 콩스버거 기술을 만들었다. 이후 Andreas Daescher는 점프 기술을 개선하기 위해 몸을 더욱 기울이고 팔을 몸 뒤쪽으로 놓은 자세로 점프했다.

주요 선수로는 시몬 암만이 있다. 그는 2002년 솔트레이크시티 동계올림픽 노머힐과 라지힐 남자 개인전에서 2관왕을 차지했으며, 2010년 밴쿠버 동계올림픽에서도 2관왕에 올랐다. 스키점프 선수로서는 처음으로 동계올림픽 통산 4개의 금메달을 목에 걸었다. 최근 떠오르는 선수로는 카밀 스톡이 있으며 1987년 6월생으로 2014년 소치 동계올림픽에서 노머힐과 라지힐 남자 개인전에서 2개의 금메달을 획득했다.

14 SNOWBOARD
스노보드

EVENTS

MEN'S EVENTS	WOMEN'S EVENTS
Giant parallel slalom men	Giant parallel slalom women
Half-pipe men	Half-pipe women
Parallel slalom men	Parallel slalom women
Slopestyle men	Slopestyle women
Snowboard Cross men	Snowboard Cross women

An Introduction to the Game

Snowboarding is a winter sport that dashes over the snow on a board. Snowboarding combines elements of surfing, skateboarding, and skiing. The snowboarder locks both feet on a board and glides down the snow covered slope while performing skills, such as the jumps, turns, and aerial stunts. These skills are fancy, active, and dynamic high-leveled techniques. Snowboarding events are composed of the halfpipe, giant slalom, parallel giant slalom, cross, slopestyle, and parallel special slalom for men and women.

Talking about the Game

KEY WORDS & EXPRESSIONS

close call: 위험할 뻔하다
look into: 조사하다
two-man: 2인
four-man: 4인
track: 트랙
weight specification: 무게 제한
sled: 썰매

Joe : Here comes winter! I have been waiting for the snow so I can go snowboarding.

겨울이다! 난 스노보드 타려고 눈이 오기만을 기다렸어.

Karen : I know you go to the ski resort every winter. By the way, did you know that snowboarding is also one of the disciplines in the Winter Olympics?

나도 네가 매 겨울마다 스키장 가는 거 알고 있지.
그런데 너 스노보드가 동계올림픽 종목 중 하나라는 거 알고 있었어?

Joe : Yes, of course. But I don't think many people know that it is an Olympic sport. Maybe that's because it is one of the more recent snow disciplines added to the Olympics. It started in Nagano in 1998.

당연히 알지. 아마 대부분의 사람들이 올림픽 종목인지 모를 거야. 왜냐하면 스노보드는 제일 최근에 올림픽 종목에 등록됐어. 1998년 나가노 올림픽이 시작이었지.

Karen : Wow, you really are a big fan. Let me ask you something. The history of snowboarding itself isn't long, then how about the history of snowboarding in Korea? Snowboarding suddenly became big in Korea.

너 진짜 스노보드 좋아하는구나. 그럼 나 궁금한 게 있어. 스노보드의 역사가 그렇게 길지 않다면 한국에서 스노보드의 역사는 어때? 한국에서 갑자기 큰 인기잖아.

Joe : It was 1995 when the Korea Snow Board Association (KSBA) was established and also when Seoung-woo Ski Resort, a paradise for boarders, opened. Before then, no ski resort accepted boarders. They didn't even sell them tickets.

1995년 사단법인 대한스노보드협회(KSBA)가 발족했으며 보더들의 천국이라고 불렸던 성우리조트가 문을 열었어. 그 전까지는 모든 스키장에서 보더들의 출입을 제한했고 보더들에게 리프트권조차도 안 팔았대.

Karen : Really? Compared to these days, that sounds really weird. Why did the boarders call Seoung-Woo Resort a paradise?

정말? 지금과 비교해볼 땐 꽤나 이해 안 되는 일이네. 그런데 왜 보더들이 성우리조트를 천국이라고 불렀어?

Joe : A son of the resort's CEO was a boarder, so the owner wanted to make his son feel free when he was snowboarding.

리조트 사장의 아들이 스노보더여서 사장이 아들의 고충을 알고 만든 거였대.

Karen : Oh, that's so sweet. But I've never heard of professional Korean boarders.

오, 진짜 멋있다. 그런데 생각해보니까 난 한국 선수들에 대해 들어본 적이 없는 것 같아.

Joe : Maybe you might have heard of Ho-jun Kim. He was the first Korean athlete to join this discipline in 2010. Pyeongchang Olympics will be the third time Korean athletes compete in this event.

아마 그럴 거야. 왜냐면 2010년 동계올림픽에서는 김호준이 국내 최초로 출전권을 획득했었지. 평창 동계올림픽이 우리나라 선수가 출전하는 세 번째 올림픽이 될 거야.

Karen : That sounds really interesting. I won't miss that match.

그렇구나. 그 경기 꼭 봐야겠어.

The History

In 1959, snowboarding first started as a game using a board to cover the flaws of skiing. However, it became a real sport in the United States in the 1960s because of a man of the name Sherman Poppen. He tried to mix the elements of mono-skiing, surfing, and skiing, calling it 'Snurfer'(a blend of the words "snow" and "surfer"). At first people used various materials and shapes of snowboards, such as wooden boards in the shape of a skateboard equipped with aluminum or plastics fins.

At the end of the 1970s, the materials and shapes of the board were developed even more, finally resulting in the modern board with a place to fix the feet, a steel edge, and with the name "snowboard." In the beginning, traditional ski resorts did not want to accept snowboarders. Skiers had conservative attitudes or were concerned about safety issues, thus they tried to exclude snowboarders from their mountains. By the 1990s, however, almost all ski resorts accepted snowboarding, which led to a large increase in the snowboarding population.

In 1983, the first National Snowboarding Championship Competition was held in the United States. Following the first competition, international competitions were founded like the US Open Championship, World Series Competition, World Snowboarding Federation (WSF) and Master World Cup Competition. This helped pave the way for snowboarding's inclusion in the 18th Olympic Winter Games in 1998 in Nagano, Japan.

Top Athletes

Shannon Dunn was small, but a giant on the slopes. She started snowboarding in 1979 and was the first American to win the bronze in the 1998 Olympics in the half-pipe competition.

Shannon Dunn은 작을지라도 슬로프 위에서는 무시할 수 없는 존재였다. 그녀는 1979년부터 스노보드를 시작했으며 1998년 올림픽에서 하프파이프 부문에서 동메달을 딴 첫 번째 미국인이다.

Terje Haakenson is called the "Michael Jordan" or the GOD of snowboarding for his wonderful tricks. Haakenson won countless number of competitions and is highly respected by many snowboarding fans.

Terje Haakenson은 현란한 트릭 때문에 마이클 조던 혹은 스노보드의 신이라고 불린다. Haakenson은 셀 수 없이 많은 경기들을 이겼고 많은 스노보딩 팬들에게 무한한 존경을 받는다.

Lesley McKenna started in skiing but became one of the top snowboarders in the world. She won many world class snowboarding competitions and is a founder of the British women's snowboarding team.

Lesley Mckenna는 비록 처음에 스키부터 시작했지만 결국 세계 정상의 스노보더 중 한 명으로 거듭났다. 그녀는 수많은 세계 스노보드 대회에서 우승을 거뒀고 영국 여자 스노보드 팀의 창설자였다.

Craig Kelly was one of the most successful snowboarders in the world holding the title of four World Championships and three U.S. Open Championships until he retired and became a backcountry guide. In 2003, at the age of 36, he was killed by an avalanche while guiding a heliskiing tour group trip in British Columbia.

Craig Kelly는 은퇴하고 오지의 가이드가 되기 전에 네 번의 월드 챔피언십과 세 번의 US 오픈 챔피언십 타이틀을 거머쥔 세상에서 가장 성공한 스노보더 중 한 명이었다. Kelly는 2003년 36살의 나이로 British Columbia에서 헬리스킹 여행 가이드를 하던 중 눈사태에 의해 죽음을 맞이했다.

Todd Richards has been riding professionally for 17 years. He is known as the best freestyle rider. His skills got him a spot on the first Olympic snowboarding event. However, his talents exceed snowboarding. In 2001, he was chosen for the main character in the movie "Out Cold"

Todd Richards는 17년 동안 전문적으로 라이딩을 했으며 최고의 프리스타일 라이더로 알려져 있다. 그의 기술들은 첫 번째 올림픽 스노보드 종목에서 주목을 받게 된다. 그는 스노보드에만 소질이 있는 것이 아니다. 2001년 그는 "Out Cold"라는 영화의 주연을 맡았었다.

Shaun White carries the nickname "flying tomato" because of his flamed red hair and airborne moves. He had his first sponsor when he was seven. Since then, he has become one of the most popular snowboarders. He has his own video game and clothing line, and was even on the cover of the "Rolling Stone" magazine wearing his Olympic gold medal and draped in an American flag.

Shaun White는 불타는 듯한 빨간 머리와 하늘에 떠있는 움직임들 때문에 "나는 토마토"라는 별명을 갖고 있다. White가 일곱 살이었을 때, 그는 이미 그의 첫 스폰서를 갖고 있었다. 그때 이후로, 그는 자국에서 가장 유명한 스노보드 선수 중 한 명이 되었다. 그는 그 자신만의 비디오 게임과 의류 상품이 있으며 올림픽 금메달을 목에 걸고 미국 국기를 걸친 채 "Rolling Stone"의 커버 모델까지도 했다.

* Photo from Wikipedia

"How did it all start?"

KEY WORDS & EXPRESSIONS

started it all (all started with): 모든 것을 시작했다(시작된 원점)

become popular: 인기를 얻다

hold on to: 꼭 잡다

quite a bit: 꽤 많은, 상당히

I personally think: 내 개인 생각에

got rid of: 없애다

Joe : There seems to be a lot more snowboarders these days.

요새 스노보드 타는 사람들이 늘어난 것 같아.

Karen : Snowboarders are lucky these days. In the 60s and 70s snowboarders weren't even allowed on the snow in the resorts because other skiers thought that it was too dangerous.

요새 스노보드 타는 사람들은 운이 좋은 거지. 60년, 70년대에는 다른 스키족들이 스노보드가 위험하다고 해서 리조트에서 금했거든.

Joe : They are also lucky for Sherman Poppen?

Sherman Poppen이 있어서 참 다행이지?

Karen : What? Who's he?

뭐라고? 그가 누군데?

Joe : He's the man who started it all. He created the snurfer. Basically, he combined mono-skiing, surfing, and skiing.

스노보드의 창시자지. 다시 말하면 스너퍼의 창시자. 그가 모노스키, 서핑, 그리고 스키를 합쳐 스너퍼라고 불렀어.

Karen : I didn't know that. All I know is that it started in the 60s in the United States.

그건 몰랐어. 나는 60년대에 미국에서 시작한 것으로만 알고 있었어.

Joe : Considering that it started in the 60s, it was adopted into the Winter Olympics quite early in 1998 at the Nagano Olympics. And it became popular so fast!

60년대에 시작한 것을 고려했을 때 동계올림픽에 채택이 빨리 된 종목이야. 1998년 나가노 올림픽에 채택되었잖아. 그리고 인기도 급속도로 상승했지.

Karen : The board changed quickly too. The snurfer looked like a long sled with a long handle in the front to hold on to and your feet were not fixed.

보드도 빨리 변했어. 스너퍼는 앞에 긴 줄 같은 손잡이가 달렸고 아주 긴 썰매같이 생겼어. 그리고 발도 고정되지 않고.

Joe : It did change quite a bit.

진짜 많이 변했구나.

Karen : I personally think the current snowboard looks a lot better and gives the snowboarder more freedom. I'm so glad they got rid of the handle in the front and created fixings for your feet.

개인적으로 현재 스노보드가 훨씬 마음에 들어. 외모상으로도 더 좋고 그리고 스노보드가 더 자유롭게 움직일 수 있는 것 같아. 앞에 그 손잡이 같은 줄을 없애고 발을 고정할 수 있게 만들어서 다행이야.

Equipment and Gear

	**Deck 데크** Basic snowboarding equipment also known as the board. Boarders fix their feet on the deck to slide down the snow. 보드라고도 알려진 기초 스노보딩 장비. 보더들은 눈위에서 미끄러져 내려올 때 발을 이 데크에 고정시킨다.
	**Boots 부츠** Boots are hard as to provide protection and support to the feet. 발을 보호하고 지지해주기 위해 단단하게 만들어졌다.
	**Bindings 바인딩** Bindings are used to fix the boots to the deck. Most bindings are attached onto the decks with three or four screws. 부츠와 데크를 고정해주는 장치이다. 대부분의 바인딩은 3~4개의 나사로 데크에 붙어있다.
	**Goggles 고글** Goggles protect eyes from the reflection of the snow or secure a clear view when the weather is bad. 눈에서 반사되는 빛으로부터 눈을 보호하거나 날씨가 흐릴 때 시야를 확보하기 위한 것.

What is this contraption?

KEY WORDS & EXPRESSIONS
deck: 데크, 보드의 윗 부분
elasticity: 탄력성
rotation: 회전
most likely: 아마도
base: 베이스, 보드의 아랫 부분
edge: 에지, 보드의 양옆
in a short while: 조만간, 금세

Joe : I heard that there are many types of boards?

보드 종류가 많다고 하던데.

Karen : Yes, you are right. Snowboarding decks are different for alpine, freestyle, and all round. The elasticity, rotation, and weight are the main differences.

응, 맞아. 스노보딩 데크는 알파인, 프리스타일, 올라운드 용이 따로 있는데 보드의 탄력성, 회로, 무게에서 주로 차이가 나지.

Joe : Can you tell me the differences between them?

그 세 가지의 차이점이 뭔지 말해줄래?

Karen : Of course. First of all, freestyle is resilient and the shapes of the front (or "nose") and back (or "switch") are the same. So it is suitable for beginners.

물론이지. 먼저, 프리스타일은 탄력성이 좋고 앞(노즈)과 뒤(스위치)의 구분이 없는 거야. 쉽게 말해 초보자들에게 알맞지.

Joe : Now, then what I rode was most likely skis for free style.

아, 그러면 지난번에 내가 탔던 것이 '프리스타일'이었구나.

Karen : Definitely! Alpines are mainly used for high speed. They resemble the equipment used for skiing rather than snowboarding. Lastly, all-mountain snowboards combine the strengths of the alpine and freestyle and this makes them suitable for all conditions.

맞아! 알파인 스타일은 주로 스피드를 위한 보드야. 스키 장비와 더 비슷하게 생겼어. 마지막으로 올마운틴 스타일은 알파인 스타일과 프리스타일의 장점을 모아 어떠한 조건에도 적합하도록 제작된 거야.

Joe : I've never heard of the all-mountain snowboard, but I've seen the alpine before.

알파인 스타일에 대해선 들어 본 것 같은데 올마운틴 스타일은 처음 들어봐.

Karen : That's weird. They are the most common type of snowboard, but they aren't the best at freestyle or alpine, though, so the pros don't use them.

이상하다. 가장 흔한 스노보드 종류지만 프리스타일과 알파인에는 가장 좋지 않기 때문에 프로들은 그 보드를 사용하지 않아.

Joe : I see. I have one more question. Can you explain the parts of the board?

그렇구나. 또 한 가지 궁금한 점이 있어. 데크는 부분별로 다양한 명칭이 있던데 그것에 대해 설명해줘.

Karen : The bottom of the board that has contact with the snow is called the base. The edge is on either side of the deck. If one can control the edge easily, that means they are at an intermediate level.

보드의 바닥이자 눈에 닿는 부분은 베이스라고 불러. 데크의 양쪽 부분은 에지라고해. 만약 에지를 잘 사용할 줄 안다면 이미 중급자라고 할 수 있어.

Joe : I was taught to use the edges as brakes, but it was difficult to do.

에지를 사용해서 브레이크를 잡아야 된다고 배웠는데 아직 나에게는 어려웠어.

Karen : It will become easier with practice. In a short while, you will be able to do the basic turns. Then snowboarding will become much more interesting.

계속 연습한다면 어렵지 않을 거야. 그렇게 된다면 기본 턴을 할 수 있고, 보드가 더 재미있어질 거야.

SPORTS FACTS

SNOWBOARDING

- First contested date in the Olympics :
  1998 Nagano Winter Olympics
- Nation of origin :
  United States
- Types of events :
  Halfpipe, Giant slalom, Parallel giant slalom, Cross, Slopestyle, and Parallel special slalom
- Country with most medals :
  United States (24 medals)
- Athlete with most medals :
  Kelly Clark (USA)

해 석

An Introduction to the Game

스노보드는 보드를 이용하여 슬로프를 질주하는 동계스포츠다. 이 종목은 서핑과 스케이트보드, 스키가 결합한 형태로서 두 발을 하나의 보드에 묶고 눈이 쌓인 비탈을 미끄러지듯 질주하면서 점프와 턴(회전), 공중묘기 등 화려하면서도 역동적이고 박진감 넘치는 고난도 기술을 펼치는 것이 특징이다. 경기는 스노보드 크로스, 하프파이프, 대회전, 평행대회전, 빅에어 등의 세부 종목으로 나누어 치른다.

The History

1959년경 미국 산악지방에서 스키의 불편함을 보완하기 위하여 널빤지를 이용한 놀이로 시작되어 1960년대에 미국에서 Sherman Poppen이라는 남자에 의해 스포츠로 발전하였다. 당시 스너퍼라 하여 모노스키와 함께 서핑을 스키에 접목하려는 노력의 일환으로 생겨났다. 초기에는 알루미늄이나 플라스틱 핀이 장착된 스케이트 보드 모양의 나무 합판을 사용하였는데, 보드의 소재와 모양도 가지각색이었다.

그 뒤 새로운 소재의 제품이 많이 개발되어 1970년대 말부터 본격적으로 등장하였다. 바인딩으로 발을 보드에 고정시키는 스타일이 등장한 것도 이 무렵이고, 스틸에지가 부착된 제품도 출시되었으며, 스노보드라는 이름이 정착된 것도 이 무렵이다. 그동안 보수적 입장과 안전을 이유로 스노보드를 금지하던 스키장들도 1990년대 들어 잇달아 문호를 개방하였으며, 세계 곳곳에서 전통적 스키 대신 스노보드를 즐기는 젊은 층이 크게 늘어났다.

1983년 미국에서 최초의 조직적 대회라고 할 수 있는 내셔널스노보딩 챔피언십대회가 열렸고, 이후 US오픈챔피언십을 비롯하여 세계스노보딩연맹(World Snowboarding Federation; WSF)이 주관하는 월드시리즈대회와 마스터월드컵대회 등 국제 규모의 대회가 잇달아 창설되었다. 이 같은 저변 확대를 바탕으로 동계올림픽에서도 1998년 일본 나가노에서 열린 제18회 대회부터 정식 종목으로 채택되었다.

15 SPEED SKATING

스피드 스케이팅

EVENTS

MEN'S EVENTS	WOMEN'S EVENTS
500m men	500m women
1,000m men	1,000m women
1,500m men	1,500m women
5,000m men	3,000m women
10,000m men	5,000m women
Team pursuit men	Team pursuit women
Mass start	Mass start

An Introduction to the Game

Speed skating is a winter sport and it is similar to short-track speed skating, but there are some differences, such as the blade of the skate, rules, and track. The skaters compete in double curved lanes with in and out courses. They alternate between the in and out course at the 200m mark, which is exactly half of the 400m rink. On the straight track it is hard to accelerate speed, so the curved course is very important to bring up the speed in order to shorten the time.

Speed skating is made up of 7 events, 10,000m men, 5,000m men/women, 3,000m women, 1,500m men/women, 1,000m men/women, 500m men/women and team pursuit men/women, and the newest event in the 2018 Pyeonchang Olympics, mass start men/women. This sport requires endurance, muscular strength, agility and lower body strength.

Talking about the Game

KEY WORDS & EXPRESSIONS

blade: 스케이트 날

half point mark: 중간 지점

Joe : Hi, welcome to Gangneung Olympic Stadium. Which events do you want to watch? Short tract, speed skating or figure skating?

안녕? 강릉 올림픽 경기장에 온 걸 환영해. 쇼트트랙, 스피드 스케이팅 또는 피겨 스케이팅, 어떤 경기를 보고 싶어?

Karen : Hm… I don't know about speed skating and I think it looks like short track speed skating. But can you explain this event?

음… 나는 스피드 스케이팅에 대해서는 잘 모르겠어. 내 생각에는 쇼트트랙이랑 비슷한 것 같은데, 설명 좀 해줄래?

Joe : Sure! You are already familiar with short track speed skating, but there are some differences. For example, in speed skating the skate's **blade** is thinner for a curved track. Also, only two skaters compete on the track. They alternate between lanes curves when they reach the **half point mark**. They do this so the skaters don't bump into each other like in short track speed skating.

물론이지! 쇼트트랙은 이미 잘 알고 있구나. 하지만 다른 점들은 있어. 예를 들면, 스케이트의 날이 쇼트트랙 스케이트보다 커브 때문에 조금 더 얇아. 그리고 트랙에서 오직 두 명의 선수가 경쟁하지. 선수들은 링크의 절반에 도달했을 때 커브 코스를 번갈아 바꿔. 따라서 선수들은 쇼트트랙처럼 다른 선수와 부딪칠 수 없지.

Karen : Thank you! I think it's really interesting. Do you know the game time? I really want to watch the game.

고마워. 매우 흥미롭다. 스피드 스케이팅 경기 시간을 아니? 나 정말로 경기를 보고 싶어.

Joe : I will check for you. Just wait a minute.

내가 확인해줄게. 잠깐만 기다려.

The History

Speed skating has a long history and goes back to Scandinavia, Northern Europe and the Netherlands. The inhabitants used skates to cross over rivers in the winter months. The blades of the skis they used were made out of bones, but the method of skating was similar to current skating. Bone blades were replaced with iron blades after the 12the century. Skating was also used as a method of communication across villages and it gradually grew into a sporting event as artificial skating rinks and clubs began to form.

Skating became popular all across the world in the 18th to 19th centuries. The first speed skating competition was held in Netherland in 1676 and the world championships in 1889, in which many countries like Russia, United States, England, and the Netherlands participated. Speed skating made its first appearance in the Chamonix Winter Olympics in 1924 at which only male players participated in. Women's events were included in 1932 in the Lake Placid Games. It was almost 28 years later in 1960 that the IOC finally included the women's events for speed skating in the Winter Olympic Games.

Top Athletes

Lidiya Skoblikova was born on March 8, 1939 in Russia. She was a successful Russian skater and holds six Olympic gold medals. Four of her gold medals are from the 1964 Innsbruck Olympics, in which she won all four races (500m, 1,000m, 1,500m, 3,000m). She retired as an athlete in 1969 and became involved in the Russian Skating Federation where she served as president for twelve years. Later in the 90s, she led the Russian team as the head coach.

Lidiya Skoblikova는 1939년 3월 8일 러시아에서 태어났다. 그는 러시아 스케이트 선수로 6개의 금메달을 보유하고 있다. 그중 4개는 1964년 인스브루크 올림픽에서 모든 종목(500m, 1,000m, 1,500m, 3,000m)을 석권하여 획득했다. 그녀는 1969년 선수 생활을 마치고 러시아 스케이트 연맹에서 12년간 회장 자리를 지켰다. 이후 90년대 들어 러시아 대표팀 코치로 활동하였다.

Claudia Pechstein was born on February 22, 1972 and is a German speed skater. She won numerous gold and silver medals in the world championships as well as five gold, two silver, and two bronze medals in the Olympics. Her main events proved to be the 5,000m and the 3,000m events where most of her medals were won. However, her success was tainted by a blood doping accusation that led to a two year ban from all competitions.

Claudia Pechstein은 1972년 2월 22일에 태어났으며 독일 스피드 스케이팅 선수다. 그녀는 세계선수권대회에서 수많은 금메달과 은메달을 따냈고 올림픽에서도 5개의 금, 2개의 은, 그리고 2개의 동메달을 획득했다. 그녀의 주 종목은 5,000m와 3,000m였으며 대다수의 메달을 이 두 종목에서 얻었다. 그러나 그녀의 성공은 혈액도핑 의혹과 2년간 경기 참가 금지령으로 오점을 남겼다.

Clas Thunberg was born on April 5, 1893 and skated for the Finnish team. He boasts gold medals in the 500m, 1,500m, 5,000m, and the combined event. He participated in the 1924 and the 1928 Olympics. Although he was strong in the short races, he was susceptible to the longer races. Despite his weakness, he still holds a long list of victories.

Clas Thunberg는 1893년 4월 5일에 태어나 핀란드팀에서 스케이트 선수로 활동했다. 그는 500m, 1,500m, 5,000m와 종합 종목에서 금메달을 땄다. Thunberg는 1924년과 1928년 올림픽에 참가했다. 단거리에 강했지만 장거리 레이스도 가능했다. 그러나 이런 약점에도 불구하고 긴 우승 기록을 보유하고 있다.

* Photo from Wikipedia

"How did it all start?"

Joe : Did you know that skating has been around for almost a millennium?

스케이트가 약 1,000년 전부터 존재했다고 알고 있었어?

Karen : I know, can you believe that? But what's more interesting is that the blades then used to be made of bones. Iron blades came much later.

그러니까, 믿어지니? 더욱 신기한 것은 그 당시 스케이트 날이 뼈로 만들어졌다는 거야. 철 날은 한참 뒤에 생겼겠지.

KEY WORDS & EXPRESSIONS

millennium: 밀레니엄, 1,000년
can you believe it: 믿을 수 있니
from what I know: 내가 알기로는
demonstration game: 시범경기
thank goodness: 다행이다

Joe : Without much of a transportation or communication system back then, natives most likely used skates to travel or send messages during the winter.

그 당시 교통과 통신 시스템이 없었기 때문에 스케이트를 이용해서 겨울철에는 이동도 하고 의사소통도 했었을 것 같아.

Karen : It got more popular though in the 18th and 19th centuries when tracks began being constructed and competitions took off. It was so popular that in the first speed skating world championships, countries like Russia, the United States, England, and the Netherlands participated.

18세기에서 19세기 사이에 스케이트장이 세워지고 경쟁 시합이 시작되면서 더욱 인기를 얻었지. 얼마나 인기가 많았던지 최초의 스피트 스케이트 세계선수권대회에서 러시아, 미국, 영국과 네덜란드와 같은 나라들이 참가했어.

Joe : Do you also know when it was added to the Olympics?

그럼 올림픽에 공식 종목으로 언제 채택됐는지 알고 있니?

Karen : From what I know, it was in 1924 in the Chamonix Winter Olympics. But it was at first a demonstration game and only men were given participating rights. The IOC eventually registered speed skating as a regular event, but the women's events were added much later in 1960.

내가 알기로는, 1924년 샤모니 동계올림픽에서 처음으로 선보였는데, 이때는 시범경기였고 남자 선수들만 참가권이 주어졌지. 결국에 IOC가 스피드 스케이트를 공식 종목으로 채택했지만, 여자 경기는 한참 후 1960년도에 인정됐어.

Joe : Well, thank goodness for that because there are so many top women speed skaters like Lidiya Skoblikova, Claudia Pechstein, and Korea's very own Sang-hwa Lee.

그것 참 다행이다. 아주 훌륭한 여성 스케이트 선수가 많이 있거든. 예를 들어 Lidiya Skoblikova, Claudia Pechstein, 그리고 대한민국의 이상화 선수.

Equipment and Gear

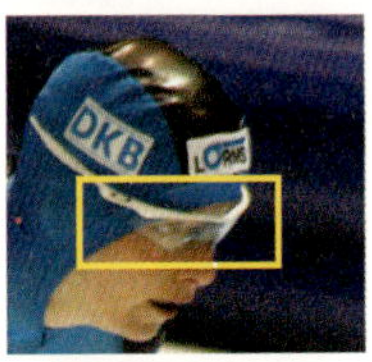	**Glasses 안경** Glasses are for clarity and to protect the eyes from ice shreds and the wind. 선명하게 보고 눈을 얼음 조각과 바람으로부터 보호하기위해 사용한다.
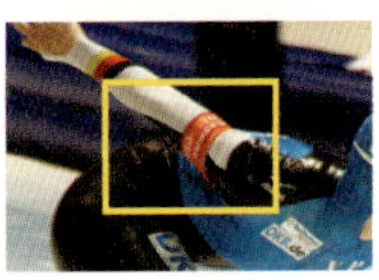	**Colored arm bands 밴드 색** Arm bands distinguish in and out course skaters. 암 밴드는 인코스와 아웃코스를 타는 선수를 구분해준다.

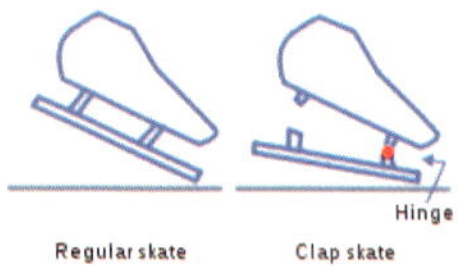

Clap blades 클랩 블레이드

Clap blads increase push off power on the ice and allow for skaters to turn easily.

클랩 블레이드는 얼음 위에서 추진력을 강하게 하고 커브를 쉽게 돌 수 있게 한다.

Racing suits 스케이트 수트

Racing suits reduce air resistance and shorten recorded times.

스케이트 수트는 공기저항에 대항하고 기록시간을 단축시킨다.

What is this contraption?

Joe : Wow! The rink is huge.

우와! 링크가 진짜 크다.

Karen : Yes! It's nearly 400m. Look there, skaters are warming up right now.

맞아! 대략 400m 정도야. 저기 봐봐, 선수들이 지금 몸 풀고 있어.

Joe : They look nervous. Um... hold on a second, you told me that short track speed skaters use different skates, right? I've never seen skates like that. It's very unique.

선수들이 긴장한 것 같아. 음... 잠깐만, 전에 나한테 쇼트트랙과 스피드 스케이팅에서 사용되는 스케이트의 차이점에 대해 설명해줬었지? 난 저런 스케이트를 본 적이 없어. 진짜 독특하다.

Karen : Yes, I told you before. The blade of the skates are definitely different. We think about normal skates as being connected with the boot. However speed skating skates disconnect with the boot.

그래. 내가 전에 설명했어. 스케이트 날이 완전히 달라. 우리가 생각하는 보통 스케이트는 부츠와 연결되어 있잖아. 그런데 스피드 스케이팅의 스케이트는 부츠와 연결되어 있지 않아.

KEY WORDS & EXPRESSIONS

warm up: 몸 풀다
connect: 연결되다
disconnect: 분리되다
push off power: 추진력
starting line: 출발점
stadium: 경기장
air resistance: 공기저항
arm band: 암 밴드, 팔에 착용하는 표시
in course: 인 코스, 안쪽 레인으로 달리는
out course: 아웃 코스, 바깥 레인으로 달리는
penalty: 페널티, 벌점

Joe : That's incredible! I understand that figure and short track skates are connected to the boot, like the ones people generally use on the ice.

신기하다. 피겨 스케이팅과 쇼트트랙은 부츠와 연결되어 있고 심지어 우리가 보통으로 스케이트장에서 신는 스케이트도 연결되어 있네.

Karen : Correct! The reason why speed skating used these types of skates is because they need push off power at the starting line.

정확해. 왜냐하면 스피드 스케이팅은 출발과 직선 주로에서 추진력이 필요하기 때문이야.

Joe : That's very interesting. The stadium is so cold right now. But skaters are only wearing a thin suit and glasses.

그거 정말 재미있다. 지금 경기장이 진짜 추운데 선수들은 안경을 쓰고 얇은 수트만 입었어.

Karen : It can't be helped. That racing suit helps them have better times. Therefore, they are fitting and thin.

어쩔 수 없어. 왜냐하면 저 경기복은 좋은 기록에 도움을 주거든. 그러나 선수들은 딱 붙고 얇은 경기복을 입어야 해.

Joe : How do racing suits improve skating times?

경기복이 왜 좋은 기록에 도움이 되지?

Karen : When skaters go fast, air resistance obstructs the skater and reduces push off power.

선수들이 빠르게 갈수록 공기저항이 선수의 진로를 방해하고 추진력을 감소시켜.

Joe : I see. So they wear racing suits to reduce air resistance.

알겠어. 그래서 공기저항을 감소시키려고 경기복을 입는구나.

Karen : That's right. They also wear glasses to protect their eyes from ice and wind and to see clearly.

맞아. 선수들은 또한 얼음과 바람으로부터 눈을 보호하고 선명하게 보기 위해 안경을 써.

Joe : The game is starting soon. The skaters have red or white bands on their arms.

경기가 곧 시작할 거야. 선수들은 팔에 빨간색이나 흰색 밴드를 차고 있어.

Karen : That's also a part of the equipment. We call that an armband.

저것도 장비야. 우리는 암 밴드라고 불러.

Joe : Does it show the skater's nationality?

저건 선수들의 국적을 나타내는 거니?

Karen : No! That distinguishes in course and out course skaters. Skaters often get confused because they go around the track so many times. If skaters incorrectly change course, there will be a penalty. So armbands are necessary for judges.

아니! 저건 우리에게 인코스와 아웃코스 선수들을 구분해줘. 선수들은 트랙을 많이 돌기 때문에 보통 그들의 방향을 헷갈려 해. 코스 변경은 실격이라 심판들에게 암 밴드는 굉장히 필요해.

SPORTS FACTS

Speed Skating

- First contested date in the Olympics :
  1924 Chamonix Winter Olympics
- Nation of origin :
  Netherlands
- Types of events :
  Men: 500m, 1,000m, 1,500m, 5,000m, 10,000m,
  team pursuit, mass start
  Women: 500m,1,000m, 1,500m, 3,000m, 5,000m,
  team pursuit, mass start
- Type of arena :
  Long track speeding skating rink (400 meters)
- Skaters in History :
  Marie Antoinette, Napoleon III
- Top Male Skater :
  Eric Heiden (United States)
- Top Female Skater :
  Karin Enke (Germany)

해 석

An Introduction to the Game

스피드 스케이팅은 동계 스포츠 게임의 일종으로 쇼트트랙과 상당히 비슷하다. 그러나 쇼트트랙과는 스케이트 날, 경기 규칙, 트랙 등이 다르다. 선수들은 인 코스와 아웃 코스로 부르는 더블 곡선 트랙에서 경쟁하는데 그들은 경기장(400m)의 반(200m)에 도달하면 코스를 번갈아 탄다. 직선 주로에서 속도를 내기 어렵기 때문에 속도를 낼 수 있는 곡선 주로에서 인 코스에서 타는 게 상대적으로 유리하다.

스피드 스케이팅은 6개의 종목(10,000m 남자/5,000m 남녀/3,000m 여자/1,500m 남녀/1,000m 남녀/500m 남녀/팀 추월 경기)으로 구성되어 있다. 이 운동은 지구력, 근력, 순발력 그리고 하체 근력을 필요로 한다.

The History

겨울에 눈을 지나가고 강을 건너야 하기 때문에 스케이트는 철기시대 전에 만든 것으로 추측한다. 당시의 스케이트는 현재의 스케이트와는 다르게 생겼다. 기존의 스케이트 날은 뼈로 만들어졌다, 그러나 스케이트 타는 방법은 오늘 날과 유사한 모습이었다. 뼈로 만든 날은 12세기 이후 폴란드인이 쇠로 스케이트 날을 만들었다. 스케이트는 마을과 마을을 이어주는 통신 역할도 했으며 점차적으로 스케이트장과 팀들이 형성되면서 스포츠로 자리를 잡기 시작했다.

18~19세기, 스케이트가 전세계에 대중화되었다. 따라서 1676년 네덜란드에서 첫 번째 스피드 스케이팅 경기가 개최되었다. 그리고 1889년 또한 네덜란드에서 많은 나라들(러시아, 미국, 영국 그리고 네덜란드)이 참여한 제1회 세계선수권이 열렸다. 이러한 과정을 통해 스피드 스케이팅은 더욱 유명해졌다. 스피드 스케이팅은 1924년 샤모니 동계올림픽 경기에서 시범경기를 가졌다. 그 당시 오직 남자 선수들만 경기에 참가할 수 있었다. 1932년 Lake placid 경기에서 여자 선수들도 참가할 수 있게 되었다. 28년 후, 즉 1960년 IOC는 마침내 동계올림픽에 여자 선수들의 참가를 허용했다.

16 South Korea in the Winter Olympics
한국의 동계올림픽

Participation in the Winter Olympics

Korea's participation began in 1936 at the Garmisch Partenkirchen Games with three Chosun athletes entering as members of the Japanese team while under Japan's rule. As an independent nation, the Republic of Korea sent three speed skaters to the 1948 St. Moritz Winter Olympics, making it the first Winter Game participation. Since then, the Republic of Korea has participated in a total of 18 Winter Olympics.

Korea achieved its first Winter Olympic victory in 1992 at Albertville. Ki-hoon Kim was able to win a gold in short track speed skating at the men's 1000m event, and again in the same event in the 1994 Winter Olympics, setting the pace for more Olympic victories in the sport. Until 2002, all of Korea's medals came from short track speed skating. Medals awarded have spread to speed skating at Turin in 2006 and then to figure skating in 2010; however, the majority of medals are still being won in short track.

Although Korea began its Olympic entry with and grew as leaders in short track speed skating, efforts have been made to diversify winter sports entries. Starting with participation in snow sports like alpine skiing and cross-country skiing in the 1960s, Korea has gradually added to the list biathlon, freestyle skiing, snowboarding, and ski jumping. In 2014, Korea competed in 13 out of 15 sports events held at the Winter Olympics.

Leading Sports

The number of Olympic medals achieved reveals Korea's definite winter strength to be short track speed skating. Out of 52 medals won by Korea in the Winter Olympics, 42 come from this sport, and 21 of the 42 are gold. The many gold medals won, however, have set greater standards for upcoming Korean skaters. Skaters undergo rigorous training at a young age and must excel in competitions to be chosen as a short track skater for Korea's National Team.

Since 2010, Korea has grown in speed skating and figure skating with skaters raking in medals and rising as stars in their field of sport. The interest in a variety of winter sports other than short track speed skating is a positive phenomenon that brings new opportunity for growth and excellence to Korea's sports culture. In conjunction with the 2018 Pyeongchang Winter Olympics, that interest is growing and propelling the country to support winter sports athletes in becoming new leaders.

Korea's Upcoming Olympians

Efforts are being made in the preparation of the 2018 Pyeongchang Olympics to train and support athletes in a variety of winter sports. With the incredible amount of hard work being done by the athletes and the support of businesses and conglomerates, Korea is preparing its next 2018 Olympian athletes.

The 2014 Sochi Winter Olympics was an eye opener for Korean sports fans. New Korean athletes and sports were brought into the light. Among the media favorites was the women's curling team. The Korean women's curling team was formed in 2012 and had since made a remarkable entrance into curling by going to the semifinals in the World Championships in the same year. The team ranks 10th in the world and has competed with top nations like Sweden and Canada. Also, in preparation for 2018, the Korean Olympic Committee and Korea Curling

Federation are inviting international teams like Switzerland's Gaggi team, Canada's team Gushue, Mongolia's women's national curling team, and Kazachstan's men's national curling team to train with the Korean team. These efforts provide opportunity for the team to improve their skills in heading for a victory at the Olympics.

Another Sochi surprise was freestyle mogul ski athlete Jae Woo Choi, the first Asian to place 5th in the World Championships in 2013 and the first Korean athlete to go to the finals in the Winter Olympics. Although he did not win a medal, he drew the attention of the media and rose as Korea's next Olympian hopeful. He is now training for the 2018 Winter Olympics and aiming for gold.

Adding to the list of Korean athletes preparing for 2018 are the figure skaters So-youn Park, Jin-Suh Kim, and Joon-hyung Lee, and the Korean Ice Hockey Team. To follow in the steps of Olympic gold medalist Yuna Kim, figure skaters are building their skills and raising scores in hopes of Olympic qualification. On one hand, the national ice hockey team was offered a place in 2018 as a generous offer by the International Ice Hockey Federation. The national team is preparing to train with the goal of entering the quarterfinals in the Pyeongchang Olympics as to raise national interest in ice hockey and expand ice hockey infrastructure in order to popularize the sport.

The hype for developing future Olympic champions is escalating with the support of Korea's biggest names like Samsung, CJ, and Shinsegae. Such conglomerates are sponsoring athletes in fields like bobsleigh, skeleton and snowboarding. Their support has led to a silver medal victory in snowboarding halfpipe in the Winter Universiad by Ho-joon Kim, 18th place in the Sochi Olympics by the bobsleigh team Yoon-jong Won and Young-woo Suh, and 16th place at Sochi by Sung-bin Yoon in the skeleton. Support is expected to continue up to the 2018 Winter Olympics in hopes of not only collecting medals, but raising awareness and interest in a variety of winter sports.

As the host nation of the next Winter Olympics, South Korea is making great efforts to train and support upcoming athletes in all types of winter sports. The nation is spreading their attention to new and fresh sports rather than focusing only on medal winners, making the wait for 2018 ever more exciting.

Republic of Korea, the Host of the Next Winter Olympics

Joe : Korea is very excited about hosting the next Winter Olympics at Pyeongchang.

한국은 평창에서 열리는 다음 동계올림픽의 개최국으로 선정된 것에 대해 매우 신이 나있어.

Karen : They have every reason to. They are the second Asian country to host the Winter Olympics.

신이 날 만해. 동계올림픽을 치르는 두 번째 아시아 국가이니까.

Joe : They've actually been participating in the Winter Olympics for quite some time. Sochi was their eighteenth entrance.

사실 동계올림픽에 오랫동안 참가하고 있었어. 소치 올림픽이 18번째 참가였어.

Karen : Wait a second. When exactly did they enter their first Winter Olympics?

잠깐. 그럼, 언제 동계올림픽에 처음으로 참가했지?

Joe : Well, it depends. If you count the colonial years, Korea's first entrance was in 1936 at the Garmisch Partenkirchen Games. They sent three athlestes, but they entered as a part of Japan's team. It was in 1948 that they entered as an independent nation.

글쎄, 어떻게 보느냐에 따라 달라. 식민지 시절까지 고려한다면 한국은 가르미슈 파르텐키르헨에 처음으로 참가했어. 그때 선수 3명을 참가시켰지만, 선수들은 모두 일본 팀으로 참가했어. 1948년이 되

KEY WORDS & EXPRESSIONS

host: 주최하다, 개최국 역할 하다
have every reason to: 그럴 만한 이유가 있다
quite some time: 꽤 오랜 시간
it depends: 무엇에 따라 달라지다
if you count: 무엇을 고려하면
independent nation: 독립 국가
paid off: 성공하다
kept on: 계속/지속적
raking in: 긁어모으다
to shine: 빛을 내다
can't leave out: 빼놓을 수 없다
diversify: 다양화하다
non-medal producing event: 메달을 얻지 못하는 종목
conglomerate: 대기업/재벌
popular interest: 대중의 관심
set the pace: 선두 하다
next thing you know: 어느 순간
stepping stone: 디딤돌

어서야 독립국가로 참가하게 됐어.

Karen : I thought they entered much later than that because I heard that Korea won its first medal in 1992 in short track.

나는 한참 나중에 참가한 것으로 알고 있었어. 아마 한국의 첫 메달을 1992년 쇼트트랙에서 얻었기 때문인 것 같아.

Joe : They did. I guess all those years of entering finally paid off. They kept on raking in the medals in short track. They won 42 medals. And 21 of them are gold medals. Up to 2002 all medals were won in short track.

맞아, 그랬어. 수많은 참가가 드디어 성공한 거야. 그 이후에도 쇼트트랙에서 메달을 휩쓸기 시작했어. 그리고 42개의 메달을 땄지. 그중 21개가 금메달이야. 2002년까지 모든 메달을 쇼트트랙에서 딴 것이었어.

Karen : They surely are strong short track skaters.

진정으로 강한 쇼트트랙 선수들이네.

Joe : But athletes in other fields have been doing well since Turin. That's when we began seeing speed skaters rise as medalists.

다른 종목의 선수들은 토리노 올림픽부터 성과를 얻기 시작했어. 그때부터 스피드 스케이트 선수들이 메달을 획득하기 시작했어.

Karen : Vancouver is where they did really well. Athletes like Sang-hwa Lee and Taebum Mo began to shine. And you can't leave out figure skater Yuna Kim. What a star!

밴쿠버에서 정말 잘했어. 이상화와 모태범 같은 선수들이 빛을 발휘하기 시작했어. 그리고 피겨 선수 김연아를 빼놓을 수 없지. 대단한 스타야!

Joe : Also, Sang-hwa Lee and Yuna Kim both received medals in 2014 also. A gold for Lee and a silver for Kim. It was good to see athletes receiving medals and doing so well in a variety of sports.

이상화와 김연아는 2014년에서도 메달을 얻었지. 이선화는 금 그리고 김연아는 은메달. 다양한 스포츠에서 메달을 따고 잘하는 모습이 보기 좋았어.

Karen : I know. Watching Sochi, I heard that Korean athletes participated in 13 out of the 15 competing sports. I even watched the women's curling team and mogul event. Korea is definitely diversifying.

그러게. 소치를 보면서 한국이 15개의 종목 중 13개에 참가했다는 것을 알게 됐어. 여자 컬링하고 모글 종목도 이번에 봤어. 한국이 정말 참가 종목을 다양화하는 것 같아.

Joe : Until now diversifying was difficult because there was no interest from investors or sponsors in non-medal producing events. But with the 2018 Pyeongchang Winter Olympic preparations, the mood has been changing. Conglomerates, like Samsung, CJ, and Shinsegae have been getting involved in supporting athletes in less popular sports like bobsleigh, skeleton and snowboarding. And they've been seeing results. This kind of support is needed to improve sports conditions in Korea.

지금까지 다양화가 어려웠던 이유는 메달을 획득하지 못하는 종목에 투자자들과 스폰서들의 관심이 없었기 때문이야. 그러나 2018 평창 동계올림픽 준비에 앞서 그 분위기가 변하고 있어. 삼성, CJ, 그리고 신세계와 같은 대기업이 비인기 종목인 봅슬레이, 스켈레톤, 그리고 스노보드 선수들을 후원하기 시작했어. 결과도 보이기 시작했지. 이런 지원이 있어야만 한국의 스포츠 환경이 향상될 것 같아.

Karen : Yes, I heard that CJ was sponsoring the mogul athlete Jae-Woo Choi and that the women's curling team has gained more popular interest. It'll be great to see more Korean athletes doing well in various sports in the Olympics.

맞아, CJ에서 모글 선수 최재우를 후원한다고 들었어. 그리고 여자 컬링 팀도 대중의 관심을 많이 얻었고. 다양한 올림픽 종목에서 한국 선수들이 잘하는 모습을 보면 참 좋을 것 같아.

Joe : I'm sure we will. Yuna Kim has already set the pace for figure skating in Korea. Next thing you know, we'll be seeing medals in curling or bobsleigh or even ice hockey.

꼭 그렇게 될 거야. 벌써 김연아가 한국의 피겨 스케이트의 길을 다져 놓고 있으니까. 어느 순간 한국이 컬링이나 봅슬레이 아니면 심지어 아이스하키에서 메달을 따는 것을 볼 수 있을 거야.

Karen : Yes! I hope Pyeongchang will be that stepping stone for diversification and improvement of winter sports in Korea.

좋지! 평창이 한국의 동계스포츠 다양성과 향상을 위한 디딤돌이 되기를 바라.

South Korea in the Winter Olympics

Winter Olympic	Participated Event	No. of Athletes	Medals
1948 St. Moritz	Speed skating	3	–
1956 Cortina d'Ampezzo	Speed skating	4	–
1960 Squaw Valley	Alpine skiing Cross-country skiing Speed skating	7	–
1964 Innsbruck	Alpine skiing Cross-country skiing Speed skating	7	–
1968 Grenoble	Alpine skiing Cross-country skiing Figure skating Speed skating	8	–
1972 Sapporo	Figure skating Speed skating	5	–
1976 Innsbruck	Figure skating Speed skating	3	–
1980 Lake Placid	Alpine skiing Cross-country skiing Figure skating Speed skating	10	–
1984 Sarajevo	Alpine skiing Biathlon Cross-country skiing Figure skating Speed skating	15	–
1988 Calgary	Alpine skiing Biathlon Cross-country skiing Figure skating Speed skating	28	–
1992 Albertville	Alpine skiing Biathlon Cross-country skiing Figure skating	23	2 gold Short track (men's 1,000m / 5,000m relay)

	Short track speed skating Speed skating		1 silver Short track (men's 1,000m) 1 bronze Short track (men's 1,000m)
1994 Lillehammer	Alpine skiing Cross–country skiing Figure skating Short track speed skating Speed skating	24	4 gold Short track (men's 1,000m/ 500m women's 1,000m/ 3,000m relay) 1 silver Short track (men's 1,000m) 1 bronze Short track (women's 1,000m)
1998 Nagano	Alpine skiing Biathlon Cross–country skiing Figure skating Luge Short track speed skating Ski Jumping Speed skating	38	3 gold Short track (men's 1,000m / Women's 1,000m/3,000m relay) 1 silver Short track (men's 5,000m relay) 2 bronze Short track (women's 1,000m/ 500m)
2002 Salt Lake City	Biathlon Cross–country skiing Figure skating Luge Short track speed skating Skeleton Ski Jumping Speed skating	48	2 gold Short track (women's 1,500m/ 3,000m relay) 2 silver Short track (women's 1,000m/ 1,500m)
2006 Turin	Alpine skiing Biathlon Cross–country skiing Freestyle skiing Luge Short track speed skating	41	7 gold Short track (women's 1,000m/ 1,500m/3,000m relay/ men's 1000m/1500m/ 5,000m relay) Speed skating (women's 2X500m)

	Skeleton Ski Jumping Speed skating		3 silver Short track (women's 1,000m/ 1,500m/men's 1,500m) 2 bronze Short track (men's 500m) Speed skating (men's 2X500m)
2010 Vancouver	Alpine skiing Biathlon Bobsleigh Cross–country skiing Figure skating Freestyle skiing Luge Short track speed skating Skeleton Ski Jumping Snowboarding Speed skating	46	6 gold Figure skating (women's individual) Short track (men's 1,000m/ 1,500m) Speed skating (men's 10,000m/ 2X500m/women's 2X500m) 6 silver Short track (men's 1,000m/ 1,500m/5,000m relay/500m) Speed skating (men's 1,000m/ 5,000m) 2 bronze Short track (1,000m/1,500m)
2014 Sochi	Alpine skiing Biathlon Bobsleigh Cross–country skiing Curling Figure skating Freestyle skiing Luge Short track speed skating Skeleton Ski Jumping Snowboarding Speed skating	71	3 gold Short track (women's 1,000m/ 3,000m relay) Speed skating (women's 2X500m) 3 silver Figure skating (women's individual) Short track (women's 1,500m) Speed skating (men's team pursuit) 2 bronze Short track (women's 1,000m/ 500m)

South Korea in the 2014 Sochi Winter Olympics

Event	Participants	Medals
Alpine Skiing	경성현 (Sung Hyung Kyung) 박제윤 (Jae Yoon Park) 정동현 (Dong Hyun Jung) 강영서 (Young Suh Kang) 김소희 (So Hee Kim)	
Biathlon	이인복 (In Bok Lee) 문지희 (Ji Hee Moon)	
Bobsleigh	원윤종 (Yoon Jong Won) 김동현 (Dong Hyun Kim) 전정린 (Jung Lin Jun) 서영우 (Young Woo Suh) 김경현 (Kyoung Hyun Kim) 김 식 (Sik Kim) 석영진 (Young Jin Suk) 오제한 (Jae Han Oh) 김선옥 (Sun Ok Kim) 신미화 (Mi Hwa Shin)	
Cross Country	화준호 (June Ho Hwa) 이채원 (Chae Won Lee)	
Curling	김지선 (Ji Sun Kim) 신미성 (Mi Sung Shin) 이슬비 (Seul Bi Lee) 김은지 (Eun Ji Kim) 엄민지 (Min Ji Um)	
Figure Skating	김연아 (Yuna Kim) 김해진 (Hae Jin Kim) 박소연 (So Youn Park)	1 silver (women's individual)
Freestyle Skiing	김광진 (Kwang Jin Kim) 최재우 (Jae Woo Choi) 박희진 (Hee Jin Park) 서정화 (Jung Hwa Suh) 서지원 (Ji Won Suh)	
Ice Hockey		
Luge	김동현 (Dong Hyun Kim) 성은령 (Eun Ryoung Sung)	

	박진용 (Jin Yong Park) 조정명 (Jung Myoung Cho)	
Nordic Combined		
Short Track Speed Skating	김윤재 (Yoon Jae Kim) 노진규 (Jin Gyu Noh) 박세영 (Saeh Young Park) 신다운 (Da Woon Shin) 이한빈 (Han Bin Lee) 공상정 (Sang Jung Kong) 김아랑 (Arang Kim) 박승희 (Seung Hee Park) 심석희 (Suk Hee Shim) 조해리 (Haeri Cho)	1 gold (women's 1,000m) 1 gold (women's relay) 1 silver (women's 1,500m) 1 bronze (women's 1,000m) 1 bronze (women's 500m)
Skeleton	윤성빈 (Sung Bin Yoon) 이한신 (Han Shin Lee)	
Ski Jumping	강칠구 (Chil Goo Kang) 김현기 (Hyun Ki Kim) 최서우 (Suh Woo Choi) 최흥철 (Heung Chul Choi)	
Snowboard	김상겸 (Sang Kyum Kim) 김호준 (Ho Jun Kim) 신봉식 (Bong Sik Shin) 이광기 (Kwang Ki Lee)	
Speed Skating	김준호 (Jun Ho Kim) 김철민 (Chul Min Kim) 김태윤 (Tae Yoon Kim) 모태범 (Tae Bum Mo) 이강석 (Kang Suk Lee) 이규혁 (Gyu Hyuk Lee) 이승훈 (Seung Hoon Lee) 주형준 (Hyung Jun Choo) 김보름 (Bo Leum Kim) 김현영 (Hyun Young Kim) 노선영 (Sun Young Noh) 박승주 (Seung Joo Park) 양신영 (Shin Young Yang) 이보라 (Bo Ra Lee) 이상화 (Sang Hwa Lee)	1 gold (women's 2X500m) 1 silver (team pursuit)

해 석

Participation in the Winter Olympics

한국은 1936년 가르미슈 파르텐키르헨 동계올림픽에 3명의 조선 선수들이 일제강점기 당시 일본 대표팀으로 참가한 경험이 있다. 독립국가로서 대한민국은 1948년 생모리츠 동계올림픽에 3명의 스피드 스케이트 선수들을 보냈으며 이것이 첫 동계올림픽 참가였다. 이후 한국은 2014년까지 총 18개의 동계올림픽에 참가했다.

한국의 첫 올림픽 메달은 1992년 알베르빌에서 얻은 것이다. 쇼트트랙 선수 김기훈 선수가 남자 1,000m 종목에서 금메달을 획득한 것인데 그는 또 다시 1994년 동계올림픽에서 같은 종목에서 금메달을 얻었다. 두 번의 승리는 추후 한국의 쇼트트랙 역사의 출발점이 되면서 2002년까지 이 종목은 한국의 효자 종목으로 자리를 잡았다. 이후에도 대다수의 메달은 쇼트트랙에서 획득되고 있었으나 2006년 스피드 스케이트와 2010년 피겨 스케이트로 점점 확산되어 갔다.

쇼트트랙의 선두주자로 동계올림픽에 진입하고 성장해왔지만 동계 스포츠 경기 주종목을 다양화하려는 노력이 경주되어 왔다. 1960년대 알파인 스키와 크로스컨트리 스키를 시작으로 참가 종목을 점차적으로 바이애슬론, 프리스타일 스키, 스노보드, 스키점프 등으로 확산해 나갔다. 그리고 2014년 소치 올림픽에서는 15개의 종목 중 13개에 참가하였다.

Leading Sports

올림픽 메달 수를 고려하면 한국이 분명한 우세를 보이는 종목은 쇼트트랙이라고 할 수 있다. 동계올림픽에서 획득한 52개의 메달 중 42개가 쇼트트랙에서 획득했으며 그중 21개가 금메달이다. 많은 금메달 획득은 미래의 한국 스케이트 선수들이 넘어야 할 기준이 높다는 것을 의미한다. 선수들은 어린 나이부터 혹독한 훈련을 견디고 경기에서 우수한 성적을 받아야 국가대표팀에 뽑힐 수 있는 기회가 주어진다.

2010년부터 한국은 쇼트트랙 외에 스피드 스케이트와 피겨 스케이트에서 메달을 획득하고 그 분야의 스타로 탄생하였다. 이렇게 쇼트트랙 외 다양한 겨울 스포츠에 대한 관심은 긍정적인 현상이며 이는 한국 스포츠 문화의 성장과 성취에 필요한 새로운 기회를 만들고 있다. 2018년 평창 동계올림픽과 함께 동계올림픽 선수들을 세계적 수

준으로 양성하는 데에 관심이 커지고 있다.

Korea's Upcoming Olympians

2018년 평창 동계올림픽 준비와 동시에 다양한 스포츠의 선수들을 훈련하고 지원하는 데에 많은 노력을 경주하고 있다. 선수 개인의 무진한 노력과 대기업의 지원으로 한국은 차기 2018년 올림픽 선수들을 준비시키고 있다.

2014년 소치 동계올림픽으로 인해 한국 팬들은 새로운 선수들과 스포츠에 눈을 뜨게 되었다. 언론이 주목한 종목은 여자 컬링이였다. 여자 컬링 대표팀은 2012년 창립해부터 놀라운 성장을 하면서 같은 해 세계선수권대회 4강까지 올라갔다. 세계 랭킹 10위인 한국 여자 컬링 팀은 스웨덴과 캐나다 같은 컬링 선진국과 경기한 경험이 있다. 2018년 준비를 위해 대한체육회와 대한컬링연맹은 스위스의 가지 팀과 캐나다의 구슈, 몽골 여자 컬링 대표팀, 그리고 카자흐스탄 남자 컬링 대표팀을 초대해 훈련한다. 이런 노력은 한국 팀이 올림픽 승리를 위해 기술과 경기력을 향상시킬 수 있는 기회로 작용할 것이다.

소치에서 놀라움을 준 또 다른 선수는 프리스타일 모글 스키 선수 최재우다. 그는 2013 세계선수권대회에서 5위를 차지한 최초의 아시아 선수이며 동계올림픽에서 결승에 진출한 최초의 한국인이다. 메달은 얻지 못했으나 언론의 주목을 받으며 차기 올림픽 유망주로 인정을 받았다. 최재우는 현재 2018년에서 금메달을 얻기 위해 훈련 중이다.

2018년을 준비하는 유망주들 중에는 피겨 선수 박소연, 김진서와 이준형, 그리고 한국 아이스하키 대표팀도 있다. 금메달 선수 김연아의 길을 따르기 위해 피겨선수들은 기술을 다지며 점수를 높여 올림픽 출전 자격을 희망하고 있다. 반면, 국가대표 아이스하키 팀은 국제아이스하키연맹(IIHF)으로부터 출전 자리를 받았다. 아이스하키 팀은 평창 올림픽에서 8강 진출을 목표로 훈련 중에 있으며 국내 아이스하키 관심을 높이고 인프라를 구축하여 종목의 대중화를 바라고 있다.

삼성, CJ, 신세계와 같은 대기업들의 참여로 차기 올림픽 선수 양성 열기가 달아오르고 있다. 이러한 대기업들은 봅슬레이, 스켈레톤, 스노보드와 같은 종목의 선수들을 지원하고 있다. 그러한 지원은 동계유니버시아드 스노보드 하프파이프 종목에서 얻은 김호준의 은메달, 소치 올림픽에서 봅슬레이 팀 원윤종과 서영우의 18위, 소치에서 스켈레톤 선수 윤성빈의 16위와 같은 성과로 이어졌다. 이와 같은 지원은 2018년 동계올림픽까지 지속될 것으로 보이고 이로 인해 메달도 얻고 겨울 스포츠 다양화에 대한 관심과 인식을 높일 것으로 기대된다.

차기 동계올림픽의 주최국으로서 한국은 동계스포츠 전 종목에 걸친 선수 양성에 많은 노력을 기울이고 있다. 한국은 메달 효자 종목에만 집중하기보다 새롭고 신선한 종목으로 관심을 넓히고 있는데, 이는 2018년 평창 동계올림픽을 더욱 기다리게 만들고 있다.

II

PARALYMPICS
THE SUMMER AND WINTER GAMES
ENGLISH CONVERSATION GUIDE

Every great dream begins with a dreamer.
Always remember, you have within you
the strength, the patience, and the passion
to reach for the stars to change the world.
Harriet Tubman

What is the Paralympics?

장애인올림픽 소개

01

New Language

- alongside: (adv.)…옆에, 나란히 / by, at, to the side of
- civilian: (n.)민간인 / citizen, commoner
- impairment: (n.)장애 / damage, illness
- incorporate: (v.)포함하다 / assimilate, mix, include
- intellectual: (adj.)지능의, 지적인 / mental, psychological, cerebral
- Paralympics: (n.)세계 장애인올림픽
- physical: (adj.)육체의 / bodily
- veteran: (n.)참전 용사, 재향 군인 / soldier, troop

The Paralympic Games is an international sports competition for athletes with various forms of physical and intellectual impairments. The term **paralympic** combines the Greek preposition *para*, meaning beside or side by side, and the name of the international sports competition, *Olympic,* to suggest a game held immediately after or alongside the Olympic Games.

- paralympic: para(나란히) + Olympic(올림픽)의 합성어로 = 올림픽과 나란히

  note) 장애인 스포츠는 최초 하지마비환자(paraplegic)의 재활 목적으로 시작하여 영어 paraplegic의 para와 olympic의 합성어로 경기를 paralympic으로 불렀다. 그러나 이 명칭은 모든 장애를 대표하지 못한다고 판단되어 그 어원의 의미를 위와 같이 개조하였다.

The movement of the games began during the late 19th century and continued into the post World War II era that experienced a flood of injured veterans and civilians. What **took off** as a form of rehabilitation for people with **spinal injuries** gradually developed into a competitive sports event.

- take off: 영어의 숙어로 다양한 의미를 갖고 있지만, 여기서는 "출발하다"와 같이 "힘 있게 시작하다"의 의미를 갖는다. 즉, begin 또는 start와 같은 단어로 대체가 가능하다.
- spinal injuries: 척추 부상

  note) 몸 특정 부위에 부상을 입었다고 표현하기 위해 spinal 대신 해당 신체 부위를 대체할 수 있다.

  ex) neck injury: 목 부상

  leg injury: 다리 부상

  head injury: 머리 부상

The first games, mainly for athletes in wheelchairs and initially called the Stoke Mandeville Games, officially began on the day of the 1948 London Olympics **opening ceremonies**. The games were decided to be **held every four years** and added winter sports in 1976. It entered the Olympic Sports **arena** when the International Olympic Committee (IOC) and the International Paralympic Committee **(IPC)** agreed to host both games in the Summer and Winter Olympic **host countries** in the same year.

- opening ceremony: 개막식

  closing ceremony: 폐막식

  note) ceremony는 엄숙하고 예의를 갖춘 국가적, 공식적, 종교적 의식을 치를 때 사용하는 용어다.
- hold every four years: 4년마다 개최하다

  note) 기간과 관련된 표현

  ex) quarterly: 분기별

  biannually: 1년에 2번

  annually: 1년마다
- arena : 경기장을 뜻하지만, territory, field, department, ground와 같이 넓은 의미로는 "영역"의 뜻으로도 사용되며, 위 문장에서는 "영역"을 의미한다.
- IOC/IPC: 이와 같은 단체의 명칭은 길기 때문에 구어에서는 단체의 이니셜만 얘기하는 경우가 많다.

- host country/host nation: 주최국

  host city: 주최 도시

  note) host의 반대는 guest 또는 visitor이다. 그러므로 초청받은 국가, 방문 중인 국가 등을 표현할 때 guest country 또는 visiting country를 사용해도 된다.

  경기 상황에서는 participating country 또는 nation이라고 표현한다.

The movement to incorporate all **disabled persons** into sports has triggered the formation of a number of other **organizations**, including the International Sport Organization for the Disabled (IOSD), Cerebral Palsy International Sports and Recreation **Association** (CPISRA), the International Blind Sports **Federation** (IBSA), the International **Committee** of the Sport for the Deaf (CISS), and the International Sports Federations for Persons with an Intellectual Disability (INAS-FID). With the coordination of these associations along with the International Stoke Mandeville Games (ISMGF) arose the International Co-coordination Committee Sports for the Disabled in the World (ICC). The development of the movement and the rise of interest from more nations **led to** the foundation of the overall governing organization, the International Paralympic Committee (IPC), on September 22, 1989.

- disabled persons: 장애인

  note) 장애인을 지칭하는 표현이 많이 존재한다, 예를 들어 handicapped와 challenged가 있다. 그러나 이와 같은 표현은 장애인들에게 모욕적으로 느껴지는 용어다. 장애인을 disabled person/people 또는 person with disability라고 부르는 것이 원칙이다.

- 단체의 성격이 이름에서 나타난다

  organization: 단체, 조직

  회사와 같이 특정한 일을 목적을 이루기 위해 구성된 조직이며 역할과 기능의 분담이 확실히 존재한다. 예를 들어, UN과 WHO 등이 있다.

  association: 협회

  같은 목적을 가진 사람, 단체, 국가가 동맹을 맺는 것이기에 우호적인 성격을 갖고 있다. 예를 들어, NATO와 ASDEAN이 있다.

federation: 연맹

여러 소규모 또는 지역적 단체의 조합으로 만들어지는 단체. 예를 들어, International Ski Federation과 International Sports Federation이 있다.

committee: 위원회

선발 또는 임명된 위원의 구성으로 특정일에 대한 법적, 계획, 기획, 보고, 등의 업무를 하는 조직. 예를 들어, IOC와 IPC

- something lead(s) to something: ~ 이어지다, A가 B를 초래하다

ex) Studying leads to good grades.

공부하는 것은 좋은 성적으로 이어진다.

Dialogue - Thoughts on the two events

Tasha : The Paralympics is such as special event, don't you think?

장애인올림픽은 굉장히 특별한 행사인 것 같지 않아?

Jared : I couldn't agree with you more.

전적으로 동감해.

Tasha : There is so much emphasis on the Olympic Games that I have never realized how meaningful the Paralympics are.

올림픽이 더 많이 강조되기 때문에 장애인올림픽이 얼마나 의미 있는 행사인지 깨닫지 못했어.

Jared : That's true, but I think both games are meaningful in their own ways. The Olympic Games, dating back to 776 B.C., are important because it helped civilizations and over time countries, come together in the name of competitive sports. The Paralympics, on the other hand, is special because it provides equal opportunity for all persons to participate in sports, despite their impairments.

맞아, 그러나 두 행사 모두 각각 의미 있다고 봐. 기원전 776년까지 거슬러 올라가는 올림픽은 문명 그리고 점차적으로 국가가 스포츠경기의 이름하에 모일 수 있도록 기여했다는 데에 의미가 있어. 반면, 장애인올림픽은 모든 사람이 장애와 무관하게 스포츠에 참여할 수 있는 평등한 기회를 제공했다는 것에 의의가 있어.

Tasha : Both events are valuable to the international community. They've evolved into a symbol of peace and equality.

두 행사 모두 국제사회에 소중하지. 두 행사 모두 평화와 평등의 상징으로 발달해왔어.

Jared : But I still think there is more room for the Paralympic events to grow.

그러나 장애인올림픽이 아직도 발달할 수 있는 여지가 남아있다고 생각해.

Tasha : Yes, but you must realize that the movement started much later than the Olympics. I think more publicity would help raise interest and awareness of the Paralympics.

맞아, 그러나 이 움직임은 올림픽보다 한참 더 늦게 시작했다는 사실을 인식해야 해. 더 많은 언론 노출이 있다면 장애인올림픽에 대한 관심과 인식을 높이는 데에 도움이 될 수 있다고 생각해.

Jared : So far, the IPC and the IOC have made great efforts in doing that. They've brought the two events together by holding them every four years in the same host city.

지금까지는 IPC와 IOC가 그러기 위해 노력을 많이 해왔어. 두 위원회는 행사를 합쳐 4년마다 한 번 같은 주최도시에서 치르지.

Tasha : I hope more work will be done in the future to make the Paralympics as big as the Olympics.

장애인올림픽이 올림픽만큼 성장할 수 있도록 나중에도 많은 노력이 있었으면 좋겠다.

Practice

Main Expressions

▸ on the other hand: 다른 한편으로는 ~, 반면에
(대조 또는 비교할 때 사용하는 표현으로 conversely, on the contrary, however 등이 있다)
ex: The USA athlete is a rookie. **On the other hand**, the athlete from Mexico is the defending champion.
미국 선수는 초보자다. **반면에,** 멕시코 선수는 전년도 우승자다.

▸ as (adjective) as: ~처럼 (형용사), ~만큼 (형용사)
(유사점을 표현하거나 무엇의 특징을 닮았다고 표현할 때 사용)
ex: The child ran **as fast as** the adult.
아이는 어른**처럼 빨리** 달렸다.

ex: The cake was **as soft as** the cloud.
케이크는 구름**만큼 부드러웠다.**

Language Focus

▸ comparative: a is (adj. + (–er)) than b // irregular adj.: a is (more + adj.) than b
비교급: a는 b보다 더 (형용사–er) // 불규칙 형용사: a는 b보다 더 (more + 형용사)
ex: Football is **bigger than** soccer in the United States.
미식축구는 미국에서 축구보다 규모가 **더 크다.**
ex: I think that soccer is **more fun** than football.
내 생각에 미식축구보다 축구가 **더 재미있다.**

A. Look at the two pictures and describe or compare them using the two expressions presented above. (on the other hand / as (adj.) as)

B. Language Focus: Make four sentences comparing the pictures above, using the comparative form. (adj. + ~er than) / (more + adj than)

1 ______________________________

2 ______________________________

3 ______________________________

4 ______________________________

02 The International Paralympic Committee (IPC): Its goals and values

장애인올림픽위원회: 목적과 가치

New Language

- coordinate: (v.) 조직화하다 / organize, regulate
- establish: (v.) 설립하다 / settle, form, create
- equal: (adj.) 동등한, 평등한 / same,
- federation: (n.) 연맹, 연합체 / association, organization
- institution: (n.) 기관 / foundation, establishment
- international: (adj.) 국제적인 / global, world
- office: (n.) 지위, 공직 / job, position, employment, duty
- locate: (v.) 위치에 두다 / placed, settled, positioned
- serve: (v.) 근무하다, 복무하다, 일하다 / work,
- succeed: (v.) 잇따르다, 승계하다, 계승하다 / come after, replace
- value: (n.) 가치관 / beliefs, ethics, ideals

The International Paralympic Committee (IPC) is an international institution coordinating twelve sports federations and various competitions **as well as** the Summer and Winter Paralympic Games.

- as well as: ~에 더하여, 게다가
  note) along with와 including은 동일한 표현이며 교체 사용이 가능하다.

It is **located in** Bonn, Germany and **was established in September 22, 1989.**

- situated in (a place): 도시 또는 특정 장소에 위치하다
  ex) The establishment is located in Seoul, Korea.
  기관은 서울에 위치하고 있다.

note) 위치를 표현하기 위해 in 외에 다른 전치사를 사용 가능하다(by, on, between).

on: The office is located on the top floor of the building.

사무실이 건물의 맨 위층에 위치하고 있다.

by: The flower vase was located by the television.

꽃병이 텔레비전 옆에 있었다.

between: The car is located between section C and E.

차는 C와 E구역 사이에 위치해 있다.

- be established in (date): (날짜)에 설립되었다.

ex) The school was established in March 3, 1999.

학교는 1999년 3월 3일에 설립되었다.

note) 날짜 또는 시간을 다양한 방법으로 표현이 가능하다

월 또는 연도: It was established in March.

It was established in 1999.

note) in 전치사 사용 안 하는 경우

date 관련 다양한 표현: last month/year/week (지난달/작년/지난주)

this month/year/week (이번 달/올해/이번 주)

decade/century (10년/100년)

ex) The hospital was established last year.

병원은 작년에 설립되었다.

ex) It was established a century ago.

기관은 100년 전에 설립됐다.

The first president of the IPC, Robert Steadward **served from 1989 to 2001** and **was succeeded by** Sir Philip Craven, who is currently in office and will **serve until 2017**.

- serve from (date) to (date): (날짜)에서 (날짜)까지 일하다

serve until (date): (날짜)까지 근무하다

serve from (date): (날짜)부터 일하다

- (person a) be succeeded by (person b): (사람 b)가 (사람 a)를 직위 또는 자리를 인계받다

(estate) be succeeded by (person): (사람)이 (재산)을 상속받다

The International Paralympic Committee was established to provide equal athletic opportunity for all persons. The IPC offers Paralympic athletes the chance to participate in sports competitions and enhance their ability from beginning to advanced levels.

This effort is to meet and enhance the values of the Paralympics, which are courage, determination, inspiration, and equality.

Dialogue - About the committee

Parker : The committee in charge of the Paralympic games is the International Paralympic Committee. Also known as the IPC. And it was established in September 22, 1989.

장애인올림픽을 담당하는 위원회는 국제장애인올림픽위원회야. 흔히 IPC라고 부르지. 그리고 1989년 9월 22일에 설립됐어.

Sheila : I would like to know more about the committee. For example, why was it set up? Where is the IPC? Who is the president? And so on.

위원회에 대해 더 알고 싶어. 예를 들어, 설립 목적이 무엇인지, IPC가 어디에 있는지, 회장은 누구인지 등등.

Parker : You would like to know all the facts?

모든 점을 알고 싶니?

Sheila : Well, yes. The basic facts would help me to gain insight on this organization.

그렇지. 기본 정보는 이 위원회에 대한 식견을 얻을 수 있게 도와줄 것 같아.

Parker : Alright, then. Answering your questions, in no order. IPC headquarters are in Bonn, Germany. The current president is Sir Phillip Craven. What was your last question?

그럼 알았어. 순서와 상관없이 너의 질문에 대한 답을 하지. IPC 본부는 독일의 본에 있어. 현재 회장은 크라벤이야. 그리고 마지막 질문이 뭐였지?

Sheila : The most crucial. Why was it set up?

가장 중요한 질문이지. 설립 목적이 뭐지?

Parker : Right. Prior to the IPC, there were various federations and organizations competing in different competitions. The IPC was established to organize these groups under one umbrella committee.

맞다. IPC 이전에 여러 협회와 단체가 다양한 경기에서 활동하고 있었어. IPC는 이 모든 단체를 하나의 우산 밑에 모으기 위해 설립됐지.

Sheila : So the IPC manages the participating federations and coordinates the Paralympic games.

그러니까, IPC는 참여하는 모든 협회를 관리하고 장애인올림픽을 조직화하네.

Parker : That's correct. They also define the rules and regulations for the competitions.

맞아. 그리고 경기 규정과 규칙도 정하지.

Practice

Main Expressions

▸ established in (date): (날짜)에 설립됐다
established to (verb): (동사)하기 위해 설립됐다
(in은 설립 날짜 또는 장소를 표현할 때 사용하는 반면, to는 설립의 목적을 표현할 때 사용)
ex: The high school was **established in** January 12, 1977.
고등학교는 **1977년 1월 12일에 설립됐다.**
It was **established in** Los Angeles, California.
고등학교는 **캘리포니아주 로스앤젤레스에서 설립됐다.**
ex: The high school was **established to provide** education for those with special needs.
고등학교는 특별한 보살핌이 필요한 자에게 교육을 **제공하기 위해 설립됐다.**

▸ in charge of: 담당하다, 책임지다
(업무에 대한 총괄 관리 및 책임을 표현할 때 사용하며 manage, responsible for와 유사)
ex: Security guards are **in charge of** doing security checks on baggage and travelers.
보안 경비원은 짐과 여행객에 대한 보안 검사를 **담당한다.**

Language Focus

- would like to ~: 무엇을 하고 싶다
  would는 will의 과거형이다
  (want to와 의미가 같으나 더욱 공손한 표현이기에 공식적인 자리는 물론 친숙하지 않은 사람에게 표현을 하거나 want to를 순화해서 표현하고자 할 때 사용한다.)
  ex: I **would like** to volunteer at the event.
  행사에서 자원봉사를 **하고 싶습니다.**

A. A few organizations have been presented below. Tell when and why they were established.

1 Organization: International Ice Hockey Fedezration

Founded: 1908

Purpose: Organize international ice hockey competitions

2 Organization: Amnesty International

Founded: 1961

Purpose: Fight injustice / promote human rights

B. Translate into English using the main expressions.

1 승무원은 승객의 안전과 쾌적한 비행을 책임진다.

(flight attendant / passenger / safety / comfort)

2 이 경기를 당신과 함께 보고 싶습니다.

(game / match / competition / event)

3 자전거 타는 것보다 인라인을 타고 싶습니다.

(ride a bike / go rollerskating)

4 중국어를 배웠기 때문에 나는 중국인 관광객을 담당했다.

(Chinese / learn / tourist)

03 Paralympic Sports
장애인올림픽 스포츠 종목

New Language

- category: (n.) 범주 / class, division, group
- competitiveness: (n.) 경쟁력, 경쟁적인 것 / ambition
- cheat: (v.) 속이다, 부정행위를 하다 / con, deceive, manipulate
- deficiency: (n.) 결핍, 부족 / imperfection, defect, lack
- discrepancy: (n.) 차이, 불일치 / difference, disparity
- eligibility: (n.) 자격 / qualification, ability, acceptability
- enhance: (v.) 향상시키다, 높이다 / increase, raise, elevate, strengthen
- limb: (n.) 팔, 다리 / arm, leg, extension
- prevent: (v.) 예방하다 / block, prohibit, restrict
- protect: (v.) 보호하다 / care for, defend, shelter, support, secure
- qualify: (v.) 자격을 얻다 / certify, permit, enable
- standard: (n.) 기준, 규범 / norm, prototype
- stature: (n.) 키 / size, height

The Paralympics, organized by the International Paralympic Committee, **consists of** twenty-five summer sports and five winter sports.

- consist of: ~로 구성되어 있다, 이루어지다 / composed of, include, made up of
  note) consist in과는 다른 의미를 갖는다
  consist in: ~에 있다/ be found in, be contained in
  ex) The spirit of the sports consists in the hard work of the athletes.

Each **sports** is divided into **events** according to specific impairments. This allows athletes with similar physical or intellectual conditions to compete fairly.

- sports와 event의 차이
  sport: 스포츠 종목 (예: 수영, 배드민턴, 스케이트)
  event: 대체적으로 하나의 스포츠 종목 안에서 치르는 경기 (예: 육상의 남자 1,000m, 남자 800m)

Athletes must **meet the criteria** set by the IPC to compete in their sports of interest. This means that the athletes must have an impairment that qualifies them for an event within the sport. Merely having an impairment does not qualify athletes into the Paralympics.

- meet the criteria: 기준을 충족하다 / 기준을 만족시키다
  criteria: criterion의 복수형
  meet: 충족시키다, 만족시키다, 만나다 등 여러 의미를 갖고 있다.
  note) meet는 다양한 idiom에 사용되고 있다.
  ex) meet the requirements / standards: 기준을 만족시키다
  meet one's match: 상대를 만나다
  meet up with someone: ~와 만나다
  meet (someone) halfway: 누구와 중간점에서 만나다 / 절충 또는 타협하다

The IPC has categorized impairments into ten categories. Athletes must **fall into** one of the categories to participate in the competitions. The eligibility standards are strict to prevent any form of unfairness or cheating.

- fall into: ~으로 나누어진다, ~에 빠지다

The ten classifications are as follows (according to the IPC):

① Impaired muscle power: the lack of ability in the muscles to contract, impairing movement
② Impaired passive range movement: the restriction of movement in one or more joints

③ Limb deficiency: loss of whole or partial bones or joints

④ Leg length discrepancy: having one shortened leg

⑤ Short stature: abnormally shortened height with unbalanced proportions in limbs or trunk

⑥ Hypertonia: the lack of ability in the muscles to stretch, impairing normal movement

⑦ Ataxia: the lack of coordination in muscle movement

⑧ Athetosis: motor dysfunction that causes involuntary muscle movement

⑨ Vision impairment: damage to the eye that restricts sight

⑩ Intellectual impairment: limited intellectual ability and behavior

Athletes eligible to participate in the Paralympics have specific needs due to their specific impairment. Therefore, unique sports techniques and methods, as well as gear and equipment have been developed to protect and assist athletes in enhancing their competitiveness.

Dialogue - Qualifying for the sport

Sharon : The Paralympics have a significant amount of competing sports. It says here that there are twenty five summer sports and five winter sports.

장애인올림픽은 상당히 많은 스포츠 종목을 포함하고 있지. 여기에 따르면, 여름 스포츠 25개의 종목과 5개의 겨울 스포츠를 포함하고 있어.

Timothy : I agree that it is a significant number, but there's quite a disparity between the two.

상당히 많은 종목이 있다는 것에 동의하지만, 두 계절에 상당한 차이도 있어.

Sharon : I know. But it is still amazing that so many people with impairments are challenging their limits in so many fields of sports.

맞아. 그러나 장애가 있는 사람들이 많은 스포츠 종목에서 자신의 한계에 도전한다는 사실이 놀라워.

Timothy : Absolutely. But don't you ever wonder how people with different abilities compete in a single event?

당연하지. 그런데 이렇게 다양한 능력을 갖고 있는 사람들이 하나의 경기에 어떻게 출전하는지에 대해 생각해 본 적 있니?

Sharon : Well, the IPC has very strict qualifications for athletes, just in case of cheating. First, the athletes must fall into one of the ten impairment categories. Then, they must confirm that the sport of their interest holds an event for their specific impairment category.

그럼. 국제장애인올림픽위원회는 부정행위를 예방하기 위해 선수들에 대한 엄격한 기준이 있어. 첫째로 선수들은 10개의 장애 종목 중 하나에 포함되어야 해. 그다음으로는, 본인이 관심이 있는 종목이 특정 장애스포츠 종목에 해당되는지 확인해야 해.

Timothy : Let me get this straight. So you are saying that the athlete can only compete if the sport includes their impairment?

다시 정리해보자. 네 말대로라면, 선수는 특정 스포츠 종목에 본인이 해당되는 장애가 포함되어야만 참여할 수 있다는 얘기야?

Sharon : Right on, Timothy. They do this to make the games fair.

맞았어, 티머시. 경기를 공평하게 만들기 위해서야.

Timothy : Is that right? I just assumed different scoring systems would be applied.

그렇다고? 그냥 다른 점수 체계를 적용할 것이라고 생각했어.

Sharon : They do have different scoring systems for different impairments. If you think about it, scoring is much more convenient when similar groups compete against one another. But mainly, it allows athletes to compete in a fairer environment.

맞아. 장애 정도에 따라 다른 점수 체계가 적용되기도 해. 잘 생각해보면, 유사한 그룹이 경기를 치른다면 점수를 매기는 것도 더욱 편리할 것이야. 그러나, 주된 목적은 더욱 공평한 환경에서 선수들이 경기를 치를 수 있도록 해주기 위해서야.

Practice

Main Expressions

- get (something) straight: 무엇을 정확히 확인하자
  (이해를 돕기 위해 무엇에 대한 내용을 확인하거나 확인시킬 때 사용하는 표현)
  ex: let me get this straight: 사실 또는 내용에 대해 정리하거나 재확인할 때 사용
  Let me get this straight, you are moving out to San Antonio?
  정확히 하자면, 넌 이제 산안토니오로 이사해?
  ex: get this straight: 확실히 이해시킬 때 사용
  Get this straight, you must finish the work by end of this month.
  확실하게 이해해, 이 일을 월말까지 반드시 끝내야 해.

Language Focus

- interjections: 감탄사
  (주로 문장 앞부분에 사용된다. 그러나 문법적으로 문장과 연결되지 않는다. 감정을 나타내는 단어를 의미하지만 이 외에도 소리와 문장 도입 단어도 속한다.)
  ex: 동의 또는 공감을 나타내는 표현
  I know: 맞아 / seriously
  Absolutely: 전적으로 동의 / completely, totally
  ex: 격려의 표현
  right on: 맞다, 대단하다 / great, you got it
  ex: 무엇을 확인할 때 사용하는 표현
  Is that right?: 맞죠? 확실하지? 그런가요? / really?
  ex: Well
  well은 큰 의미가 없거나, 화제를 바꾸거나, 감탄을 표현할 때 다양하게 사용된다

A. Use the main expression to rephrase the sentences below. (use : get something straight)

1 A person with impaired muscle power has difficulty moving because the muscles do no contract.

2 The car accident was very serious, causing damage to the eyes, and may

lead to vision problems.

3 Today's game has been cancelled and will be postponed due to the weather.

B. Add an interjection

1 ______________________, I'm more interested in winter sports than summer sports.

2 ______________________, she's the most famous Olympian in our country.

3 ______________________, let's go see the games tomorrow.

4 ______________________, didn't you enjoy the watching the athletes?

5 ______________________, you got the technique down perfectly.

04 List of Summer Sports and Winter Sports
여름 스포츠와 겨울 스포츠 종목

New Language

- adapted: (adj.) 개조된 / altered, adjusted, reformed
- assist: (v.) 돕다 / aid, support
- classification: (n.) 범주, 분류 / category, group
- control: (n.) 통제력 / command, power
- discipline: (n.) 운동경기의 종목 / method, practice
- doubles: (n.) 2인 / dual
- equipment: (n.) 장비 / tools
- event: (n.) 경기 / competition
- gate: (n.) 스키 게이트
- mild: (adj.) 약간의, 가벼운 / benign, moderate
- minimal: (adj.) 최소의 / light
- moderate: (adj.) 보통의, 중간의 / mild
- modified: (adj.) 변경된, 수정된 / altered, adjusted, fitted
- partial: (adj.) 부분적인 / limited
- player: (n.) 선수 / athlete
- reduced: (adj.) 감소한, 축소한 / decreased, diminished
- run: (n.) 경주 / race
- severe: (adj.) 극심한, 심각한 / serious, acute, critical
- slope: (n.) 스키 슬로프 또는 연습장
- standard: (adj.) 보통의, 표준 / normal, typical
- tally: (v.) 기록 / score
- target: (n.) 표적, 목표 / aim, goal
- total: (adj.) 전체의 / complete, full, entire

Summer Sports	Description
Archery 양궁  (source: https://en.wikipedia.org)	**Introduction:** Archery is a game played with a bow and arrow. The archer shoots an arrow at a target from a designated distance. Scores are tallied according to the rings shot on the target. This form of archery is called target archery and it requires accuracy, steadiness, and focus. **소개:** 양궁은 활과 화살을 사용하는 경기다. 양궁 선수는 정해진 거리에서 활로 목표를 쏜다. 과녁을 쏘면 점수가 매겨진다. 양궁의 종목은 표적경기이며 정확도, 꾸준함, 그리고 집중력을 요구하는 종목이다. **Events:** Men's events – 90m, 70m, 50m, 30m Women and W1 – 70m, 60m, 50m, 30m **경기:** 남자 – 90m, 70m, 50m, 30m 여자 및 W1 – 70m, 60m, 50m, 30m **Classification:** W1 Archers – have a disability in both their upper and lower body with functional defects in their hands or arms. (Equipment: compound bows without magnifying sights) W2 Archers – use a wheelchair, but have ability in their hands and arms. (Equipment: recurve bows and wheelchairs) Standing Archers – can stand but have a physical disability. (Equipment: recurve bows and stools) Open Compound – fall into one of the above categories (Equipment: compound bow, magnifying sight, and mechanical release) **장애분류:** W1 – 상반신 및 하반신에 장애가 있으며 손과 팔에 기능적 장애가 존재 (장비: 확대기가 없는 컴파운드 보) W2 – 휠체어를 사용하지만 손과 팔에 기능 존재 (장비: 휜 활) 서는 선수 – 설 수 있지만 신체적 장애 존재 (장비: 휜 활 및 스툴 또는 의자) 오픈 컴파운드 (Open Compound) – 위 분류 중 하나에 해당됨 (장비: 컴파운드 보, 확대기, 및 자동 쏘기 기능)
IPC Athletics 육상	**Introduction:** IPC athletics is a combination of many competitions described below. The competitions are open for all impairment groups, specific impairment groups use special equipment to support them during a competition. **소개:** 육상은 다양한 경기를 조합한 경기다. 모든 장애분류에 속한 선수들이 참여 가능하며 특정 장애에 따라 지지하는 장비를 사용한다. **Events:** Track events – sprint (100m, 200m, 400m), middle distance (800m, 1,500m), long distance (5,000m, 10,000m), relay races (4X100m, 4X400m)

(source: zimbio.com)

Road event – marathon

Field events – high jump, long jump, triple jump, discus, shot put, javelin

Combined events – pentathlon.

경기: 트랙 경주 – 단거리(100m, 200m, 400m), 중거리(800m, 1,500m), 장거리(5,000m, 10,000m), 계주(4X100m, 4X400m)

로드 경기 – 마라톤

필드 경기 – 높이뛰기, 멀리뛰기, 세단뛰기, 원반던지기, 포환던지기, 창던지기

복합 경기 – 근대5종 경기

Classification: T/F 11–13 – visual impairment (11–13: lowest vision to best vision)

T/F20 – intellectual impairment

T32–38 and F31–38 – athetosis, ataxia, hypertonia (lowest is the most severe/31–34 are in a seated position/35–38 better trunk and leg function and can stand)

F40–41 – short stature

T42–47 and F42–46 – limb deficiencies (42–44 have leg impairment/45–47 have arm impairment)

T51–54 and F51–57 – wheelchair users (T51–54 have poor arm and leg function/T54 have partial trunk and leg function/F51–54 have limited arm and leg function / F54 have normal function in arm and hands/F55–57 mild trunk and leg impairment)

장애분류: T/F 11–13 – 시각장애 (11–13: 가장 낮은 시각능력에서 가장 좋은 시각능력)

T/F20 – 지적장애

T32–38 및 F31–38 – 무정위운동증, 운동실조증, 긴장항진 (가장 양호한 상태에서 가장 심각한 상태/31–34는 앉을 수 있는 자세/35–38은 몸통 통제가 더 좋고 다리 기능이 양호해서 설 수 있음)

F40–41 – 단신

T42–47 및 F42–46 – 팔과 다리 장애 (42–44는 다리 장애 / 45–47은 팔 장애)

T51–54 및 F51–57 – 휠체어 사용자 (T51–54는 낮은 팔다리 기능/T54는 일부 몸과 다리 기능 가능/F51–54 제한된 팔과 다리 기능/F54는 정상적인 팔과 손 기능 가능/F55–57는 경미한 몸과 다리 장애 존재)

Badminton
배드민턴

Introduction: Badminton is a sport played in singles or doubles with a racquet and shuttlecock, or a feathered ball. Players must pass and strike the shuttlecock over the net and strike the floor of the opposing player's court.

소개: 배드민턴은 싱글과 더블로 하는 경기이며 라켓과 셔틀콕을 사용한다. 선수는 네트 너머로 셔틀콕을 패스하고 반대편 선수의 코트에 스트라이크

(source: paralympic.org)

하여야 한다.

Events: Men – singles, doubles, mixed doubles
Women – singles, doubles, mixed doubles
경기: 남자 – 싱글, 더블, 혼합복식
여자 – 싱글, 더블, 혼합복식

Classification: WH1 and WH2 – wheelchair use
SL3, SL4, SU5 – standing
SS6 – Short stature
장애분류: WH1 및 WH2 – 휠체어 사용
SL3, SL4, SU5 – 서서 경기 가능
SS6 – 단신

Boccia
보치아

(source: theguardian.com)

Introduction: Boccia is a game played by throwing red and blue leather balls closely towards a white target ball. The team throwing their ball closest to the target ball scores.
소개: 보치아는 빨간 또는 파란 가죽 공을 하얀 목표 공에 가장 가까이 던지는 것이다. 목표 공에 가장 가까이 던지는 팀이 이긴다.

Events: Mixed gender – Individual, pairs, or teams of three
경기: 혼합팀 – 개인, 페어, 3인 팀

Classification: BC1 – use their hand or foot to throw the ball (Equipment: wheelchair, assistant)
BC2 – use hand to throw the ball (no assistant allowed)
BC3 – players with severe locomotor dysfunction that disables them from throwing the ball (Equipment: wheelchair, ramp, assistant)
BC4 – players with severe locomotor dysfunction and poor trunk control (no assistant allowed) (Equipment: wheelchair, no assistant allowed)
장애분류: BC1 – 손 또는 발을 사용하여 공을 던질 수 있다 (장비: 휠체어, 보조원)
BC2 – 손을 사용하여 공을 던질 수 있다 (보조원 사용 불가능)
BC3 – 심각한 운동 장애로 인해 공을 던질 수 없음 (장비: 휠체어, 경사, 보조원)
BC4 – 심각한 운동 장애 및 낮은 몸 기능 통제 (보조원 사용 불가능) (장비: 휠체어, 보조원 사용 불가능)

Canoe
카누

Introduction: Canoe is a race done in kayak boats that are propelled by racers rowing with paddles.
소개: 카누는 선수들이 패들로 카약을 저어서 경주하는 경기다.

(source: paralympic.org)

Events: Men and Women – single kayak (200m sprints)

경기: 남자 및 여자 – 1인승 카약 (200m 단거리)

Classification: KL1 – have limited trunk function and no leg function (Equipment: high backrest seat)

KL2 – have partial trunk and leg function, but is limited (Equipment: backrest)

KL3 – have trunk and partial leg function (Equipment: one prosthesis)

장애분류: KL1 – 제한된 몸 통제 및 다리 기능 (장비: 높은 등받이 자리)

KL2 – 몸통과 다리에 일부 기능이 가능하지만 제한됐다 (장비: 등받이)

KL3 – 몸통 및 일부 다리 기능 가능 (장비: 의족 하나)

Cycling
사이클링

(source: paralympic.org)

Introduction: Cycling is a race done on regular bicycles or other special cycles.

소개: 사이클링은 표준 사이클 또는 특수 사이클로 진행되는 경주다.

Events: Road events – road race, individual time trial, handcycling relay

Track events – tandem sprint, team sprint, 500m time trial, kilometer time trial, individual pursuit

경기: 로드 경기 – 로드 경주, 도로독주 및 핸드사이클링 계주

트랙 경기 – 2인 단거리, 팀 단거리, 500m 타임트라이얼, 1km 타임트라이얼, 개인 추발경주

Classification: blind and visually impaired (Equipment: tandem – two person cycle)

Cerebral palsy and locomotor disabilities (Equipment: standard cycle or tricycle – three wheels)

Handcycling – for those with lower limb impairments (Equipment: hand-operated cycles)

장애분류: 맹인 및 시각 장애 (장비: 2인 사이클)

뇌성마비 및 운동 장애 (장비: 표준 사이클 또는 세 발 사이클)

핸드사이클링 – 하지 장애 (장비: 손으로 작동되는 사이클)

Equestrian
승마

(source: telegraph.co.uk)

Introduction: Equestrian Dressage is the only type of discipline that is included in the paralympics. Dressage is a type of equestrian discipline in which riders prompt their horse to perform specific movements.

소개: 마장마술 경연은 승마 중에서 유일하게 장애인올림픽에 출전되는 종목이다. 마술은 말의 특정 움직임을 기술로 선보이는 종목이다.

Events: Dressage (Grade 1a to Grade 3: use 40 X 20 meter arena)

Grade 1a – Walk only

Grade 1b – Walk and trot

Grade 2 – Walk and trot but canter allowed in freestyle

	Grade 3 – Walk, trot and canter, freestyle (Grade 4: use 60×20 meter arena) Grade 4 – Walk, trot, canter, center half-pirouettes, 3 and 4 sequence changes and lateral work **경기:** 마장마술 (Grade 1a 에서 Grade 3: 40m×20m 경기장 사용) Grade 1a – 평보 Grade 1b – 평보 및 경속보 Grade 2 – 평보 및 경속보, 프리스타일에서는 구보가 가능 Grade 3 – 평보, 경속보, 및 구보, 프리스타일 (Grade 4: 60m×20m 경기장 사용) Grade 4 – 평보, 경속보, 구보, 센터 하프피루에트, 3과 4 연속 변화 및 사횡보 **Classification:** range from Grade 1a (severely impaired) to Grade IV (least impaired) **장애분류:** Grade 1a (심각한 장애)에서 Grade IV (경미한 장애)
Football 5-a-side 시각 축구  (source: londontown.com)	**Introduction:** Football that is modified for the visually impaired. There are five players who wear eye shades and use noise-making balls to score. Goalkeepers and guides may be sighted. **소개:** 시각장애인을 위해 개조된 축구. 눈가리개와 소리 나는 공을 사용하여 5명의 선수가 하는 경기다. 골키퍼와 가이드는 정상적인 시각을 가진 선수가 뛰어도 된다. **Classification:** B1 – complete blindness B2 – partial blindness B3 – partial vision **장애분류:** B1 – 완전한 실명 B2 – 부분적 실명 B3 – 부분적 시각
Football 7-a-side 뇌성 축구  (source: zimbio.com)	**Introduction:** Football that is modified for those with cerebral palsy and other neurological disorders. There are seven players on each team. **소개:** 뇌성마비와 신경장애를 가진 사람들을 위해 개조된 축구다. 각 팀에 7명의 선수가 경기를 한다. **Classification:** C5 – inability to walk or run C6 – lack of control and co-ordination in upper limbs C7 – hemiplegia C8 – sufficient impairment that affects playing football **장애분류:** C5 – 걷거나 뛰기가 불가능 C6 – 상지의 통제 및 조화가 불능 C7 – 반신불수 C8 – 축구를 할 수 없을 정도의 장애

Goalball **골볼**  (source: https://en.wikipedia.org)	**Introduction:** Goalball is a sport where three players on each team, all wearing eye shades, roll or throw a noise-making ball to the opposite team's goal. Players try to defend their goal by pushing the ball with their bodies away from the goal. **소개:** 골볼은 눈가리개를 착용한 선수 3명이 소리 나는 공을 상대편 골에 굴리거나 던지는 경기다. 선수들은 몸으로 공을 골에서부터 밀어내면서 방어한다. **Classification:** Visually impaired **장애분류:** 시각적 장애
Judo **유도**  (source: zimbio.com)	**Introduction:** Japanese martial art adapted for the visually impaired. Athletes compete according to weight categories. **소개:** 시각적 장애를 가진 선수들을 위해 개조된 일본 무술. 선수들은 체중 범주에 따라 경쟁한다. **Events:** Men – (60kg, 66kg, 73kg, 81kg, 90kg, 100kg, 100+kg) Women – (48kg, 52kg, 57kg, 63kg, 70kg, 70+kg) **경기:** 남자 – (60kg, 66kg, 73kg, 81kg, 90kg, 100kg, 100+kg) 여자 – (48kg, 52kg, 57kg, 63kg, 70kg, 70+kg) **Classification:** B1 – complete blindness B2 – partial blindness B3 – partial vision **장애분류:** B1 – 완전한 실명 B2 – 부분적 실명 B3 – 부분적 시각
IPC Powerlifting **역도**  (source: paralympics.org.uk)	**Introduction:** Powerlifting requires athletes to test their strength by lifting weight three times their body weight in the bench press. **소개:** 역도 선수는 자신의 몸무게 3배가 되는 바를 벤치 프레스하면서 시합을 진행한다. **Events:** Men – (49kg, 54kg, 59kg, 65kg, 72kg, 80kg, 88kg, 97kg, 107kg, +107kg) Women – (41kg, 45kg, 50kg, 55kg, 61kg, 67kg, 73kg, 79kg, 86kg, +86kg) **경기:** 남자 – (49kg, 54kg, 59kg, 65kg, 72kg, 80kg, 88kg, 97kg, 107kg, +107kg) 여자 – (41kg, 45kg, 50kg, 55kg, 61kg, 67kg, 73kg, 79kg, 86kg, +86kg) **Classification:** Physical impairments – impaired muscle power, impaired passive range of movement, limb deficiency, leg length difference,

short stature, hypertonia, ataxia, athetosis, cerebral palsy, spinal cord injuries, lower limb amputation, poliomyelitis

장애분류: 신체장애 – 근력 손상, 가동 범위 운동, 팔다리 결핍, 다리 길이 차이, 단신, 고긴장, 운동실조, 무정위운동형, 뇌성마비, 척수 손상, 하지 절단, 소아마비

Rowing
조정

(source: zimbio.com)

Introduction: Rowing is a boat race involving single, double, or four rowers to row the boat over a 1,000 meter distance. The rowers are adapted to the sport with special equipment to assist them in the race.

소개: 조정은 싱글(1인), 더블(2인), 또는 4인의 선수가 스컬(배)을 1,000m 거리에서 경기를 치른다. 특별한 보조 장치를 착용하여 선수들은 조정이라는 스포츠에 적응한다.

Events: LTA mixed coxed four (+1,000m)
LTA mixed double sculls (+1,000m)
TA mixed double sculls (+1,000m)
AS women's single sculls (+1,000m)
AS men's single sculls (+1,000m)

경기: 혼성 콕스 4인 (+1,000m)
혼성 더블스컬 (+1,000m)
여자 싱글스컬 (+1,000m)
남자 싱글스컬 (+1,000m)

Classification: LTA (Leg, trunk, and arm) – PD (Physical disability)
VI (Visual Impairment) and ID (Intellectual Disability)
TA (Trunk and Arms)
AS (Arms and Shoulders)

장애분류: LTA (다리, 몸통, 팔) – PD (신체장애)
VI (시각 장애) 및 ID (지적 장애)
TA (몸통 및 팔)
AS (팔 및 어깨)

Sailing
요트

(source: paralympic.org)

Introduction: Sailing is a sport in which athletes race boats using sails and the wind to propel the boat forward.

소개: 요트는 돛이 있는 배를 사용하는 스포츠이며 바람을 이용해서 배를 앞으로 추진시킨다.

Events: Open Single-Person Keelboat (Boat: 2.4mR)
Two-Person Keelboat (Boat: SKUD 18)
Open Three-Person Keelboat (Boat: Sonar)

경기: 1인 킬보트 (요트: 2.4mR)
2인 킬보트 (요트: 스커드 18)
3인 킬보트 (요트: 소나)

<table>
<tr><td></td><td>Classification: Amputation and limb loss
blindness and visual impairment
spinal cord injury and wheelchair-users
cerebral palsy, brain injury, and stroke
장애분류: 절단 및 팔다리 소실
맹인 및 시각 장애
척수 손상 및 휠체어 사용자
뇌성 마비, 뇌 손상 및 뇌졸중</td></tr>
<tr><td>IPC Shooting
사격

(source: zimbio.com)</td><td>Introduction: Shooting is a sport that uses rifles or pistols to shoot a target. This sport requires great accuracy to aim at the center of the target to obtain the highest score possible.
소개: 사격은 피스톨 또는 라이플총을 사용해서 과녁을 쏘는 스포츠다. 이 종목은 가장 높은 점수를 얻기 위해 과녁 중심을 겨누기 때문에 높은 정확성을 요구한다.

Events: Men, Women, and Mixed – 10m, 25m, 50m
경기: 남자, 여자 및 혼합 – 10m, 25m, 50m

Classification: SH1 – lower limb and or upper limb impairments, but are able to support weight of rifle or pistol (Equipment: stool, chair, or wheelchair)
SH2 – severe upper limb impairments that prevents athletes from supporting weight of rifle or pistol (Equipment: spring mounted stand, support assistant)
장애분류: SH1 – 하지 또는 상지 손상, 그러나 라이플과 피스톨의 무게를 지탱할 수 있다 (장비: 스툴, 의자, 또는 휠체어)
SH2 – 심각한 상지 손상으로 선수가 라이플 또는 피스톨의 무게를 지탱할 수 없다 (장비: 스프링으로 지지된 스탠드, 보조원)</td></tr>
<tr><td>Sitting Volleyball
좌식 배구

(source:https://en.wikipedia.org)</td><td>Introduction: Much like standard volleyball, sitting volleyball is a sport that requires six players on each team passing a ball over a net. Players must have some part of their torso touching the ground. The court is also smaller at 10m by 6m and the net lower at 1.15m for men and 1.05m for women.
소개: 표준 배구와 같이 좌식 배구는 6명으로 이뤄진 두 팀이 공을 패스해서 네트를 넘긴다. 선수는 몸통 일부를 반드시 코트 바닥에 닿게 해야 한다. 표준 코트보다 작은 사이즈인 10m에 6m이며 남자 경기 네트는 1.15m, 그리고 여자 경기 네트는 1.05m로 규정됐다.

Events: Men and Women
경기: 남자 및 여자

Classification: MD (Minimal Disability) – most physically able</td></tr>
</table>

	D (disabled) – least physically able **장애분류:** MD (최소의 장애) – 대부분 신체적 기능이 정상적이다. D (장애) – 신체적으로 기능이 가장 떨어진다.
IPC Swimming 수영  (source: zimbio.com)	**Introduction:** IPC Swimming is done in a standard eight-lane 50m pool, where swimmers compete in freestyle, backstroke, butterfly, breaststroke, and medley events. **소개:** 수영은 표준 50m의 8레인 수영장에서 자유형, 배영, 접영, 평영, 그리고 혼형 경기가 치러진다. **Events:** S – Freestyle, Butterfly and Backstroke SM – Individual Medley SB – Breaststroke **경기:** S – 자유형, 접영, 및 배영 SM – 개인 혼형 SB – 평영 **Classification:** S1 SB1 SM1 – significant loss of muscle power in legs, arms, and hands S2 SB1 SM2 – able to use their arms but not their hands, legs or trunk, also severe coordination problems in four limbs S3 SB2 SM3 – amputations of all four limbs S4 SB3 SM4 – ability in arms with minimal ability in hands, but can not use their trunk or legs S5 SB4 SM5 – short stature with one additional impairment and hemiplegia or paraplegia S6 SB5 SM6 – short stature, amputations of both arms or moderate co-ordination problems on one side of their body S7 SB6 SM7 – one leg and one arm amputation on opposite sides, double leg amputations or paralysis of one arm and one leg on the same side. S8 SB7 SM8 – loss of either both hands or one arm and severe restrictions in joints of lower limbs S9 SB8 SM9 – joint restrictions in one leg, double below-the-knee amputations or one leg amputation S10 SB9 SM10 – minimal physical impairments, loss of a hand or both feet, and significant limitations in one hip joint Sport Classes 11-13 – visual impairment Sport Class 14 – Intellectual impairment **장애분류:** S1 SB1 SM1 – 다리, 팔과 손에 심각한 근력 손상 S2 SB1 SM2 – 팔은 사용 가능하지만 손, 다리 또는 몸통의 사용은 불가능하며 사지에 심각한 조정력 문제가 있다.

S3 SB2 SM3 – 사지 절단

S4 SB3 SM4 – 팔의 사용은 가능하지만 손 사용은 제한되었고 몸통 또는 다리는 사용 불가능하다.

S5 SB4 SM5 – 장애 하나 및 반신불수 또는 양측 하지 마비를 포함한 단신

S6 SB5 SM6 – 단신, 양팔 절단, 그리고 신체 한쪽의 조정력 문제 존재

S7 SB6 SM7 – 반대쪽 다리와 팔 한쪽 절단, 양다리 절단 또는 같은 쪽의 팔과 다리 마비

S8 SB7 SM8 – 양손 또는 팔 손실 그리고 하지 관절에 심각한 제한

S9 SB8 SM9 – 다리 한쪽에 관절 제한, 양 무릎 아래로 절단 또는 다리 하나 절단

S10 SB9 SM10 – 최소의 신체적 장애, 손 또는 양쪽 발 손실 그리고 심각한 고관절의 제한

Sport Classes 11–13 – 시각 장애

Sport Class 14 – 지적 장애

Table Tennis
탁구

(source: https://www.paralympic.org)

Introduction: Para table tennis is table tennis following the International Table Tennis Federation rules for athletes with physical or intellectual impairments.

소개: 장애인 탁구는 신체적 또는 지적 장애인을 위한 국제탁구협회의 규칙을 따르는 종목이다.

Events: Men and women – individual, doubles, team events

경기: 남자 및 여자 – 개인, 더블, 팀 경기

Classification:

Sitting Classes from Class 1 to Class 5 (Equipment: use wheelchairs)

Class 1 – reduced function in arm and inability in sitting up

Class 2 – inability to sit up with little ability in the arm

Class 3 – limited ability to sit up with limited motor loss in the hand

Class 4 – limited ability in sitting up

Class 5 – normal trunk muscle power

Standing classes from Class 6 to Class 11

Class 6 – Severe impairment in leg and arms

Class 7 – Severe leg or arm impairment or impairment in both limbs

Class 8 – Moderate impairments in legs or arms moderate cerebral palsy, hemiplegia, diplegia with arm ability

Class 9 – mild impairment of leg, playing and nonplaying arm mild cerebral palsy, hemiparesis, monoplegia

Class 10 – mild impairment in legs, arms, and trunk

Class 11 – intellectual disability

장애분류 :

앉은 분류 Class 1에서 Class 5 (장비: 휠체어 사용)

Class 1 – 감소된 팔 기능 및 불능한 앉는 기능
Class 2 – 앉을 수 없으며 제한된 팔 사용
Class 3 – 앉을 수 없으며 제한된 손 기능
Class 4 – 앉을 수 없다
Class 5 – 정상적인 몸통 근력

서는 분류 Class 6에서 Class 11

Class 6 – 다리와 팔에 심각한 장애
Class 7 – 다리와 팔에 심각한 장애 또는 사지에 장애
Class 8 – 팔 또는 다리에 장애, 경미한 뇌성마비, 반신 불수, 양측 마비, 단마비
Class 10 – 다리, 팔, 그리고 몸통에 경미한 장애
Class 11 – 지적 장애

Taekwondo
태권도

(source: sportsfeatures.com)

Introduction: Taekwondo is a Korean martial arts discipline that mainly uses the legs, fist, and foot in sparing and form. The discipline is continually being modified for paralympic athletes.

소개: 태권도는 겨루기와 품세에 주로 다리, 주먹과 발을 사용하는 한국의 무술이다. 이 종목은 장애인올림픽 선수를 위해 지속적으로 개조되고 있다.

Events: Kyorugi (sparring)
Poomsae (martial arts form)

경기: 겨루기
품세

Impairment Groups: Neurological Impairment
ID(Intellectual Disabilities)
VI(Visually Impaired)

장애분류: 신경 장애
ID (지적 장애)
VI (시각 장애)

Triathlon
트라이애슬론 (철인 3종 경기)

(source: www.triathlon .org)

Introduction: Paratriathlon is a race where athletes participate in three athletic disciplines; swimming, cycling, and running.

소개: 장애인 트라이애슬론은 선수들이 수영, 사이클링, 그리고 러닝 종목에 참여하면서 경주하는 경기다.

Events: Swimming – sprint paratriathlon (750m)
Cycling – hand bike or tandem (20km)
Running – racing wheelchair (5km)

경기: 수영 – 단거리 장애인 트라이애슬론 (750m)
사이클링 – 손으로 작동하는 사이클 (20km)
러닝 – 휠체어 경주 (5km)

Classification: PT1 – wheelchair users with physical impairment but able to safely ride a bike and run

	PT2 through PT4 – from severe to mild limb deficiency, hypertonia, ataxia and or athetosis, impaired muscle power or range of movement (Equipment: prosthesis and other supportive devices) PT5 – total or partial visual impairment **장애분류:** PT1 – 안전하게 사이클을 하거나 달릴 수 있으나 휠체어를 사용하며 신체장애가 있다 PT2에서 PT4 – 심각한 정도에서 경미한 사지 장애, 고긴장, 운동 실조 또는 무정위운동, 근력 장애 또는 제한된 움직임 (장비: 보철 및 기타 보조 장치) PT5 – 전체 또는 일부 시각 장애
Wheelchair Basketball **장애인 농구**  (source: zimbio.com)	**Introduction:** Wheelchair basketball is a modified form of basketball using the same court size and basket heights. However, due to impairment, all players use wheelchairs. **소개:** 휠체어 농구는 표준 농구에서 개조됐지만 같은 코트 크기 및 농구대 높이는 동일하다. 단, 장애 때문에 모든 선수는 휠체어를 사용한다. **Events:** Men's and Women's Team **경기:** 남자 및 여자 팀 **Classification:** physical impairment with difficulty in running, jumping, and pivoting **장애분류:** 달리기, 점프 및 피벗을 제한하는 신체적 장애
IPC Wheelchair Dance Sport **장애인 댄스스포츠**  (source: paralympic.org)	**Introduction:** Wheelchair dance sport is a partner or group formation dance that performs the waltz, tango, cha-cha, samba, freestyle, and other forms of dance. **소개:** 장애인 댄스스포츠는 파트너 또는 그룹으로 왈츠, 탱고, 차차, 삼바, 프리스타일, 그리고 기타 무용 형태를 선보이는 종목이다. **Events:** Combi – partner dancing with an able-bodied partner Duo – two wheelchair users in a partner dance Formation – group formation dance of four, six or eight couples **경기:** 콤비 – 비장애인 파트너와 춤추는 파트너 춤 듀오 – 휠체어 사용자 2명이 하는 파트너 춤 그룹 – 4, 6, 8인 커플이 그룹으로 하는 춤 **Classification:** Physical impairment of the lower limbs **장애분류:** 하지에 신체장애
Wheelchair Fencing **장애인 펜싱**	**Introduction:** Wheelchair fencing is fencing modified on wheelchairs that are locked to the floor. **소개:** 장애인 펜싱은 바닥에 고정한 휠체어를 위해 표준 펜싱을 개조한 스포츠다. **Events:** Foil epee – men and women

(source: paralympic.org)

Saber – men

경기: 플러레, 에뻬 – 남자 및 여자

사브르 – 남자

Classification: Amputations, spinal–cord injuries, cerebral palsy

Class A – full trunk movement and good balance

Class B – no leg movement and impaired trunk with balance functions

Class C – disability in all four limbs

장애분류: 절단, 척수 손상, 뇌성마비

Class A – 몸통 움직임이 가능하며 좋은 균형

Class B – 다리 움직임이 없고 몸통의 조정기능 장애

Class C – 사지에 장애

Wheelchair Rugby
장애인 럭비

(source: paralympic.org)

Introduction: Wheelchair rugby is a sport mainly played by quadriplegic athletes. To accompany wheelchairs the game is played indoors on a basketball court. A mixed gender team of four play on each team.

소개: 장애인 럭비는 주로 사지마비 선수들로 이뤄졌다. 휠체어를 고려하여 이 종목은 실내 농구코트에서 경기를 진행한다. 한 팀은 남녀 혼합이며 각 팀은 4명의 선수로 이뤄졌다.

Events: Male and female mixed team event

경기: 남자 및 여자 혼합 경기

Classification: Quadriplegic, cerebral palsy, muscular dystrophy, amputations, polio and neurological conditions

장애분류: 사지마비, 뇌성마비, 근위축증, 절단, 소아마비, 그리고 신경 질환

Wheelchair Tennis
장애인 테니스

(source: paralympic.org)

Introduction: Tennis for those with impairment in the legs. The game is played according to the same rules as able–bodied tennis, with the exception that the ball can bounce twice.

소개: 다리 장애를 가진 선수를 위한 테니스다. 이 종목은 표준 테니스와 같은 규칙을 따르지만 공을 두 번 튕길 수 있다.

Events: Mens – singles, doubles

Ladies – singles, doubles

Quads – singles, doubles

경기: 남자 – 싱글, 더블

여자 – 싱글, 더블

쿼드 – 싱글, 더블

Classification: Physical impairment (loss of function in one or both legs)

장애분류: 신체장애 (한쪽 또는 양쪽 다리에 기능 손실)

Winter Sports	Description
IPC Alpine Skiing **알파인 스키**  (source: wikipedia)	**Introduction:** Alpine skiing is a sport that involves racing down a slope to determine the skier with the fastest record. There are seven types of events: the downhill, slalom, giant slalom, super-G, super combined, team events, and snowboard. Athletes compete according to their impairment group and may use special equipment to assist them. **소개:** 알파인 스키는 스키 슬로프에서 경주하여 가장 빠른 기록을 결정하는 종목이다. 이 종목은 7개의 경기가 있다. 활강 스키, 슬랄롬, 자이언트 슬랄롬, 슈퍼 대회전, 슈퍼 복합, 팀 경기와 스노보드. 선수는 장애분류에 따라 경기하며 특별한 보조 장비를 사용한다. **Events:** Downhill – Skiing down a slope while passing through gates Slalom – Distinguished from other events with its shorter slope and greater amount of gates. Skiers must run twice to determine scores. Giant slalom – Longer slope with fewer gates than the slalom. Skiers cannot miss a gate, or else may be disqualified. Skiers must run twice to determine scores. Super-G – Shorter than the downhill slope, skiers must race down a slope. Super combined – A discipline combining a downhill or super-G with the slalom. The athlete is required to make two runs down the slope to determine their time. Snowboard – Riders snowboard on a man-made course while doing a number of stunts. **경기:** 활강 스키 – 게이트를 통과하며 슬로프를 활강한다. 슬랄롬 – 짧은 슬로프와 많은 수의 게이트가 이 종목을 구별시킨다. 성적은 선수가 두 번 달린 후 결정된다. 자이언트 슬랄롬 – 슬랄롬보다 긴 슬로프이며 게이트가 적다. 스키 선수는 게이트를 통과 못 하면 실격된다. 성적은 선수가 두 번 달린 후 결정된다. 슈퍼 대회전 – 활강보다 짧은 슬로프를 활강한다. 슈퍼 복합 – 알파인 스키 경기 하나와 활강 스키 또는 슈퍼 대회전을 슬랄롬과 함께 행하는 종목이다. 선수는 두 번 활강하여 최종 시간이 결정된다. 스노보드 – 선수는 인공 코스에서 다양한 스턴트를 연기한다. **Classification:** Alpine Skiers Standing Skiers – Leg Impairments LW 1 – severe impairment in both legs LW 2 – severe impairment in one leg LW 3 – moderate impairment in both legs

LW 4 – moderate impairment in one leg

Arm Impairments

LW 5/7 – impairment in both arms

LW 6/8 – impairment in one arm

Combined arm and leg impairments

LW 9 – impairments in both arms and legs

Sitting Skiers

LW 10 – minimal trunk stability

LW 11 – limited control in lower trunk and hips

LW 12 – normal or slight inability in trunk and leg

Visual Impairment

B1 to B3, where B1 is the most severe visual impairment and B3 the least visual inability

Snowboard

SB-LL1 – severe impairment in one leg

SB-LL2 – moderate impairment in one or both legs

SB-UL – upper limb impairment

장애분류: 알파인 스키 선수

스탠딩 스키 선수 – 다리 장애

LW 1 – 양다리에 심각한 장애

LW 2 – 한 다리에 심각한 장애

LW 3 – 양다리에 장애

LW 4 – 한 다리에 장애

팔 장애

LW 5/7 – 양팔에 장애

LW 6/8 – 한 팔에 장애

팔과 다리 장애

LW 9 – 팔과 다리 모두에 장애

싯 스키 선수

LW 10 – 최소한의 몸통 안정감

LW 11 – 몸통 아래와 힙에 제한된 통제

LW 12 – 몸통과 다리에 경미한 장애

시각 장애

B1에서 B3가 있으며 B1은 가장 심각한 시각 장애이며 B3는 가장 경미한 시각 장애다.

스노보드

SB-LL1 – 한 다리에 심각한 장애

SB-LL2 – 한 다리 또는 양다리에 장애

SB-UL – 상지 장애

IPC Biathlon
바이애슬론

(source: wikipedia)

Introduction: Biathlon consists of shooting a rifle at two designated points while skiing to the finish line. A missed shot is deducted from the athlete's overall time.

소개: 바이애슬론은 선수가 스키를 타며 지정된 2개의 지점에서 라이플로 사격을 하여 결승전까지 가는 경기다. 실격한 타격은 선수의 전체시간에서 점수가 공제된다.

Events: Sitting, Standing, and Visually Impaired

Men's – 7.5km, 12.5km, 15km

Women's – 6km, 10km, 12.5km

경기: 싯, 스탠드, 시각 장애

남자 – 7.5km, 12.5km, 15km

여자 – 6km, 10km, 12.5km

Classification: Standing Skiers

Leg Impairments

LW2 – impairment in one leg (Equipment : prosthesis, two skis)

LW3 – impairment in both legs

LW4 – impairment in one lower leg

Arm Impairments

LW5/7 – impairment in both arms, thus skiing without poles

LW 6 – severe impairment in one arm

LW 8 – moderate impairment in one arm, thus using one pole

Arm and Leg Impairment

LW9 – impairment in both arms and legs

Sit Skiers

LW 10 – impairment affecting leg and trunk control

LW 10.5 – lack trunk control, but have sitting balance

LW 11 – impairment in leg and have some trunk control with ability to keep balance when moving sideways

LW 11.5 – some trunk control

LW 12 – impairment in leg with normal trunk control. Able to participate in either standing or sitting events.

Visual Impairment

B1 – severe visual impairment

(Equipment : eyeshades, ski guide)

B2 – better acuity than B1, but still have severe

B3 – moderate visual impairment

장애분류: 좌식 및 스탠드 스키 선수

다리 장애

LW2 – 다리 한쪽 장애

(장비: 보철, 스키 두 쪽)

LW 3 – 양쪽 다리에 장애

LW 4 – 한쪽 다리에 장애

팔 장애

LW 5/7 – 양팔에 장애가 있어 폴을 사용 안 한다

LW 6 – 한쪽 팔에 심각한 장애

LW 8 – 한쪽 팔에 장애가 있어 폴 하나를 사용한다

팔과 다리 장애

LW 9 – 양팔과 다리 장애

싯(좌식) 스키 선수

LW 10 – 다리 및 몸통 통제 장애

LW 10.5 – 몸통 통제가 불가능하지만 앉는 균형이 있다

LW 11 – 다리 장애 및 몸통 통제가 있으며 옆으로 이동할 때 균형 유지 가능

LW 11.5 – 일부 몸통 통제력 존재

LW 12 – 다리 장애가 있지만 몸통 통제력은 정상적이다. 스탠드 또는 싯 경기 중 하나에 참석 가능하다.

시각 장애

B1 – 심각한 시각 장애

(장비: 눈가리개, 스키 가이드)

B2 – B1에 비해 시각이 좋지만 심각한 시각 장애

B3 – 시각 장애

IPC Cross-country Skiing

크로스컨트리 스키

(Source: wikipedia)

Introduction: Skiers of cross-country skiing ski along snow tracks to race to the finish line.

소개: 크로스컨트리 스키는 설원을 가로지르며 결승점까지 경주하는 종목이다.

Events:

Standing Skiers

Men's – 1,200m, 10km, 20km,

Women's – 1,200m, 5km, 15km

Sitting Skiers

Men's – 800m, 10km, 15km

Women's – 800m, 5km, 12km

경기:

스탠드 스키

남자 – 1,200m, 10km, 20km,

여자 – 1,200m, 5km, 15km

싯(좌식) 스키

남자 – 800m, 10km, 15km

여자 – 800m, 5km, 12km

Classification: Sitting and Standing Skiers

Leg Impairments

LW2 – impairment in one leg

(Equipment : prosthesis, two skis)

LW3 – impairment in both legs

LW4 – impairment in one lower leg

Arm Impairments

LW5/7 – impairment in both arms, thus skiing without poles

LW 6 – severe impairment in one arm

LW 8 – moderate impairment in one arm, thus using one pole

Arm and Leg Impairment

LW9 – impairment in both arms and legs

Sitting Skiers

LW 10 – impairment affecting leg and trunk control

LW 10.5 – lack trunk control, but have sitting balance

LW 11 – impairment in leg and have some trunk control with ability to keep balance when moving sideways

LW 11.5 – some trunk control

LW 12 – impairment in leg with normal trunk control.

able to participate in either standing or sitting events.

Visual Impairment

B1 – severe visual impairment

(Equipment : eyeshades, ski guide)

B2 – better acuity than B1, but still have severe

B3 – moderate visual impairment

장애분류: 좌식 및 스탠드 스키 선수

다리 장애

LW2 – 다리 한 쪽장애

(장비: 보철, 스키 두 쪽)

LW3 – 양쪽 다리에 장애

LW4 – 한쪽 다리에 장애

팔 장애

LW5/7 – 양팔에 장애가 있어 폴을 사용 안 한다

LW 6 – 한쪽 팔에 심각한 장애

LW 8 – 한쪽 팔에 장애가 있어 폴 하나를 사용한다

팔과 다리 장애

LW9 – 양팔과 다리 장애

싯(좌식) 스키 선수

LW 10 – 다리 및 몸통 통제 장애

LW 10.5 – 몸통 통제가 불가능하지만 앉는 균형이 있다

LW 11 – 다리 장애 및 몸통 통제가 있으며 옆으로 이동할 때

	균형 유지 가능 LW 11.5 – 일부 몸통 통제력 존재 LW 12 – 다리 장애가 있지만 몸통 통제력은 정상적이다 스탠드 또는 싯 경기 중 하나에 참석 가능하다. **시각 장애** B1 – 심각한 시각 장애 (장비: 눈가리개, 스키 가이드) B2 – B1에 비해 시각이 좋지만 심각한 시각 장애 B3 – 시각 장애
IPC Ice Sledge Hockey **아이스슬레지하키**  (source: https://en.wikipedia.org)	**Introduction:** Ice Sledge Hockey has been adapted from Ice Hockey for those with a disability in the lower part of their body. Six players on each team compete on sledges to strike the puck into the goal. **소개:** 아이스슬레지하키는 하지에 장애가 있는 선수를 위해 표준 아이스하키에서 개조됐다. 슬레지를 탄 선수 6명이 퍽을 골대에 넣기 위해 경기를 펼친다. **Classification:** Impairment to the legs **장애분류:** 다리 장애
Wheelchair Curling **장애인 컬링**  (source: https://en.wikipedia.org)	**Introduction:** Wheelchair curling is curling that has been adapted to those with a leg impairment. **소개:** 장애인 컬링은 다리 장애를 가진 선수를 위해 표준 컬링을 개조한 종목이다. **Classification:** Impairment to the legs **장애분류:** 다리 장애

Dialogue - Paralympic Sports

Jeff : I've heard of most of these sports, but they seem to be played differently. Why did I assume the rules would be the same?

여기 있는 종목 대부분은 한 번쯤 들어봤지만 다르게 느껴져. 왜 규칙이 비슷하다고 생각했을까?

Teresa : Actually, the basic rules are the same. But the games have been tweaked a bit. Like tennis, the ball is allowed to be bounced twice before passing it to the other court.

사실, 기본 규칙은 비슷해. 그러나 종목이 조금은 수정됐어. 예를 들어 테니스에서는 공을 반대편 코트에 넘기기 전에 두 번 튕길 수 있어.

Jeff : Tweaked? More like transformed!

조금 수정? 완전히 변형된 것과 같은데!

Teresa : It just feels that way because of all the special equipment.

특별한 장비가 많아서 그렇게 느껴지는 거야.

Jeff : That must be it. It's not only the prosthetics and wheelchairs. There are eyeshades, stools, and bells.

그래, 바로 그거야. 의족하고 휠체어뿐이 아니야. 눈가리개, 스툴과 종도 있어.

Teresa : If you look closer, the games are played in different positions too. The most obvious change is the sitting equipment that are used in the games, as in ice sledge hockey, or sit-skis used in IPC alpine, biathlon, and cross-country.

더 자세히 보면, 종목은 다른 자세로도 경기가 진행돼. 가장 두드러진 변화는 아이스슬레지하키 또는 좌식 스키와 같이 경기에서 사용되는 앉는 장비야.

Jeff : Teresa, it's the actual sitting players as in goalball or volleyball that's quite amazing.

테레사, 골볼과 좌식 배구에서 실제로 앉아서 경기하는 선수들이 진짜 대단하다고 생각해.

Teresa : For me it's the eyeshades the visually impaired players use and the guides that help them that I like. Anyhow, all those little changes make up the transformation you are talking about.

나는 시각장애인 선수들이 사용하는 눈가리개와 돕는 사람이 가장 좋아. 아무튼, 이 모든 수정사항이 네가 말하는 완전한 변화를 이뤄지게 하는 거야.

Jeff : I hope more and more sports continue to adapt the games for the disabled.

계속해서 더 많은 스포츠 종목이 장애인을 위해 경기를 개조하면 좋겠다.

Teresa : Yes, for all types of impairments.

맞아, 모든 장애의 유형을 위해 그랬으면 좋겠어.

Practice

Main Expressions

▸ I've heard of (something / someone): (무엇 또는 누구에 대해) 들어본 적이 있다.

ex: **I've heard of** wheelchair curling before.

이전에 장애인 컬링**에 대해 들어본 적 있어.**

ex: **I've heard of** the athlete through a friend of mine.

친구를 통해 그 선수**에 대해 들어본 적 있어.**

▸ tweak: 약간 수정하다 / adjust, tune

(아주 작은 수정에 대해 말할 때 사용하는 표현)

ex: The repairman **tweaked** the phone, so it works like new.

수리사가 전화기에 작은 수정을 해서 이제 새것 같이 작동된다.

Language Focus

▸ like: 유사한, 처럼(같이), 좋아하다

(like는 여러 가지 의미가 있다.)

ex: The event is **like** soccer, but much more thrilling.

경기는 축구와 **유사**하지만 훨씬 더 흥미롭다.

(A가 B와 비슷하다고 표현할 때 사용)

ex: Some skiers **like** to ski without prosthetics.

일부 스키 선수는 의족을 사용하지 않고 스키 타는 것을 **좋아한다.**

(무엇을 좋아한다고 표현할 때 사용)

ex: Wheelchair basketball is played with standard hoop heights, **like** in standard basketball.

휠체어 농구는 표준 농구처럼 표준 높이의 농구대를 사용한다.

(as와 동의어로 '무엇처럼'을 표현할 때 사용)

A. Appropriately use the expressions "have heard of" and "tweak" to describe the photos below.

1. 

2. 

3. 

4. 

B. Use ***like*** in different ways. Make three types of sentences using the various meanings of like.

1 좋아하다: ______________________________

2 유사하다: ______________________________

3 무엇처럼, 무엇과 같이: ______________________

05 The Paralympians
장애인올림픽 선수

New Language

- challenger: (n.) 도전자 / contender, contestant, player
- compete: (v.) 경쟁하다 / battle, challenge
- effort: (n.) 노력 / feat, endeavor
- endeavor: (n.) 시도, 애씀 / effort, struggle, undertaking
- field: (n.) 종목, 분야 / area, division
- incorporation: (n.) 포함하는 행위 / addition, joining, connection
- inspiration: (n.) 영감 / encouragement, motivation, stimulation
- paralympian: (n.) 국제장애인올림픽에 참가한 선수 / athlete
- rigorously: (adv.) 엄격하게, 혹독하게 / fiercely, vigorously, powerfully
- serviceman: (n.) 군인 / soldier
- sportsman: (n.) 운동선수 / athlete
- train: (v.) 훈련하다 / practice, discipline
- triumph: (n.) 업적, 승리 / accomplishment, achievement

Paralympians are athletes who compete in the Paralympic Games. Paralympians possess a particular physical disability that qualifies them for the Games. Like able-bodies athletes, these are competitive athletes who train rigorously to become the best sportsman in their field.

The effort **put forth** by paralympians tells us that there is not one challenger who is lacking. Rather, their participation, their impairments, and their endeavor have become an inspiration to everyone. Paralympians are no longer just **ex-servicemen** in rehabilitation sessions; they are symbols of triumph, strength, courage, and incorporation.

- put forth: 보이다, 제시하다 / present, propose, exert, exercise
- ex-servicemen: 퇴역 군인

note) ex: 이전의 (예를 들어: ex-girlfriend - 전 여자 친구 / ex-convict - 전과자)

ex를 홀로 사용할 경우 전에 사귀었던 사람 또는 결혼했던 사람을 의미

ex) His ex left him because of his drinking habit.

그의 전 여자 친구는 그의 음주습관 때문에 그를 떠났다.

Some Famous Paralympians

(photo: parasport-news.com)

Seung Hwan Jung

- **Event:** Sledge Ice Hockey
- **Impairment:** Loss of left leg due to an accident in 1990
- **Record in the Paralympics:** Participated in the 2010 Paralympic Winter Games and is preparing to enter the 2018 Paralympic Games, which is scheduled to be held in his home country, South Korea.
- **Interesting Story:** He lost his leg at the age of five. And although he is small, he is known for his speed.

(photo: zimbio.com)

Lee Pearson

- **Event:** Dressage (Equestrian)
- **Impairment:** Arthrogryposis multiplex congenita (limited movement)
- **Record in the Paralympics:** 3 gold medals in 2000, 3 gold medals in 2004, 3 gold medals in Beijing, 1 gold, 1 silver, and 1 bronze in London
- **Interesting Story:** Pearson is allergic to horses and was skeptical about disability sports, but went on to become a successful athlete.

(photo: eticaesport.it)

Paola Fantato

- **Event:** Archery
- **Impairment:** Poliomyelitis
- **Record in the Paralympics:** Total of five gold, one silver, and two bronze medals in a total of 5 Paralympic games from 1988 to 2004.
- **Interesting Story:** Paola Fantato has competed not only in the Paralympics, but also in the 1996 Summer Olympics.

(photo: espanol.upi.com)

Augusto Perez

- **Event:** Wheelchair Curling
- **Impairment:** Hip disarticulation of left leg due to cancer
- **Record in the Paralympics:** Participated in the 2006 and 2010 Winter Paraplympics in the field of Wheelchair curling.
- **Interesting Story:** Suffering from cancer and undergoing many treatments, Perez has competed in curling, canoe, and biathlon.

(photo: nydailynews.com)

Caitlin Sarubbi

- **Event:** Apline Skiing
- **Impairment:** Albepharon Macrostomia (cause visual impairment)
- **Record in the Paralympics:** Participating in the 2010 Vancouver Games, Sarubbi placed 6th and 8th in different events.
- **Interesting Story;** Her sister supports her as her guide. Sarubbi is also a pre-med student at Harvard University.

Dialogue - Getting to know the athlete

Ashley : I read an article yesterday about a Paralympian who is now in prison. I can't remember his name, but I thought you might know. Do you know who he is?

어제 수감된 장애인올림픽선수에 대한 기사를 읽었어. 이름이 기억이 안 나는데, 네가 알 수 있을 것 같아서 그래. 혹시 그 사람에 대해 알고 있니?

Toby : Of course, he is a really famous sprinter. His name is Oscar Pistorius. He is so fast that he's also known as "Blade Runner."

당연하지, 엄청 유명한 단거리 선수야. 이름은 오스카 피스토리어스야. 얼마나 빠른지 "블레이드 러너"라고도 불려왔어.

Ashley : How do you think he decided to become a sprinter? It's amazing if you think about it. He has lost both of his legs.

그런데 어떻게 단거리 선수가 되기로 결정했을까? 생각해보면 정말 대단한 것 같아. 양쪽 다리 모두 절단됐으니까.

Toby : I know, who would've thought about running without legs, right? Well, obviously if you're Oscar Pistorius you do more than just running without legs.

그렇지? 절단된 다리로 누가 달리기를 할 생각을 했겠어? 그런데, 오스카 피스토리어스라면 다리 없이도 달리기 말고도 할 수 있는 것이 많은 것 같아.

Ashley : What do you mean?

그게 무슨 말이야?

Toby : He was born without the fibula in both his legs, so he had to get them amputated below the knees when he was only 11 months old. But despite the loss of his limbs, he grew up to be active in competitive sports like wrestling, water polo, and rugby.

피스토리어스는 양다리에 종아리뼈가 없이 태어났어. 그래서 11개월밖에 안 된 나이에 무릎 밑으로 양쪽 다리를 절단해야 했어. 그런데 다리를 절단했음에도 불구하고 레슬링, 수구, 럭비와 같은 스포츠를 하면서 자랐어.

Ashley : Oh, I get it. He was naturally athletic.

오, 알겠다. 타고난 운동 실력이 있었구나.

Toby : Right, but then he got a knee injury that forced him out of these sports. What was next? Running.

맞아, 그런데 무릎 부상 때문에 이런 운동을 그만두게 됐지. 이후에는 달리기를 시작했어.

Ashley : Running all the way to the Paralympic games, I guess. What country does he represent?

달리다 보니 장애인올림픽까지 출전하게 된 거네. 어느 나라의 대표 선수야?

Toby : He's a South African athlete. I think he was born and raised there.

남아프리카 선수야. 거기서 태어나고 자란 것으로 알고 있어.

Ashley : He must have been very good to be so famous.

이렇게 유명할 정도면 엄청 잘했겠네.

Toby : Yes, very good. He has several gold medals in the 100m, 200m, 400m, and relay at the Paralympics. And he challenged able-bodied athletes by qualifying and participating at the 2012 London Olympics. He wasn't able to get a medal, but he became the first person with double amputations to compete in the Summer Olympics.

그럼, 무척 잘했지. 장애인올림픽 100m, 200m, 400m, 그리고 계주 종목에서 금메달 여러 개를 얻었어. 피스토리어스는 2012년 런던 올림픽에 참가할 자격을 얻고 참가하면서 일반 달리기 선수들에게 도전했어. 메달은 못 얻었지만 하계올림픽에 최초로 참가한 양지 절단 선수가 됐어.

Ashley : That's some feat. But, how did he fall from grace?

대단한 업적이다. 그런데 어떻게 그 자리에서 몰락하게 됐어?

Toby : He was convicted of shooting and killing his girlfriend.

여자 친구 총살 사건으로 유죄판결이 났어.

Ashley : Yes, I read that he was in prison and finally coping with his situation. But when did this happen? I was so unaware.

그래, 감옥에서 드디어 자신의 상태에 적응하기 시작했다고 읽었어. 그런데 언제 이런 사태가 일어났어? 나는 그것도 모르고 있었네.

Toby : It happened on Valentine's day of 2013. He was sentenced for 5 years in jail.

2013년 발렌타인 날에 일어났어. 5년을 선고받았어.

Ashley : It's all very unfortunate.

참 안타까운 일이야.

Practice

Main Expressions

- born and raised (in + place): (장소 +에서) 태어나고 자라다 / grow up
  (한 장소에서 계속 자랐다는 의미/장소가 다를 경우 born (in +place) but raised (in +place)로 표현 가능)
  ex: I was **born and raised in Seoul.**
  서울에서 태어나고 자랐다.
  ex: I was **born in Seoul, but grew up in Los Angeles.**
  서울에서 태어났지만 로스앤젤레스에서 자랐다.
- feat: (n) 위업, 개가 / accomplishment, deed, achievement, performance
  ex: Winning a gold medal in a Paralympic event is a great feat.
  장애인올림픽 경기에서 금메달을 획득하는 것은 엄청난 위업이다.
- fall from grace: 몰락, 신임을 잃다, 실추 / disgraced
  ex: The gold medalist fell from grace after being convicted of using drugs.
  마약 복용 유죄판결을 받은 후 금메달리스트는 신임을 잃었다.

Language Focus

- question starters: who(누구), what(무엇), when(언제), where(어디), why(왜), how(어떻게)
  (일반적으로 질문할 때 동사 이전에 위의 단어들로 시작할 수 있다.)
  ex: (사람에 대해 질문할 때): Who is this person?
  ex: (물건에 대해 질문할 때): What did he get for Christmas?
  ex: (시간에 대해 질문할 때): When will you go on vacation?
  ex: (장소에 대해 질문할 때): Where can I buy that?
  ex: (이유에 대해 질문할 때): Why are you still here?
  ex: (방법에 대해 질문할 때): How do you untie this?
- Do you know ~: ~ 알고 있니
  (사람, 장소, 물건, 시간, 이유, 방법 등과 관련된 지식 또는 정보에 대해 질문할 때 사용)
  Do you know the way out of here?
  이곳에서 나가는 길을 **알고 있니?**
- What do you mean?: 무슨 뜻이야? / 무슨 말이야? / 무슨 의미야?
  (말의 의미를 다시 확인하거나 내용을 더욱 명확하게 하기 원할 때 사용하는 질문)
  ex: **What do you mean** by disqualification?
  자격 박탈이라니, 그게 **무슨 의미야?**

A. Read the following paragraph about Kelly Marie Gallagher.

Kelly Marie Gallagher is Great Britain's first Paralympic apline skier that won a gold medal in the Paralympics. She was born in Northern Ireland on May 18, 1985. Gallagher was born with oculocutaneous albinism, which is a type of albinism that affects the eyes, skin, and hair. As for the effect in the eyes, it decreases acuity in vision and raises sensitivity to light. She was also not particularly athletic in her younger years, standing out awkwardly in a regular school environment. However, she showed excellence in skiing during her first ski lesson at the age of 17. She continued on to participate in her first Paralympics in the 2010 Vancouver Paralympics where she came in 6th. Kelly Gallagher trained for the next Paralympics that led to a series of bruises, injuries, and concussions. These injuries forced her to stay home, during which her father passed to cancer. To support her through these tough times was her sighted guide, Charlotte Evans, who trained with her, guiding Gallagher with an audio commentary through a Bluetooth earpiece. Despite the rough times, she received her first gold in the Women's Super-G for the visually impaired in the 2014 Sochi Paralympics. Kelly Gallagher is currently supporting the movement for spreading education for all disabled children. Recently, she went to a school for blind students in Senegal to share her life experience as a blind child growing up in a regular school setting and encouraged those similar to herself.

B. Imagine you are unfamiliar with the Paralympian in the above reading. Make some questions about the athlete, beginning with the question starters.

06 Upcoming Pyeongchang Paralympic Games
평창 장애인올림픽을 앞두고

New Language

- emblem: (n.) 상징 / symbol, logo, marker
- embody: (v.) 상징하다 / represent, manifest, exhibit
- identical: (adj.) 동일한, 똑같은 / same, similar
- initiate: (v.) 개시되게 하다 / trigger, activate
- location: (n.) 장소, 위치 / area, region, venue
- possibility: (n.) 가능성 / opportunity
- project: (n.) 계획, 프로젝트 / program
- promote: (v.) 장려하다, 촉진하다 / encourage, support
- slogan: (n.) 표어, 구호 / phrase, saying
- symbolize: (v.) 상징하다 / embody, represent
- upcoming: (adj.) 다가오는 / approaching, nearing, impending
- venue: (n.) 장소 / place, site, ground

The upcoming 2018 Winter Paralympics will be held in Pyeongchang, South Korea from March 9th to March 18th. The **ten-day-long** competition consists of eighty events in six sports categories that include alpine skiing, biathlon, cross country skiing, ice sledge hockey, snowboard, and wheelchair curling.

- ten-day-long: 10일 동안을 의미하며 '며칠 동안'을 표현하기 위해 숫자와 day long을 함께 사용한다.
  note) 이와 유사한 표현은 all day long이 있으며 아침부터 밤까지, 하루 종일을 의미한다.

The **venues** for the 2018 Games will be held in the three locations of Jeongseon, Pyeongchang, and Gangneung. All ski events will be held in Jeongseon and

Pyeongchang, and Gangneung will host ice sledge hockey and wheelchair curling.

- venue: (n.) location, place / 장소
  note) 일반적인 장소와는 달리 특성 행사가 진행되는 장소를 지칭할 때 사용하는 용어다.
  ex) The venue for opening ceremony is the grand stadium.
  개막식의 장소는 대형 경기장이다.

Pyeongchang Paralympics has presented "Passion and Connected" as its slogan. This slogan embodies the spirit of the Paralympics in bringing people together and connected. The aim is to connect people **regardless of** age and nationality, bring new possibilities to all athletes, and to spread peace throughout the world.

- opening ceremony: 개막식
  closing ceremony: 폐막식
  note) ceremony는 엄숙하고 예의를 갖춘 국가적, 공식적, 종교적 의식을 치를 때 사용하는 용어다.
- hold every four years: 4년마다 개최하다
  note) 기간과 관련된 표현
  ex) quarterly: 분기별
  biannually: 1년에 2번
  annually: 1년마다

The emblem describes a world where peolpe with and without impairment, athletes, spectators, and people of the world get together

PyeongChang 2018
PARALYMPIC GAMES

The emblem of the Paralympics symbolizes snow, ice, and the paralympians. The identical symbols are set beside one another to represent equality. Lastly, the five colors **stand for** the uniqueness of every individual.

- stand for: ~을 나타내다, 의미하다 / represent, symbolize

  ex) The bear is a mascot that stands for this team.

  마스코트인 곰은 이 팀을 나타낸다.

In preparation for 2018, the city of Pyeongchang has initiated a project called Dream Programme. The project's goal is to promote and **raise awareness for** the Paralympics by presenting winter sports to youth. Another aim of the project is to encourage **social inclusion**. This means being aware of all types of people and realizing that everyone is connected.

- raise awareness for: ~에 대한 인식을 고취시키다

  note) 일반적으로 어떠한 사건, 혹은 정치적, 사회적 운동에 대한 인식을 높인다고 말할 때 사용한다.

  ex) The feminists held a street demonstration to raise awareness for abortion rights.

  여성운동가들은 낙태권에 대한 인식을 높이기 위해 집회시위를 열었다.

- social inclusion: 사회적 통합

  note) 모든 인간이 사회적 활동에 참여할 권리를 말한다.

  ex) The Paralympics is a social inclusion for all athletes despite their impairment.

  장애인올림픽은 장애와 상관없이 모든 선수들을 사회적으로 통합시키는 경기다.

Dialogue - What's in 2018?

Grace : 2018 is only a couple of years away. I'm so excited about the Paralympics.

2018년은 이제 몇 년밖에 안 남았어. 장애인올림픽에 대해 너무 신이 난다.

Asher : So am I. We're so lucky that it's going to be held in Gangneung.

나도 그래. 강릉에서 치르게 되다니 참 행운이야.

Grace : But only ice sledge hockey and wheelchair curling are going to be held here.

그런데 아이스슬레지하키하고 휠체어 컬링만 진행되잖아.

Asher : At least there are some events taking place here. And don't forget that the location for other places are also close by in Pyeongchang and

Jeongseon.

그래도 일부 경기라도 여기서 열리잖아. 그리고 다른 장소도 평창과 정선에 위치한 장소에서 열리기도 하고.

Grace : By the way, do you know what this symbol means? It kind of looks like a snowflake.

참, 이 상징이 무슨 의미인 것 같아? 눈송이처럼 생긴 것 같아.

Asher : That's the emblem for the upcoming Paralympics. It's supposed to **stand for** ice, snow, and the Paralympians. There are two identical symbols to **show** equality. And the five colors **represent** all individuals.

그것은 다가올 장애인올림픽에 대한 상징이야. 얼음, 눈, 그리고 선수들을 나타내는 엠블럼이야. 두 개의 동일한 그림은 평등을 보여주지. 그리고 5개의 색은 각 개인을 의미해.

Grace : The Paralympics are all about social inclusion, so I guess representing equality in the emblem is expected.

장애인올림픽은 사회적 통합을 중요시하니까 엠블럼이 평등을 상징하는 것은 당연하지.

Asher : Yeah, and they've also put that **train of thought** into the slogan.

그래서 그 생각을 바로 표어에도 넣었어.

Grace : How do you know all this?

이것을 어떻게 다 알고 있어?

Asher : I read about it. The slogan is "Passion and Connected." It's all about connecting people, possibilities, and spreading peace.

읽었지. 표어는 "열정과 연결"이야. 이 표어는 사람과 기회를 연결시키고 평화를 확산시키는 것을 나타내.

Grace : It seems like **everything is under way** for March. They've got the venue, the emblem, the slogan; all they need now are the athletes and the fans.

3월을 위해 모든 것이 진행 중인 것 같아. 장소도, 엠블럼도 표어도. 이제 필요한 것은 선수와 관객들인 것 같아.

Practice

Main Expressions

- a couple of years away: 몇 년밖에 안 남았다 / 몇 년만 떨어졌다

  ex: The competition is only a couple of years away.

  경기는 몇 년밖에 안 남았어.

- train of thought: 생각의 흐름, 이어지는 생각

  (논리 또는 생각의 연결에 대해 표현할 때 사용)

  ex: My train of thought was disturbed when the starting gun was shot.

  신호총 소리가 났을 때 생각의 흐름이 흩어졌다.

- under way: 시작되어 진행 중

  ex: The preparations for the project is under way.

  프로젝트를 위한 준비는 진행 중이다.

Language Focus

- using synonyms) stand for, represent, show, symbolize, mean

  ex: The lion on the flag is a family mark that (stands for) bravery.

  국기에 있는 사자는 가문이며 용맹함을 (상징한다).

  note: 가로 안에 있는 단어는 위에서 제시한 유사어와 바꾸어 사용할 수 있다.

A. Use the following expressions in a sentence.

1 a couple of years away: ______________________________

2 train of thought: ______________________________

3 under way: ______________________________

B. Language Focus: Look at the photos below and use the synonyms from above to tell what it represents.

1. 

2. 

3. 

4. 

5. 

해 석

What is the Paralympics?

장애인올림픽은 여러 신체적 · 인지적 능력이 손상된 운동선수를 위한 국제적인 스포츠 경기다. 장애인올림픽을 지칭하는 용어인 Paralympic은 옆에, 나란히, 또는 함께를 의미하는 그리스어의 전치사 para와 국제스포츠경기인 Olympic의 합성어로서 올림픽 경기와 나란히 치르는 대회를 뜻한다.

장애인올림픽 운동은 19세기 말부터 시작하여 수많은 병사와 일반인의 부상을 낳은 2차 대전 이후까지 이어졌다. 척추부상자들을 위해 운동재활치료의 한 형태로 시작하였다가 점차적으로 스포츠 경기의 형태를 갖추게 되었다. 당시 휠체어를 이용하는 선수를 위한 경기이자 스토케 맨드빌 경기(Stoke Mandeville Games)로 불렸던 장애인 경기는 공식적으로 1948년 런던 올림픽 개막식 날에 맞추어 시작했다. 경기는 4년마다 개최하기로 결정되었으며 이후 1976년 동계스포츠 종목으로 추가됐다. 국제장애인올림픽위원회(IPC)와 국제올림픽위원회(IOC)가 하계 및 동계올림픽 주최국에서 두 경기를 동시에 개최하기로 결정하면서부터 올림픽 행사에 포함되게 되었다.

모든 장애인을 스포츠에 포함하기 위한 이 움직임은 여러 협회를 탄생시켰다. 그중 국제장애인 스포츠협회(IOSD), 국제뇌성마비 스포츠 레크리에이션협회(CPISRA), 국제시각장애인 스포츠연맹(IBSA), 국제청각장애인 스포츠위원회(CISS), 그리고 국제지적장애인 스포츠연맹(INAS-FID)이 있다. 국제스토크 맨더빌 경기대회(ISMGF)를 포함한 단체들의 협력은 국제장애인 스포츠 협력위원회(ICC)를 만들었다. 장애인 스포츠의 발전과 더불어 더 많은 국가의 관심이 증가함에 따라 총괄 조직인 국제장애인올림픽위원회(IPC)가 1989년 9월 22일 설립되기에 이른다.

The International Paralympic Committee (IPC): Its goals and values

국제장애인올림픽위원회(IPC)는 국제적인 기구로서 12개의 경기연맹과 각종 대회를 포함한 하계 그리고 동계 장애인올림픽 경기를 총괄하고 있다. 위원회는 독일에 본부를 두고 있으며 1989년 9월 22일에 설립되었다.

위원회의 초대 위원장인 로버트 스테드워드(Robert Steadward)는 1989년에서 2001년까지 임기를 맡았고, 추후 필립 크레벤(Sir Philip Craven)이 뒤를 이어 위원회의 위원장 자리를 2017년까지 맡았다.

국제장애인올림픽위원회는 모든 사람에게 스포츠를 할 수 있는 기회를 만들어 주기 위해 만들어졌다. IPC는 장애인올림픽 선수들이 경기에 참가하여 초급에서 고급 수준으로 능력을 향상시킬 수 있는 기회를 제공한다. 용기, 결정, 불굴의 의지, 영감, 그리고 평등이라는 장애인올림픽의 가치들에 부응하고 이를 증진시키기 위한 노력이다.

Paralympic Sports

장애인올림픽은 국제장애인올림픽위원회(IPC)가 주관하며 25개의 여름 스포츠 종목과 5개의 겨울 스포츠 종목으로 구성되어 있다. 각 종목은 특정 장애에 따라 여러 경기로 구분된다. 유사한 신체적 또는 지적 조건을 가진 선수들이 공정하게 경기를 할 수 있도록 만들어준다. 선수는 국제장애인올림픽위원회의 기준에 해당되어야 특정 종목에 참가할 수 있다. 즉, 선수는 해당 스포츠 종목의 경기에 적합한 장애가 존재해야 시합에 참가할 수 있다. 단순히 장애를 가진 것만으로 장애인올림픽에 참가할 수 있는 자격이 주어지지 않는다.

국제장애인올림픽위원회는 장애를 10개의 범주로 구분하였다. 선수는 최소 하나의 범주 안에 해당되어야 경기에 참가할 수 있다. 불공평한 그리고 부정한 행위를 예방하기 위해 자격 기준은 매우 엄격하다.

10개의 범주는 다음과 같다(국제장애인올림픽위원회가 명시).

① 손상된 근력: 근육을 수축하는 능력이 없어 움직임이 저하된 상태
② 손상된 수동관절 가동범위: 하나 이상의 관절의 움직임의 제약이 있는 상태
③ 사지 결핍: 뼈 또는 관절의 전체적 또는 부분적 결핍
④ 다리 길이 불일치: 한쪽 다리가 짧아진 상태
⑤ 불균형적인 단신: 비정상적으로 키가 작고 불균형적인 팔다리 또는 몸통을 갖고 있는 상태
⑥ 긴장 항진: 근육을 늘릴 수 없어 정상적인 움직임이 저하된 상태
⑦ 운동 실조증: 근육 공동 작용이 저하된 상태
⑧ 아테토시스(무정위운동): 운동장애의 일종으로 불수의 근육 움직임을 유발하는 상태
⑨ 시각 장애: 눈 손상으로 시각에 이상이 있는 상태
⑩ 지적 장애: 제한된 지적 능력 및 행동

장애인올림픽에 참가할 수 있는 자격을 얻은 선수들은 특정 장애로 인해 특정한 요구들이 존재한다. 그러므로 경기 실력을 향상시키도록 선수들을 보호하고 도울 수 있는 스포츠 기술과 방법 그리고 장비와 도구가 개발되었다.

The Paralympians

Paralympian(패럴림피언) 또는 장애인올림픽 선수는 국제장애인올림픽에서 경기를 펼치는 선수를 지칭하는 용어다. 선수들은 참가할 수 있는 특정 신체장애를 갖고 있다. 일반 선수들과 같이 패럴림피언은 경쟁심이 강한 선수들이며 각 종목에서 최고의 선수가 되기 위해 엄격한 훈련을 견뎌낸다.

장애인 선수가 보여주는 노력은 경쟁자 한 명도 부족함이 없다는 것을 보여주고 있다. 선수들의 참가, 그들의 장애, 그리고 그들의 노력은 모두에게 영감을 주고 있다. 패럴림피언들은 더 이상 재활하는 퇴역 군인이 아닌 승리, 힘, 용기, 그리고 함께함의 상징이다.

Upcoming Pyeongchang Paralympic Games

다가오는 2018년 동계 국제장애인올림픽은 대한민국 평창에서 열리며 3월 9일에서 18일까지 진행된다. 10일 동안 6개의 종목, 즉 알파인 스키, 바이애슬론, 크로스컨트리 스키, 아이스 슬레지하키, 스노보드, 그리고 휠체어 컬링에서 총 80개의 경기가 치러지게 된다.

2018년 올림픽은 3개의 장소인 정선, 용평, 강릉에서 열린다. 모든 스키 종목은 정선과 평창에서 이루어지며 강릉은 아이스슬레지하키와 휠체어 컬링을 주최하게 된다.

평창 장애인올림픽은 표어로 "열정(Passion)과 연결(Connected)"을 제시했다. 이 표어는 모든 사람을 연결하고 하나가 된다는 장애인올림픽의 정신을 상징한다. 나이와 국적에 상관없이 사람을 연결시키고 선수에게 새로운 기회를 주고 전 세계에 평화를 넓히는 것이 이 경기의 목적이다.

국제장애인올림픽의 엠블럼은 눈, 얼음, 그리고 선수를 상징한다. 동일한 모양의 두 표가 나란히 놓여 있는 것은 평등을 나타낸다. 마지막으로, 5개의 색은 각 개인의 독특함을 표현한다.

2018년 준비를 위해 평창시는 드림 프로그램 프로젝트를 개시했다. 이 프로젝트는 겨울 스포츠를 청소년에게 소개하고 장애인올림픽에 대한 인식을 높이는 데 목표를 둔다. 또 다른 목적은 사회통합을 고취하는 것이다. 즉, 다양한 사람들이 존재하고 있다는 것을 인식하고 모두가 연결되어 있음을 깨닫는 것이 필요하다.

Glosary
용어집

A

adapted [ədǽptid] (adj.) 개조된 / altered, adjusted, reformed
alongside [əˌlɔːŋˈsaɪd] (adv.) …옆에, 나란히 / by, at, to the side of
assist [əˈsɪst] (v.) 돕다 / aid, support

C

category [ˈkætəgɔːri] (n.) 범주 / class, division, group
challenger [ˈtʃælɪndʒə(r)] (n.) 도전자 / contender, contestant, player
cheat [tʃiːt] (v.) 속이다, 부정행위를 하다 / con, deceive, manipulate
civilian [səˈvɪliən] (n.) 민간인 / citizen, commoner
classification [ˌklæsɪfɪˈkeɪʃn] (n.) 범주, 분류 / category, group
compete [kəmˈpiːt] (v.) 경쟁하다 / battle, challenge
competition [ˌkɑːmpəˈtɪʃn] (n.) 경기 / game, match, tournament
competitiveness (n.) 경쟁력, 경쟁적인 것 / ambition
control [kənˈtroʊl] (n.) 통제력 / command, power
coordinate [koʊˈɔːrdɪneɪt] (v.) 조직화하다 / organize, regulate

D

deficiency [dɪˈfɪʃnsi] (n.) 결핍, 부족 / imperfection, defect, lack
disability [ˌdɪsəˈbɪləti] (n.) 장애 / impairment, ailment, inability
disabled [dɪsˈeɪbld] (adj.) 장애를 가진 / impaired (n.) 장애인 / handicapped
discipline [ˈdɪsəplɪn] (n.) 운동경기의 종목 / method, practice
discrepancy [dɪsˈkrepənsi] (n.) 차이, 불일치 / difference, disparity
doubles [ˈdʌbl] (n.) 2인 경기 / dual

E

effort [ˈefərt] (n.) 노력 / feat, endeavor
eligibility [èlidʒəbíləti] (n.) 자격 / qualification, ability, acceptability
emblem [ˈembləm] (n.) 상징 / symbol, logo, marker
embody [ɪmˈbɑːdi] (v.) 상징하다 / represent, manifest, exhibit
endeavor [indévər,en-] (n.) 시도, 애씀 / effort, struggle, undertaking
enhance [ɪnˈhæns] (v.) 향상시키다, 높이다 / increase, raise, elevate, strengthen
equal [ˈiːkwəl] (adj.) 동등한, 평등한 / same,
equipment [ɪˈkwɪpmənt] (n.) 장비 / tools
establish [ɪˈstæblɪʃ] (v.) 설립 / settle, form, create
event [ɪˈvent] (n.) 경기 / competition

F

federation [ˌfedəˈreɪʃn] (n.) 연맹, 연합체 / association, organization
field [fiːld] (n.) 종목, 분야 / area, division

G

gate [geɪt] (n.) 스키 게이트

H

hold [hoʊld] (v.) 개최하다 / accommodate, entertain
host [hoʊst] (v.) 주최하다 / arrange, assemble (n.)주인 / owner, presenter

I

identical [aɪˈdentɪkl] (adj.) 동일한, 똑같은 / same, similar
impairment [ɪmˈpermənt] (n.) 장애 / disability
incorporate [ɪnˈkɔːrpəreɪt] (v.) 포함하다 / assimilate, mix, include
incorporation [inkɔ́ːrpəréiʃən] (n.) 포함하는 행위 / addition, joining, connection
initiate [ɪˈnɪʃieɪt] (v.) 개시하다 / trigger, activate
injured [ˈɪnddʒərd] (adj.) 부상을 입은 / damaged, wounded, hurt
inspiration [ˌɪnspəˈreɪʃn] (n.) 영감 / encouragement, motivation, stimulation
institution [ˌɪnstɪˈtuːʃn] (n.) 기관 / foundation, establishment
intellectual [ˌɪntəˈlektʃuəl] (adj.) 지적 / mental
international [ˌɪntərˈnæʃnəl] (adj.) 국제적인 / global, world

L

limb [lɪm] (n.) 팔, 다리 / arm, leg, extension

location [loʊˈkeɪʃn] (n.) 장소, 위치 / area, region, venue

M

mild [maɪld] (adj.) 약간의, 가벼운 / benign, moderate

minimal [ˈmɪnɪməl] (adj.) 최소의 / light

moderate [ˈmɑ:dərət] (adj.) 보통의, 중간의 / mild

modified [ˈmɑ:dɪfaɪd] (adj.) 변경된, 수정된 / altered, adjusted, fitted

movement [ˈmu:vmənt] (n.) 움직임, 운동 / campaign, operation

O

office [ˈɔ:fɪs] (n.) 지위, 공직 / job, position, employment, duty

P

paralympian [ˌpærəˈlɪmpɪən] (n.) 국제장애인올림픽에 참가한 선수 / athlete

Paralympics [ˌpærəˈlɪmpɪks] (n.) 세계 장애인올림픽

partial [ˈpɑ:rʃl] (adj.) 부분적인 / limited

physical [ˈfɪzɪkl] (adj.) 신체적 /

player [ˈpleɪə(r)] (n.) 선수 / athlete

possibility [ˌpɑ:səˈbɪləti] (n.) 가능성 / opportunity

prevent [prɪˈvent] (v.) 예방하다 / block, prohibit, restrict

project [ˈprɑ:dʒekt] (n.) 계획, 프로젝트 / program

promote [prəˈmoʊt] (v.) 장려하다, 촉진하다 / encourage, support

protect [prəˈtekt] (v.) 보호하다 / care for, defend, shelter, support, secure

Q

qualify [ˈkwɑ:lɪfaɪ] (v.) 자격을 얻다 / certify, permit, enable

R

reduced [ridjú:st] (adj.) 감소한, 축소한 / decreased, diminished

rehabilitation [rì:həbìlətéiʃən] (n.) 재활 / recovery, improvement rigorously [ˈrɪgərəsli] (adv.) 엄격하게, 혹독하게 / fiercely, vigorously, powerfully

run [rʌn] (n.) 경주 / race

S

serve [sɜ:rv] (v.) 근무하다, 복무하다, 일하다 / work,

serviceman [ˈsɜ:rvɪsmən] (n.) 군인 / soldier

severe [sɪˈvɪr] (adj.) 극심한, 심각한 / serious, acute, critical

situate [ˈsɪtʃueɪt] (v.) 위치에 두다 / placed, settled, positioned

slogan [ˈsloʊgən] (n.) 표어, 구호 / phrase, saying

slope [sloʊp] (n.) 스키 슬로프 또는 연습장

sportsman [ˈspɔ:rtsmən] (n.) 운동선수 / athlete

standard [ˈstændərd] (adj.) 보통의, 표준 / normal, typical

standard [ˈstændərd] (n.) 기준, 규범 / norm, prototype

stature [ˈstætʃə(r)] (n.) 키 / size, height

succeed [səkˈsi:d] (v.) 잇따름, 승계, 계승 / come after, replace

symbolize [ˈsɪmbəlaɪz] (v.) 상징하다 / embody, represent

T

tally [ˈtæli] (v.) 기록 / score

target [ˈtɑ:rgɪt] (n.) 표적, 목표 / aim, goal

total [ˈtoʊtl] (adj.) 전체의 / complete, full, entire

train [treɪn] (v.) 훈련하다 / practice, discipline

triumph [ˈtraɪʌmf] (n.) 업적, 승리 / accomplishment, achievement

U

upcoming [ˈʌpkʌmɪŋ] (adj.) 다가오는 / approaching, nearing, impending

V

value [ˈvælju:] (n.) 가치관 / beliefs, ethics, ideals

venue [ˈvenju:] (n.) 장소 / place, site, ground

veteran [ˈvetərən] (n.) 참전 용사, 재향 군인 / soldier, troop

Source
참고자료

BOOKS :

Johnson, Robin. *Winter Olympic Sports Paralympic Sports Events.* New York: Crabtree Publishing Company, 2010.

WEB SITES :

Badminton World Federation	http://www.bwfbadminton.org/page.aspx?id=15437
Boccia International Sports Federation	http://www.bisfed.com/
federation equestre internationale	http://www.fei.org/
International Blind sports federation	http://www.ibsasport.org/
International canoe federation	http://www.canoeicf.com/icf/
International Paralympic Committee	http://www.paralympic.org
International Rowing Federation	http://www.worldrowing.com/
International Sailing Federation	http://www.sailing.org/disabled/
International Table Tennis Federation	http://www.ittf.com/
International Tennis Federation	http://www.itftennis.com/wheelchair/home.aspx
International Triathlon Union	http://www.triathlon.org/paratriathlon
International Wheelchair & Amputee Sports Federation	http://www.iwasf.com/
International Wheelchair Basketball Federation	http://www.iwbf.org/
International Wheelchair Rugby Federation	http://www.iwrf.com/
PyeongChang 2018 Paralympic Games	http://pyeongchang2018.com/horizon/eng
Team USA	http://www.teamusa.org
Union Cycliste Internationale	http://www.uci.ch/
US Rowing	http://www.usrowing.org/
World Archery	http://archery.org/Archery
World Curling Federation	http://www.worldcurling.org/
World ParaVolley	http://www.worldparavolley.org/